CONTEMPLATIVE

Autobiography of the Early Years

By
Bernadette Roberts

ContemplativeChristians.com

Published by ContemplativeChristians.com
June 2018
P.O. Box 164202
Austin, TX 78716

Contemplative: Autobiography of the Early Years

Library of Congress Cataloging-in-Publication Data

Roberts, Bernadette (1931 – 2017)
Contemplative: Autobiography of the Early Years
ISBN: 978-0-692-12517-5

1. Spiritual life – Christianity. 2. Contemplative Journey. I. Title.

About the Cover:
THE MONK

Before I was born my father acquired a 7 x 9" photo of this painting. It hung on a wall of our home and had great meaning for me. I recently learned it was painted in Munich, Germany, by Thure Nikolaus Freiherr von Cedentrom (1843-1924, born in Sweden). Its last known whereabouts was the Magdeburg museum, Germany, which was damaged in the war (1945) and the picture never seen again. (There is a similar painting, however, in the Cleveland museum entitled "The Sunlight"). Special thanks to Fred Fuentes for his extensive research tracking down my monk.

CONTEMPLATIVE

CONTENTS

INTRODUCTION

This book is an account of my spiritual journey from birth to seventeen. Since my earlier work, *The Path to No-Self*, begins at seventeen, the present book covers the earlier years and my initial steps in the contemplative path. The purpose of this writing is not only to give background to my previous works, but to give witness to God's work in a single soul. Since God is at work in every soul, each individual must give his own account, no one else can do this for him. At an early age I was convinced my experiences were not given for myself alone, and though I never figured out how they could affect others, at least I could tell the story. My hope is that people will relate to these experiences the better to discern God's work in themselves.

While every child is a product of genes and environment–family, culture, religion, and so on–this can never be the whole story of one's life. Without denying these influences, priority must be given to God's graced work in the soul, because grace is no respecter of persons, genes, environment, family, culture and so on. God does not wait for better circumstances or pamper individual temperaments, nothing can inhibit or deter His work in the soul, and thus no life is complete without this graced accounting. But if it is relatively easy to account for heritage and environment, it is not so easy to describe the working of grace and a genuine supernatural experience. As its cause, God .does not communicate to the senses, intellect, emotions, or use words, thus the mind is at a loss to account for how it even knows this communication. About all we can account for is our reactions which can never be a true description of the event itself. The nature of a supernatural communication, however, is knowledge, in fact the whole purpose and end of an experience is to learn something, which means an experience is only as important as what is learned from it. To communicate this knowledge to others, however, re quires it be filtered through the intellect and put into verbal form, which can never be satisfying because we know what is communicated is not it.

Be this as it may, the focus of this narrative is a description of those spiritual experiences that shaped and molded my psychological and intellectual development. It is a mistake to think that spiritual and psychological development are one and the same or no different. While the two are not wholly separable, spiritual development always leads the way so that any lag in spiritual development results in a lag in psychological development. We do not first develop psychologically and then spiritually, rather it is the other way around: the effect of a graced experience is bound to define our particular mentality, psyche, and all we are. Since I have not found in the literature an account of these developmental experiences, I hope these pages will help fill a gap in our knowledge of this twofold and simultaneous development of man's spiritual-psychological life. Whatever the inadequacies of my account, I hope these pages will act as a reflection for those who seek insight into the experiential truth of the mystery that dwells in themselves, a mystery that reveals itself to one and all.

My entrance to the traditional Christian contemplative path began at fifteen with a particular "conversion" experience, after which, all the experiences and major turning points of my journey were pretty much par for the course—that is, well known and accounted for in the Christian tradition. For this reason, the primary focus of the present narrative is on those experiences that led up to my conversion experience. Without an account of these early experiences my conversion to the traditional path can never be rightly understood. So another purpose of this book is to account for those spiritual experiences that preceded my entering the more traditional Christian contemplative path. Since these early experiences are not part of the traditional path and were not even typically Christian, I do not believe an account of such experiences will be found in other books on the Christian contemplative life. In these pages I have refrained from superimposing any retrospective interpretation or understanding on these early experiences. If there is anything unique in this story, it is a child's (and adolescent's) account without overlay of adult commentary.

Although my family life was rich in diversity of experiences, I have had to be selective in tracing the development of but one of its members–myself. This meant omitting a great deal about other members, as well as all the family activities, lest the narrative turn into a family saga with little direct bearing on my "extra-family" experiences. I have included enough about family life, however, to make it obvious I did not grow up in a vacuum or was anything but a most ordinary child of my day and age.

The predominant atmosphere of our home was rooted in my parents' extraordinary love of God and Catholic faith. The traditional practices of this faith were so incorporated into everyday life it would be impossible to treat them separately or apart from the flow of ordinary home life. Thus from birth I attended all variety of religious services .and festivities, listened to religious talk at the table, was surrounded by religious articles, people and books. In short, home life was a reflection of my parents' deepest convictions: their love of God and one another. It should not be imagined, however, we were a household of pious, restricted souls, on the contrary, life was a free flow of totally independent, out-spoken, free spirits, a fact I valued all my life.

Despite this enriched milieu, however, I found no immediate religious context for my early spiritual experiences. It was the failure to find such a context that sent me on a quest for answers not forthcoming from my religious environment, practices and education. Had there been ready answers or had my experiences fit into the context of my faith, there would have been immediate understanding and no need to search for the truth of what I experienced. Without this quest, however, my life would have been very different and not what it was. So despite being raised in an extraordinarily religious environment, I had to find my own answers and go my own way.

A major concern in relating this story is that I may have given my parents short shrift, not deliberately, but due to space and time. This is a problem because it is not possible to get a true glimpse of the home in which I was raised without giving a more complete portrait of the two people responsible for it. To do them justice, however, would take a book in itself, a short history or character sketch would not suffice. I must leave this project, however, for another time. While mother would not be too difficult to describe–because she was near perfect, even-tempered, and predictable–my father was so complex, no brief sketch could approach a true portrait. In every way the two were opposites, yet I don't think there could be found a more loving couple or compatible marriage–as dad always said, their marriage was "made in heaven." It would be impossible, however, to tell my story without them, and while there were times we were at odds, this was all part of growing up. My concern is that I seem to relate more of the tougher times we had than of the best of times, of which there were so many. Perhaps I can best sum up my parents by saying: I regard them as the most intelligent, holiest individuals I ever met. Without doubt, God's first great grace to me was the two of them–my parents.

Age 8 months

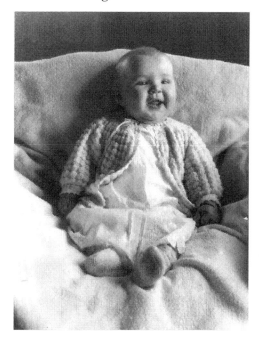

Age 2

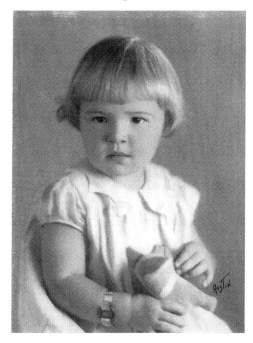

BIRTH THROUGH AGE TWO

Mom: There was such a fuss at your baptism I thought it might never happen.

Me: What was all that about?

Mom: To tell the truth, I never understood what it was about.

Me: Well, what happened?

Mom: We were all ready to start, Father asked the name you were to be given. When dad told him, (Bernadette), your godfather objected. That's when all the fuss started.

Me: Why did he object?

Mom: All I know is that he thought your name should be Therese, his favorite saint–the Little Flower. He and dad argued, at one point they left church for about ten minutes to consult some book or other. What I could never understand is why Father King didn't put his foot down.

Me: How long did this go on?

Mom: At least a half hour or more.

Me: And Father just stood there waiting?

Mom: Yes!

If mother did not understand the reason for the fuss, I did. It was a Catholic tradition to give every child a saint's name, a saint they could look up to as their special patron in heaven. At that time, Bernadette, the seer at Lourdes, had not yet been canonized, which is why my godfather, Mr. Vaughan, wanted to insert St. Therese for a saint's name. Even after dad agreed, there was a fuss about which name should be first, the Saint or the merely Blessed. Since my father intended to call me Bernadette, it only made sense to put it first, but Mr. Vaughan insisted on the protocol of putting the Saint's name first. And so after all the wrangling I was finally baptized, Therese Bernadette, June, 28, 1931.

How I got the name Bernadette is another story. My father had a life-long devotion to Our Lady, and during the First World War, unmarried and stationed in France, any time he could get leave, he would go to Lourdes and help carry the sick from the train station to the grotto. Dad told us some wonderful stories about this time in his life–the most spectacular being his surviving the sinking of the Tuscania. After he married, because of his devotion to Lourdes, he always wanted to name one of his girls Bernadette. Mother objected. She said the name was too long and difficult for a child to pronounce; and besides, she had never heard the name before she met dad. The truth is, she didn't like either of my names–sticking her child with two French names was a bit much. It turns out, mother would never care for Saint Therese–"It was her sisters who canonized her," she used to say. Dad, however, knew Therese through his long friendship with the Discalced Carmelites (Therese's religious Order) whom he met when their community first arrived in Los Angeles to establish a monastery. Mother told me, "Since I knew you were to be our last child, I consented to the name Bernadette, I knew it would please your father." Mother, however, had no intention of calling me either name, early on she came up with a nickname. While I was not overly fond of "Bernadette," I positively hated my nickname.

Actually, my Baptism in Church had been only a formality because I had already been baptized the moment I was born–which was the cause of a far bigger fuss than the one in Church. At any rate, at five weeks of age, Therese Bernadette Roberts was inscribed in the ledger of St. Mark's Catholic Church in Venice, California. I would never know my godparents or what happened to them, they played no part in my life. Whatever their prior acquaintance with my parents, it seems my Baptism was the end of it.

I was the fourth and last of my parents children. At the time of my birth, Gert was eleven, Lee was nine, and the day Marge turned six, I was born—and ruined her party. Apart from the family, I remember almost nothing before the age of two. A few weeks after my second birthday, however, we moved to a large home my parents had built a block from Venice beach. From that time on, I remember everything, even the day we moved in.

The house was situated on a trolley-way, thus its address, 800 Trolleyway. The trolley car ran from downtown Los Angeles, where my father had his law office, to a car-barn a block from our house. To get to the beach we walked across the car tracks and down Park Avenue in front of our home. There is nothing like growing up at the beach; the sea as one's horizon imparts a sense of expansiveness and freedom of spirit forever imprinted on the soul. Needless to say, we spent a great deal of time at the beach; in summer, we only came home to eat.

For mother, our home was her ideal house, she had dictated every nook and cranny of the architect's plans. From several of the windows we could see the beach; there was an office (or library) for dad; and a special bedroom and bath downstairs for grandpa—who my parents thought might live with us some day. We even had a large outdoor shower to rinse off the sand before coming indoors. On the second floor, to the right of the stairs was a large square hall where dad had an altar built into its free corner. The altar had several tiers and was topped by the most beautiful statue of Our Lady I would ever see. The statue had been given to dad at my birth by the Claretian priests, to whom dad was both friend and attorney. At least two feet high, possibly made of paper and plaster, it was beautifully painted, had a fragile alabaster face and hands, and glass eyes that looked at you wherever you stood. This shrine was really the center of our home, you could not pass by and not be aware of Mary. Sometimes the family would say the rosary kneeling in front of this altar. Behind its sliding front door were kept all kinds of religious goods, I loved sitting on the altar step going through its contents. This is where dad kept his imported wicker jug of Lourdes water—which he was never without—and there were my parents' childhood Bibles, dad's a Douay version, mom's, a King James. On one of the walls in this hall hung a large wooden crucifix, an unusual work of art, hand carved in China and sent to my parents by a Maryknoll priest—dad was also friend and attorney to the Maryknoll Community in Los Angeles where they served a Japanese parish.

My earliest remembrance was one day being called to the couch where my parents were seated. Mom put me on her lap sideways so I faced dad sitting next to her, she said, "We have something special to tell you, and we want you always to remember it. We are not your real parents. Your real Parent is God. He made you and gave you to us to raise for Him."

These were her exact words, if she said anything else, I do not remember. Although the words must have stuck, I know for sure they meant nothing to me, I did not understand and never gave them a thought. Sometime later, however, (days, weeks, months, I don't know) I was scolded for something and feeling dejected, when suddenly mother's words popped into mind. Instantly my spirits revived—I understood! This sudden reversal of spirit I thought marvelous, and when something works once, you use it again and again. So from then on, whenever my parents were upset with me or got after me for anything, I'd shrug my shoulders and say to myself, "They're not my real parents anyway!" and go on my merry way.

I figured that since they were not my real parents, I shouldn't expect them to understand me. It was impossible. The only One who could really know and understand me was the One who made me, not my parents. At best, they only knew me from the outside, which is why they got upset with me, whereas God knew me from above and never got upset with me—all that petty stuff that irked others was beneath God. So from here on, knowing my parents could never really know or understand me, I never expected them to. This conviction or truth stood me well my whole life: nobody but God had access to my mind, heart and soul, nobody could know me like God, not even myself.

Years later when I asked mom how old I was when she told me about God being my real parent, she said she didn't know because she and dad had told this to all of us many times. "We didn't know at what age you children would be able to grasp it, so we decided to start early and keep telling you until you got it. We wanted you to grow up never remembering a time you did not know God made you and given you to us to raise for Him." This explains why it was my earliest remembrance. Though initially I did not comprehend, the words stuck. I only "got it" later. What I got was not just the meaning, but also the reason for my parents well intended, but sometimes failed, attempts on my behalf.

My parents, of course, never suspected their words to an uncomprehending child would work to countermand their attempts to shape my mind and behaviors, much less enable me to shrug off their intended good lessons. At the same time this partially explains why, from the first, I had a dauntless feeling of freedom and independence—for sure, the Truth will set you free. What also contributed to this feeling of freedom and independence was the fact that ours was not a child-centered home. My parents' first consideration and love was one another, and while they certainly loved and wanted us, they never depended on us for anything—which left us free. Then too, living by the expansive sea, running free on its shores, also promoted feelings of freedom and independence. Whatever innate or God-given sense of freedom we are born with, parents can either promote or demote it. Fortunately I had parents who promoted it, even without their knowing.

So before I was three, I had this much down pat: I knew God was the One who made me, and that just as my parents knew and cared for me on a practical level in this world, God knew and cared for me from a higher level—in heaven. (At this age I was not aware of any psychological dichotomy between "within or without", for me the major dichotomy was "heaven and earth"). At the same time, this made me aware of the difference between how I appeared to others and how I really was—that is, my own thoughts, feelings, intentions, desires and so on—which only God and I were privy to, no one else.

About this time I was told that when I died I would see God and live happily with him forever in heaven. From this I concluded that the day I died would be the happiest day of my life—a conviction that never left me. Once, when thinking about what life in heaven would be like, I wondered if they had peanut butter sandwiches. Since this was about all I could eat at the time, I was concerned and went to ask mom about this. "Of course!" she replied, "In heaven you will have everything you ever wanted–and more." I was greatly relieved, "It's a good thing," I said, "Because if they didn't have peanut butter sandwiches I couldn't live there." (For years mom fretted over my poor eating habits, several times she took me to the doctor complaining, "She doesn't eat enough to keep a bird alive!" So naturally I was concerned about the heavenly cuisine.)

A little later I was told that God knew me so well He even knew my most secret thoughts, words and deeds, which got me thinking. While God (like everyone else) could hear my words and see my deeds, yet He would have to be in my head to know what I was thinking–how could this be? How could God be in heaven and in my head at the same time? If this were true, it meant God had to be as close to me as my own thoughts, an idea that not only boggled my mind, but bothered it–somehow it robbed me of my privacy. On the other hand, however, I wanted God to know when I was thinking of Him, so I decided God only knew our thoughts about Him, and not our thoughts about anything else–He wasn't concerned about all that stuff anyway.

After moving to the new house, one of my first remembrances was mom driving me to Santa Monica to have my picture taken–a delayed second birthday picture. After sitting me on a stool, some man put on a stunning performance, making odd faces, shaking things, jumping up and down, playing peek-a-boo, in short, went crazy before my very eyes. Never in my life had I seen such an odd fellow or such mad antics. If mom had not stood close by I'd have been downright frightened. From the sidelines, however, mom kept saying, "Smile, smile!", but what was I to smile at? That man wasn't funny, he was the oddest, craziest human being I'd ever seen. I could only stare at him skeptically, not sure what he would do next. Finally he took a picture of a rather serious watchful face. Mom was so disgusted, all the way back to the car she walked ahead of me instead of holding my hand as usual; then she put me in the back seat, not the front as usual. On the way home she said nothing, and after driving the car into the garage she got out, shut her door, walked into the house and left me in the back seat. It seemed she wanted to forget I was there. Though I waited and waited she never returned.

Now I had never opened a car door by myself, always others did it for me. Pretty soon, however, I began to worry about how long I'd be stuck in the car before somebody found me. When I gingerly gave the door handle a try and nothing happened, my spirits sank, probably I began to cry. After a time, however, I tried the door again and by pushing and pulling every which way, lo and behold, it opened–I did it, I opened the door all by myself! After that I regretted I hadn't tried that hard sooner. This is all I recall of the story except that the sober looking picture that crazy man snapped, ended up in our living room where, for years, it re-called this unhappy incident.

Several years down the road when I brought up this incident to mom, she denied it, "You were too young to remember–and I never left you in the car!" This was not the first time mom had denied my early remembrances–though her denial of this one, especially bugged me. On occasion when the family reminisced about someone or some place, if I chimed in with "I remember!" mom would wave me down, "You were too little." Once I asked her, "Well if l didn't remember, then how come I remembered?" to which she replied, "You must have heard us talking about it or perhaps seen a picture." For a while she made me doubt my own remembrances–was I really there, or did I just hear about it from others? Granted I only remembered things after others brought them up, but so what? How could I remember if I didn't? This whole issue so both-ered me, I deliberately set my mind to remembering things, and then put-ting them to mom, like–"Did grandpa ever walk out of a restaurant be-cause they didn't have waffles?" "Was there a man who used to walk by the house and give us kids pennies?" I came up with all kinds of things and people. If she didn't say "You couldn't possibly have remembered that," she'd say, "But that was just a few weeks (or months) ago," as if that remembrance didn't count. Once I asked, "How long ago was I too little to remember–a week, a month?" "Longer than that," is all she an-swered.

It seems mom had her mind set on some age limit for remembering, a limit I was already questioning by age three. I didn't like being waved down, denied and disbelieved; furthermore, it was disconcerting to be granted no past–as if I only existed today. After a while, however, I gave up racking my memory to try and vindicate myself. I decided I didn't need mom's affirmation for anything, what I knew I knew, and that was that. From the age of two I was perfectly aware of everything going on around me. If there is anything I was not aware of, it obviously played no part in my life, in which case, it wasn't worth remembering anyway.

My parents frequently reminisced about their early days together. They especially enjoyed going over the things we kids did when we were little, which always set them laughing. For our part, we enjoyed hearing these stories because they filled in a part of our history we would never have known otherwise. With few exceptions, everything mom recalled of my first two years I remembered quite vividly—but only after she brought them up. Sometimes I could fill in a few details she either left out or had not been privy to. This always bothered her, she could never believe I remembered anything prior to the age of five.

An example of one of mom's reminiscences which I recalled after she told the story, is as follows. After Mass, dad always stayed in Church to make a thanksgiving while we kids ran around outside. Usually mom went out with us and talked with other parents until dad came out. But this Sunday she decided to pray at the altar rail before the Blessed Sacrament, have a few quiet moments of prayer without us kids around. After a few minutes, however, I came and stood on the step beside her, she put her arm around me, pointed to the tabernacle and whispered, "Jesus is in there." I looked and looked, then whispered back, "How can he fit?" Obviously I had in mind the life size Jesus on the crucifix to the right of the altar. Mother just smiled and went back to her prayers. But I persisted, "How can he breathe? What does he do in there?" But mother just shook her head for me to be quiet and went back to her prayers. After that, leaning on the altar rail, I slid down to the end of it, stretching my neck to try and see behind the altar. After a bit I slid back to mom and whispered, "I think his feet are sticking out the back." That was it! Mom left Church in a hurry before she laughed out loud.

When mom first went over this story it sparked an added remembrance. I used to wonder what was going on behind the altar before Mass started. The Priest and altar boys would scurry back and forth between the sacristy and behind the altar, carrying things, whispering, there were odd noises, sometimes banging–things dropped on the floor perhaps–I couldn't help but wonder what all that hustle and bustle was about. But after mom told me Jesus was in the tabernacle, this solved the mystery. Of course, they were stuffing Jesus into the tabernacle! It made sense, now I knew.

Mom and dad had a lot of stories about us kids in Church, the best one, however, was when Lee, hardly a year old, started to wail in the middle of Fr. Patrick's sermon. Immediately dad got up to take him out, when suddenly Father pointed at dad and shouted, "You down there with the baby, sit down! This is a children's Mass, if anybody doesn't like it they can leave!" Mom and dad would roar whenever they recounted this story.

It seems Fr. Patrick made it known loud and clear that the 9 o'clock Mass was for children, not only the school children, but the little ones as well. He didn't care if they ran around or squawked, if it bothered anyone, they should go to another Mass. At this Mass he never talked from the pulpit, but paced the isle between the school children up front–boys on one side, girls on the other–asking them questions, everyone quaking in their boots lest they be called on. Sometimes their answers provoked titters from the congregation, it was always a stressful time. It was also not beyond Father Patrick to abruptly usher a clumsy altar boy off the altar by the seat of his pants.

Mom used to say she felt sorry for us kids going to Mass when we were little. Like most tots we were restless, inattentive, often squawking, in short, just didn't get what was going on. Raised Protestant, mother couldn't say enough about the happy years she spent at her Sunday school and how she wished we could have had her same wonderful experiences. When she told me this, all I could say was, "I'm glad I don't have to go to school on Sundays, five days a week is enough!" Mass was a totally different experience than our daily religion classes. I would much rather go to Mass than spend another day in school.

"When you children were little," mom used to say, "I never had any time to pray, I couldn't even receive communion in peace. Dad and I took turns going to communion so one of us could watch you children, but your dad was too absorbed in his prayers to be any help. I'll never forget the time Father was just about to give me communion (in those days kneeling at the altar rail with hands under the communion cloth) when Lee tapped me on the shoulder, stuck a pencil in my face and said, "Mamma, sharpen my pencil!" He kept insisting! I just managed communion and took him back to the pew." Then addressing dad, mom said, "You know, Mark Roberts, there are other people in Church who want to pray besides yourself!" Dad smiled a bit sheepishly, but never changed his ways. Always after communion, with his elbow on the pew and right hand covering his face–like the statue of the Thinker on his knees–he remained in that stance unmoved until one of us poked him. Once I clocked him unmoved for over half an hour.

When I was 11 or 12, we once waited for dad so long after Mass, everyone else had gone home. Mom told me, "Go tell dad it's time to go." Though I had delivered this message many times, that day, when I saw him unmoved in the empty church, for some reason I didn't want to disturb him. Standing beside him I cleared my throat, but no response, then I gently tapped him on the shoulder. When he looked up I was shocked, I hardly recognized him. It was the look of someone who did not know where he was or who I was, a look of wonderment or innocence, I'd never seen anything like it. Without a word I turned and hurried out of Church knowing I would never again disturb my father in Church, there was something wrong about it. After this, whenever mom told me to fetch him, I refused.

In keeping with this, mom often remarked on dad's extraordinary powers of concentration. It seems he could write a legal brief undisturbed with noisy children running around, a baby crying, people at the door or whatever the hubbub. When she tried to keep us quiet he said that her getting after us was the only thing that honestly disturbed him. Even late in life with a TV going, it would irk mom when, after some program was over, dad would look up from his book and ask, "What happened?" "If you were interested," she'd reply, "you'd have watched it, but since you weren't, just go back to your book."

* * * * * *

Every year around June or July, a group of newly ordained Maryknoll priests would arrive in Los Angles from New York to embark for China. Dad would invite the group to spend a day at our home–to swim or go to the amusement pier–and after dinner we all gathered round the piano for a songfest. It was during their first visit to our home at the beach, sitting on the lap of one of the young priests, I heard the word "pagan" mentioned. Now I had already heard this word because Marge sometimes brought home a cardboard piggy bank to collect coins for the "pagan babies"–money for the missions. When there was a pause in the young priest's conversation I asked him "What is a pagan?" He thought a moment and said, "Someone who prays to idols–to statues." Excitedly I said, "We do too!" He gave me a shocked look and said, "I hope not!" I jumped off his lap and pulled him by the hand, "Yes we do, come upstairs, I'll show you Our Lady!" "Oh, but that's not Our Lady!" he said. "Yes it is," I insisted, "come and see!" He just smiled, let go my hand and went back to his conversation. I couldn't understand his denial, of course it was Our Lady. I went upstairs by myself to be sure she was still there.

For a while I stood looking at her. "If this statue is not Our Lady, then where is she?" It occurred to me she might be behind the statue. With great effort I dragged a stool from my parents' room and climbed up to look behind the statue, all I saw, however, was the wall and an empty space. Looking at her some more, another idea came to mind, "She is on the inside, that's where she is!" The more I considered this the more sense it made. Our Lady was not what we saw on the outside, rather, she was hidden from our eyes because she was inside the statue. So the young Priest was right, what we saw was not Mary because Mary was inside. For me this resolved the dilemma. At the same time, it was my first intuition of what I would later know as a "soul"–something unseen on the outside, but nevertheless present on the inside (of the body, that is).

Obviously, when my parents had pointed to the crucifix or statue and told me it was Mary or Jesus, I took it at face value. Had they told me it was only a representation of Mary or Jesus I don't know if it would have made any difference. I had already seen photographs of myself and family and knew the difference between ourselves and our pictures–though I could not have explained it–yet, between photographs of people I knew and 3D statues of people I didn't know, I obviously made no similar distinction. I was not, however, the brightest of kids. That sooner or later I somehow got things straight, is pretty much the story of my life.

I do not remember ever being without my own little Sunday prayer book–similar to the ones children receive at their first communion, with colored pictures of Mass and Christ's life. Like everyone else in the family, I had some holy cards tucked into it. One Saturday, however, I decided I needed more cards and began looking through drawers and other Missals in the house until I collected a pile of them. When I discovered I had enough for almost every page of my prayer book, I decided I might as well have one for every page. So I scrounged around some more until every page had its holy card. Altogether, this project took me most the day. I was delighted with my success until I discovered I couldn't shut the book. With a card in every page, the book looked like an open fan, it would not close. I had to pick it up very carefully with both hands so the cards wouldn't fall out.

The next morning when we were getting into the car to go to Mass and mom saw my book, she gasped, "Oh no, you can't take that to Mass, go put it back in the house." After all my trouble? No way! There ensued a big fuss with everyone chiming in: Marge: "Just shake out the cards;" Gert, "Leave it in the car;" dad, "Do as your mother says!" But I clung to the book and didn't budge. Finally Lee said "I've got an idea!" He jumped out of the car, ran into the house and came back with a big fat rubber band–the same he used for his rubber-gun-shooter. Taking my prayer book he snapped the rubber band around it–a perfect fit! Mom told Lee, "If those cards end up all over the floor in Church, you're the one who has to pick them up," and off we went.

In Church Lee positioned me at the end of the pew and sat down next to me. He carefully took off the rubber band, put the book in my lap and whispered, "Now don't move until Mass is over!" Everything went perfectly, one by one I took out each card, looked it over thoroughly and put it back, always trying to decide which ones I liked best. Going from front to back took all of Mass. Afterwards, Lee put the rubber back on and we got home without a spill. Once at home, however, everybody converged on my little prayer book and took all their holy cards back. A whole day's work–gone in a minute!

Shortly after we moved into the new house I noticed a continuous hum in the air, an unfamiliar sound that seemed louder in the morning and evening than during the day. I couldn't help but wonder what it was. Sometimes I deliberately listened out my bedroom window to try and figure it out. One day I was standing on the front porch with mom when I became aware of this sound, I asked her what it was. She listened a moment and said, "I don't hear anything, there is just silence." I understood this to mean that what she heard (the sound I heard) was silence, so from then on, whenever I was aware of the sound I thought I was hearing silence. Often I would deliberately be quiet so I could listen to be sure the silence was still there.

One day I had my head out the window listening to the silence when mom came into the room, I called to her, "Come and listen." She came and stuck her head out the window for a minute. "I don't hear a thing," she said. "But don't you hear the silence?" I insisted. She smiled and patted me on the head, "Sometimes you are the strangest child," and went back to her work. I couldn't understand why she said this, but then, she didn't understand me anyway.

Initially, I thought that what might be making the sound of silence was the hills in the distance, because I noticed that away from home where there were no hills, I never heard it. Things began to dawn on me when the first big storm hit our shores. We could all hear the roar of the waves pounding on shore, and walked down to see them. It was exciting to see the gigantic waves spewing water over the beach, sometimes even flooding the shops along the ocean front. At home we could tell by the sound of the waves when things began to get calmer, and that's when I wondered if the sea was not the sound I had been hearing all the time. One morning, lying in bed listening to the silence, I asked my sister in the other bed, "Do you hear that sound?" She said, "You mean the ocean?" That's when I knew, all this time I had been hearing the sea but didn't know it. Although the mystery was solved I never lost the habit of deliberately listening for silence; I became sensitive to any kind of noise or sound that could block out the silence. For the rest of my life I would listen for silence, seek it out, prize it, even need it. That I became aware of silence at an early age, however, was all due to the sea.

One house and an empty lot from our home was Miss Farrow's Kindergarten, a small school of about 8 children or so. I attended this school for three years starting when I was 2 1/2 and ending when I turned 5. Though known in 1933 as a Kindergarten, today it would be regarded as a Preschool–in those days there were no public Kindergartens. If I had to rate Miss Farrow's on an academic scale, I'd give it a zero, but for providing an enjoyable structured time that made for a happy childhood, I'd rate it a 10.

Miss Farrow lived in a big house alone with her mother. The only room used for the school, however, was her bare living room. All the children except myself came from her Christian Science Church. None of them lived in our neighborhood. Miss Farrow was probably in her 50's, a dignified lady commanding respect; I never recall a sign of impatience from her, nor did she ever utter a single reprimand. Everything was mapped out, she told us what to do and we did it. I believe school went from 9 to noon every day; all we were required to bring was a single piece of fruit. The day went as follows:

In the morning we sat on the steps outside until everyone arrived, then we lined up and marched into the house to the tune of her mother playing a march on the piano. After that we recited the Pledge of Allegiance before a flag. In the course of a year we acted out every nursery rhyme in the book. Prancing in a circle on stick horses we sang Ride-a-cock-horse and Yankee Doodle. She'd put a candlestick in the center of the room and we'd all "Jump over the Candlestick," we might gather around her grandfather clock as she pulled a mouse on a string up and down to Hickory-Dickory-Dock, and so we acted out, sang or recited all the nursery rhymes. We also played all the children games–Farmer in the Dell, London Bridges, Tisket-a-Tasket and many others. We learned to color, trace, cut out and paste.

Every Monday morning we walked three blocks to her Christian Science Church where we flipped up the Church seats–several hundred of them. Running around banging up the seats was great fun, the job was done in no time. Also, every week we walked to the beach and fed bread crumbs to the pigeons and gulls, then looked for shells and rocks on the shore.

Other days we walked around the neighborhood and sometimes went to the dime-store where she'd buy something for everyone, a pinwheel, flag, pencil or some trinket. If it rained she read us stories instead of going for a walk. There was no attempt, however, at teaching the ABC's, in fact, no direct teaching at all. There were no toys, no free time or free play, nor much free chatter. Our interaction was pretty much everyone doing the same thing at the same time, yet there was no boredom, no friction or competition, everything went smoothly, peacefully, in short, there was something healthy about the whole routine. 1 cannot imagine any little child in the world who would not have enjoyed Miss Farrow's Kindergarten.

When I got home from school, after lunch I had a nap. About 3 o'clock mom would put a nice dress on me and we'd usually go out to some store or other. When the older ones got home from school my peaceful routine ended and the real learning began. From Gert's teaching me the piano to the wooden box of ABC's dad bought and taught me, I was read to and played with, above all, allowed to join the older ones in every kind of (sometimes wild) indoor and outdoor games. When it was hot we often went for a swim after dinner, and when it was cold, dad sometimes took us in the car to the Venice indoor plunge, which was always followed by hot chocolate and milk-toast. Most days after dinner, however, when the older ones finished the dishes they went to their rooms to do homework—or so my parents thought. Gert would write in her diary, Lee whittled away at his airplanes, and Marge always had her nose in some novel. Meanwhile mom and dad were in the living room talking, reading and sometimes listening to the radio—on weekends the whole family would listen to radio programs. Because Marge and I shared a room, I never got to sleep before she did, so there was no early-to-bed for me. Though I napped until I was four, I rarely slept, but lay there listening to the sea.

Age 3

AGES 3 & 4

It was a beautiful day at the beach. I sat alone near the shore watching the waves break when something indistinct seemed to emerge from the waters in front of me. Though visibly unseen, it was so huge and close that the waves seemed far in the background. It remained there unmoved for some time, seemingly staring at me as if it wanted to be sure I saw it. At first I broke out in goose bumps and was poised to get up and run. What verged on fear was not so much its sudden appearance, but its deliberate sustained focus on me. I had a sense it wanted to communicate something or expected something of me, but not a thought came to mind. Then as suddenly as it appeared it vanished, and once again I was watching the waves breaking on shore.

As to "what" I saw, since it was not visual, it left no image in mind for me to think about or get hold of Even later, with an adult's vocabulary, I could never have described it or given it a name. Despite this, however, I knew something had appeared in front of me: that it seemed to emerge from the waters, that it had deliberately looked at me, and that it lived somewhere in the ocean, this much I knew. For the rest, it was mine to try and figure out what did I see? Why did it look at me? Later in life, recalling this experience I would think of it as an invisible face with large serious dark eyes staring at me.

In some ways I felt burdened with the mystery of this experience. Apart from pondering "what" it was, the fact it evidently wanted me to see it and wanted me to know that it saw me, set up a personal connectedness, as if there was something between us, something it wanted me to know. Perhaps just my knowing it was "there" was all there was to know.

From this time on, however, I knew this mystery was present in the sea, of this there was never a doubt. At the beach I often went off by myself to sit in the same spot to see if it might appear again. Though I never saw it as before, somehow I knew it was there, and there for me, so from that time on, whenever I went to the beach–often every day–the first thing I'd do was run down and greet it "Here I am! I don't see you, but I know you see me, I know you are there!" and then I'd experience a keen happiness, like two friends seeing each other again. I would spend many hours sitting by the sea, aware of its mystery, pondering my attraction to it, even addressing my thoughts to it.

In the days and months that followed I often put questions to my friend in the sea: What are you? Why did you look at me? What are you to me? But when I tried to think up some possible answers, my mind was a blank. To my knowledge, this experience was the first instance of deliberately trying to "think" about something, to question an experience, try to figure it out. It was also my first awareness of not being able to think and coming up against a blank mind–the end of thinking, that is. Initially I excused this blank mind remembering what I was so often told, "You're too little," meaning–too young to understand, not old enough to do this or go there; always I had to wait until I was "older." As the youngest, I always wanted to do whatever the others were doing, to follow them everywhere, but was often put off with "You're too little." Sometimes, of course, this excuse came in handy. It allowed me to get away with a lot of things because I knew I'd be excused for being "too little." At any rate, when I couldn't find answers to my questions, I figured they would come when I got older, and let it go at that.

After a while, however, the excuse that I was too young didn't work anymore, it didn't satisfy, I needed some answers **now.** Besides, how long would I have to wait, how much older would I have to be- and just how old is "older?" Would I have to wait until I was as old as dad? Come to think of it, I didn't know how old he was; since I was in bed at the time, I got out and hollered downstairs to the living room:

Me: Dad, how old are you?

Dad: Why do you want to know?

Me: I want to know how old I have to be before I'll know something.

Dad: (laughing) I'm 44—how's that?

Me: (I was shocked – 44? why I might be dead by then!) That's too old, I can't wait 'til then! (And went back to bed).

The idea of living my whole life with unanswered questions was unacceptable. I felt my whole future depended on finding out, and right now; without answers my life was on hold, a matter of continuous waiting.

Then and there I determined to keep at the questions, keep thinking about them over and over, because if I didn't figure things out for myself, nobody was going to do it for me. From the beginning, then, I put my whole heart and soul into a quest for answers, a quest that would become the driving force of my life—I wanted to know!

One day at the dinner table I overheard dad say to Lee, "We Roberts have the sea in our blood." That was it! That explained my mysterious attraction to the sea—it was in my blood—and with this notion of physical identity I was satisfied, it seemed to explain everything, for a while at least. Sometimes when I thought about the sea's presence in me I knew it had some connection with the mysterious "presence" I had seen in the sea. One day sitting on the beach thinking about this, something clearly broke into my mind: "what" I had seen was not only in the sea but also in me! This meant the mystery was not just the sea water in my veins, rather, "what" I had seen was in me as well. But where was it in me? How could anything so huge fit into me? Although I dismissed the notion, the message stuck; two or three years later I would know where it was in me.

The sea played a large part in the development of my spiritual life, it had a magnetic attraction, almost a physical pull. I was sure this personal attraction was on both sides, a kind of mutual bond I would come to know as "love." With this initial experience by the sea, my spiritual journey began, the first piece of a puzzle had been laid down. Though I would never count this as an extraordinary experience—because others would overshadow it—it was an important beginning that colored everything that followed. Around this initial piece other pieces would emerge until one day, down the road, they would all miraculously fit together.

The most quiet room in our home was my father's study. In the afternoon, the sun streamed through its bay windows to light up its office furnishings. Behind the large mahogany desk was a wall of books, and to the side, a stand with a typewriter. In front of the bay window was a carved table with a glass bowl in which mom arranged the pretty shells and rocks I collected at the beach. After a days' work, mom could usually be found here sitting in the big leather chair either reading or doing her nails. Although the older ones frequently used the typewriter or looked up things in books, it was the least used room in the house. On week-ends, however, when dad had to do some work at home, it was his undisturbed territory.

Although we had been told not to disturb dad when he was working, I learned that if I didn't say a word or make any noise, I could tip-toe in, sit in the big chair awhile, and then leave without his ever knowing I was there–or so I thought. In time, however, I learned that if l sat in the chair long enough, dad would eventually look up, smile at me and say something. If he really didn't want me there he'd say cheerfully, "Come and give me a big kiss" and then send me out to play. Usually, however, I could sit there as long as I wanted. It was a deep comfortable chair, my feet didn't even reach the edge of it, so I would settle back, watch dad write, listened to the sea and try to think about things.

On one of these occasions, my attention became focused on a picture hanging on the wall opposite me. It was the picture of a man in a long white robe leaning against an open stone window, he was just standing there looking out over a hillside. I determined that when dad spoke to me I'd ask him who he was. When dad finally looked up at me and smiled, I pointed to the picture,

Me: Who's that?

Dad: He is a monk.

Me: What's a monk?

Dad: He is someone who has dedicated his whole life to God.

Me: What's he doing there?

Dad: He's contemplating

Me: What's that?

(Dad leaned back in his chair and thought a moment).

Dad: To contemplate means to gaze, to look.

Me: What's he looking at?

Dad: That monk is looking at God–contemplating God.

Me: That's what he's doing?

Dad: Yes.

I said nothing more, but continued looking at the picture while Dad went back to work. After a bit it occurred to me to see if I could gaze at God too; to do this I would do just what the monk was doing. Since the window in Gert's room was the only one low enough for me to lean against, I went to her room, opened the window, leaned back against the frame and assumed the same pose as the monk in the picture. I stood there awhile just looking over the tops of the trees at the sky and clouds, after a bit I said to myself, "The monk is right, I see God too."

This was not an experience of any kind, but a knowledge as simple and obvious as the sky itself I never doubted I was seeing God, I took it for granted, never thought it unusual or anything other people were not also seeing. I might add, I never thought the tree, clouds or sky was God, which would have been a lot of gods. Somehow I knew God was what I did not visibly see in nature. From then on, to see God I had only to look out the window, or, if I was already outside, "just stand quietly for a while and look–"gaze", as dad put it. With this new knowledge I was certain that what I had seen in the ocean was God. This now seemed perfectly obvious. Now I knew God was not only in the sea (invisibly of course), but in the clouds, sky, trees, hills–all over nature. I was very happy with this new knowledge of God, indeed, the monk had answered my questions!

Despite identifying God as what I had seen in the sea, the difference between actually "seeing" God and "gazing" at God (contemplating) was never lost on me, they were obviously very different. In the beach experience it was not merely me seeing God, but God seeing me, a seeing that set up a personal bond between us. Simply "gazing" at God, on the other hand, affected no such bond, for all I knew He didn't even know I was gazing at Him, thus God seemed more aloof and distant. At the same time, however, I took the seeing at the beach as a kind of proof that "what" I was looking at (contemplating) in nature, was God. Had I not first "seen" God, I don't know that by merely "gazing" at nature I would have known I was seeing Him at all. It seems one first has to see God before they can contemplate God, otherwise, they don't really know what they're looking at.

If this sounds like I thought all this through, reasoned it out and came to these conclusions, this would not be true. I never used my head at all, instead, it was just a simple ordinary knowing. It's only when you have to communicate these things to others you have to use your head. At three, however, I would have been incapable of communicating this to anyone, still, the knowledge was there, it was in place, simple, assured, and quite taken for granted. The upshot of all this is that, for the rest of my life, I never looked at nature that I did not see God's mysterious presence–never. This knowledge was mine forever.

After this I always felt a special affinity with the monk and wanted to find out all I could about him. Whenever I was alone with dad in the study and he paused to look up, I'd ask him more questions about the monk: "Where does he live–could we go see him?" I had all kinds of questions. After explaining that the picture was a copy of some old painting and not an actual photograph of a living monk, he told me what a monastery was, and that it took a special vocation–a calling from God–to live in one. On one occasion, after going over the different religious orders in the Church and their particular missions, he looked at the picture and said, "I think that monk is probably a Carthusian, which means he is a hermit and probably lives in the mountains somewhere." On another occasion he told me that as soon as I learned to read I could read about this monk's life in the Catholic Encyclopedia–pointing to a shelf full of heavy tomes. "Which book is it?" I asked. Dad got out the "C" volume, found the article on the Carthusians, took a piece of paper and stuck it in place, "Here, this will mark the place so you can find it when you learn to read." "How soon can I learn?" I asked. "It won't be long," he answered, putting the marked book back in place.

A few years later when I asked mom how they had acquired the picture, she told me this story: "When your dad got his own law office downtown (before I was born) we had to furnish it and find things to hang on the wall. One week-end he made a special trip downtown to look around some art and picture shops. I couldn't go with him that day, but I just knew he'd come home with a bunch of religious pictures and nothing suitable for his office. Sure enough, that's all he brought home, and the Monk was one of those pictures. After that I went with him and we got everything that's in his office now." As to why dad picked out that picture, I'm not sure. Years later, however, putting two and two together I'm sure it had to do with his Irish grandfather who, as a young man, thought he had a vocation to be a monk. In later life this grandfather actually left his family (in his 60's) to become a monk and was never heard from again. Before he ran off, however, his faith and piety had already made a lifelong impression on his grandson–my dad.

It was not long after I asked dad when I could learn to read, he came home with a heavy wooden box under his arm, a present for me, he said. It was a box of large wooden letters that I instantly treasured. That first night I learned five of them. Once I knew them all, Gert invented the next step. She printed everyone's name on paper and had me find the letters and line them up. Since there were no duplicates, however, she had to come and check every name before I could go on, which was a constant interruption for her. After that she decided to show me how to type these names on the typewriter. Though naturally delighted, it was a big leap to those small letters on the typewriter–I spent most my time just hunting them down. With her list of names, however, I started this project early one Saturday morning and never left the typewriter until dinner at six when I handed her my completed paper. Although it was messy, Gert duly praised me. I was so tired, however, I almost fell asleep at the table.

Once I had learned my lower case letters, Gert gave me a book in big print and had me copy one of the paragraphs on the typewriter. After another day's work, she looked at it and gasped, it seems she forgot to show me how to use the spacer. The paper was unreadable. At any rate, I was on my way learning to read, and though it would still be another two years or so, I credit Gert for it all. When she read me stories from the Book House Series–the first volume was in large print–she would run her finger under the words so I not only listened, but looked at the words as well–more than anything, this is what did it. During these years, however, I often went to dad's study to be sure his marker in the "C" volume was still in place.

One summer evening at the dinner table Lee announced that next Saturday there was to be a parade down the ocean front. It would travel between the Venice and Ocean Park piers–we lived mid-way between the two–and would start with Neptune coming out of the ocean at the end of the Venice pier Saturday morning. I asked, "Who's Neptune?" Lee answered, "He's god of the sea." I jumped out of my seat, "I knew God was in the sea! I just knew it, I was sure of it!" The family laughed–at my excitement, or so I thought. Lee turned to me, "Well, if you want to see god, I'll take you there Saturday morning." I threw my arms around him in sheer delight, "Oh, yes! You promise you'll take me? Promise?" "Of course," he responded, "now sit down and eat your dinner." I counted the days to the following Saturday, the anticipation of seeing God again could not have been higher, and Lee, of course, made the most of this. Every day he reminded me to prepare myself for the great day of vision and revelation, because, he said, "We are going to be very privileged people." I could hardly sleep at night waiting for the great day to arrive.

The morning of the great day we set out for the pier hand in hand. When we got near the pier, however, we could see it was already crowded with people. I began to complain I'd never be able to see, but Lee assured me otherwise. Putting me on his shoulders he slowly squeezed and elbowed his way to the very spot on the railing where we could look directly down to see Neptune's arrival. Putting me down, he pointed to the water below and told me to keep my eye on it so I wouldn't miss a thing. Too short to look over the rail, I stuck my head between the rails. The appointed time went by and nothing happened. It seemed like an hour before a low roar swelled up from the crowd–Neptune was about to appear! Lee bent over me looking down, "Oh see, look there, something's under the water, look, here he comes!" First there appeared a clump of seaweed,

and under it a head, then up popped a bearded face! Immediately I recognized him as one of Venice's beach bums. Totally draped in seaweed, the
crowd roared and cheered as he climb up the pier's ladder.

First I was shocked, then let down, then madder than I'd ever been
in my life. Over the roar of the crowd I shouted angrily at my brother,
"That's not God! That's not God!" The people around us heard me and
laughed, on my brother's face was a sheepish grin that said, "Ha Ha, I
fooled ya!" The only way I knew to get even with him was to get lost in
the crowd, I knew it would worry him because he wouldn't dare go home
without me. So I dived into a sea of legs and just kept going. Immediately
I lost my sense of direction, I couldn't see anything but legs. There were
a few tense moments when I was afraid I'd never get to an open space
because the air down there was getting pretty thin; for all I knew I was
only going in circles–going nowhere. It was a big relief when I suddenly
came to an open space and discovered I was near the foot of the pier. I
could see my way home from there. Because I thought Lee might look
for me along the ocean front, I took another route home.

On the way home I realized I was not angry at Lee, I was really
angry at myself. What had I expected to see? How could I have been so
stupid? I already knew God was not in the sea like a fish or a man, so
why did I think He could come out of the water or that I could physically
see Him? What had I been thinking? When I got home I went to my room,
sat by the window and tried to figure myself out. I could not answer my
own question–"what had I expected to see?"–because if I didn't know the
answer beforehand, it was too late afterwards.

Perhaps the only good thing to come from this horrible incident
was my never being tempted to regard God as anything that could be seen
with the eyes, or for that matter, heard with the ears or touched with the
hands. If I had not been clear on this before, I was now. Though I had
not yet heard God defined as "Spirit", somehow I knew it all along. As to
how I could have been so duped and stupid I never figured out.

The only small consolation that day was thinking of my brother
running around frantically looking for me–which is exactly what happened. He didn't get home until almost dinner and as soon as he came in

I heard him anxiously ask mom, "Is she here?" Mom answered, "She was home before lunch, but where have **you** been?!" When I heard him stomping up the stairs I greeted him at the top with the same smug "Ha, ha" face he had given me. After an angry look he went to his room and slammed the door. I was relieved when nobody brought up the Neptune subject at the dinner table. Obviously, what had been a big thing to me, was nothing to them.

Later in life I wondered why I had such an automatic abhorrence of mythology. I could never make sense of it, had no mind for it at all. Possibly this Neptune affair is part of the reason. Seeing how stupid I had been to believe it, I assumed anybody who believed it was stupid. This fact, however, may also tie in with something mom told me when I was much older. In her own words:

Mom: After Gert was born (the oldest) I wanted to buy a book of Nursery Rhymes and some Fairy Tales to read to her, but your father said he would never allow such books in the house. He didn't want his children's minds filled with lies, nonsense–garbage. I was absolutely shocked! I said, 'Well, what do you think little children should read?'

Dad: The lives of the saints, true stories of great people–remember, truth is stranger than fiction.

Mom: But what harm is there in a fairy tale?

Dad: To fill their minds with such stuff before they are able to discern right from wrong, true from false, fact from fiction, can't but mess up their minds, confuse them. Only after they know the difference can they read fairy tales–if they still want to.

Mom: I told him that when I was little I thoroughly enjoyed reading fairy tales, even thought they enriched my young life. So I asked him, 'Mark, do you think I have a messed up mind?'

As usual, mom had the last word–always she had the last word, regardless of the topic. Mom got her fairy tales, the beautifully bound Book House Series of seven or eight volumes. They were the only tales in the house–which, I might add, were not near as fantastic as dad's Lives of the

Desert Fathers, which I would read later on. As soon as we kids could read by ourselves, we never touched the Fairy Tale books again, we had more interesting books around. Sometimes parents think children like fairy tales when, in fact, children prefer others stories, I know I did. It seems the only difference between fairy tales and mythology is that the former is for children, the latter for adults, but where children quickly outlive fairy tales, some adults never outlive their myths. It goes without saying, in our home we never believed in Santa Claus, the Easter Bunny, Tooth Fairy or any of that stuff I don't know if any of this actually effected my developing mind, but I do know I never developed an imagination and could not hold a mental image in mind for more than a few seconds. My mind never worked in images, which is probably why I was always going blank or coming up against a blank wall. While this had nothing to do with no Santa Claus—can't miss what doesn't exist—yet dad's insistent stress on the truth and nothing but the truth definitely affected me. Though I don't think this accounts for my particular mentality—since other members of the family were not so affected—nevertheless, it may have reinforced some innate proclivity, who knows?

Whenever my brother or sisters got upset with me, called me names, told me to get lost, or said something to hurt my feelings, I'd go and complain to mom. Initially she brushed it off, "They didn't mean it, don't pay any attention to them ...they were just teasing." Sometimes she'd make an excuse for them like "They are too busy, or can't be bothered right now", whatever. After a while, however, she told me this: "When they say something you don't like, just say to yourself sticks and stones may break my bones, but words will never hurt me"'. I didn't understand what that meant, and mom didn't explain, yet she insisted it would help if I learned it and said it whenever I was feeling hurt. So I memorized the ditty and went out to test it. Either that day or the next I went into my brother's room for something when suddenly he jumped up and shouted "Get out of here!" and slammed the door in my face. With my nose still next to the door I quickly said mom's words and then waited for a miracle. But nothing happened. I ran and told mom it didn't work. "Just keep saying it, some day it will work," she said.

Finally, one day the meaning dawned on me, and it helped for a few days, but when I thought about why it helped, it got me thinking: words may not be able to hurt you physically, but still, they can hurt your feelings, why is that?. It seemed to me that if words can't hurt you, they also can't help you, so what are words anyway? Well, for one thing you can't see or touch them, they are like air–they're nothing! But if they are nothing, how is it they can make you happy or mad? I didn't know, but there had to be an answer–maybe when I got older.

This problem was resolved a bit later when mom said to me one day, "You talk so much it just goes in one ear and out the other." This confirmed my view that words were nothing but air, they could pass right through your head–in one ear and out the other. As long as they went straight on through, no problem, it's when they went in and didn't come out the other ear that made for problems. My understanding of this was that anything retained in your mind is what could make for bad feelings, or good feelings. So to avoid bad feelings all I had to do was just let words pass right on through, and this, I discovered, really worked. From then on I developed the habit of checking up on my mind to be sure nothing got stuck in it. In time I discovered it was only when hearing something absolutely true that words ever stuck–a rare occurrence I might add– whereas everything else went right on through.

There is no underestimating what this early discovery meant for my life–that words were so much air. I'm convinced that by the age of four, and for the rest of my life, I never believed a single word I heard or anything I was ever told, it would have been impossible. But if I was not a believer, I was also not a disbeliever. Between the two lies the tester, someone who has to find out the truth for themselves, and this was me. Although it may seem I reasoned all this out, or deliberately determined not to believe or play the skeptic, this was not the case. It was all in the process of my mental, psychological development, so much so, I never even thought about it until I was older and wondered how I got that way. For sure I was never an easy believer–in anything.

An early example of unbelief had to do with our bedtime prayers. Every night before we got into bed we knelt beside it to say our prayers. Mom, of course, would kneel beside me to teach them to me, one prayer being "Angel of God, my guardian dear." I knew it by heart some time before I questioned her about actually having a guardian angel. Mom explained that even though I could not see it, an angel was always beside me watching to be sure nothing bad happened to me and to help me out when needed. When I asked, "How come I have never felt anybody there helping me?" She replied, "Well you have an angel there whether you know it or not." "But," I replied, "If I don't know it, don't see it, then what good is it to me?" In other words, if I didn't experience any outside help, then how did I know any such help existed? Mom assured me, however, the angel was here with me, and left it at that. I would always wonder how she could believe that, sometimes wondered if she honestly believed it herself.

Now it seemed to me that to attribute help to something you never saw, didn't know, never experienced, and felt no need for, made absolutely no sense. Unless you know something is really there, all you are doing is pretending. From the get-go dad had never allowed us to believe in Santa Claus and the like, so what about a guardian angel, what was the difference? For me, at least, it was too late, I couldn't believe it. I knew that unless I had first-hand knowledge, I would never be able to honestly believe in a guardian angel. Should I ever experience one, then I'd know it for myself and wouldn't have to believe something I didn't honestly know. So if down the road one showed up, good, if not, nothing lost. This is simply another example of what I meant when saying that from this age onward I never honestly believed anything anybody ever told me. It was not a deliberate decision not to believe, it was just a simple matter of self-honesty and truth.

Another factor to account for my view of words as so much hot air, was due to my brother who was a consummate tease. To be teased or tricked, you are either being lied to, or the truth has been withheld, and when someone teases you enough, there comes a point at which you can no longer believe anything they say. With my brother, I simply got to that point. He could upset me so much, to survive there was no choice but to take his words and antics with a grain of salt, let it pass, never take him seriously. One of my earliest remembrances of his teasing was when he called me into the kitchen one evening while he and Gert were doing the dishes. What I saw was my precious baby doll, Toddles, her mouth to the faucet and water pouring out her rear end. I screamed with the horror of the sight, it was positively grotesque. Mom ran in but could hardly reprimand Lee for laughing–for some reason, mom always got a kick out of things Lee did, but not the rest of us.

I have to say, however, Lee paid more attention to me than anyone else in the family. I was his "baby sister" and, according to mom, from the day I was born he thought I was the cutest thing in the world. He showed me off to everybody and wanted to take me everywhere with him–which pretty much he did. I had so many good times with Lee I can't image a happy childhood without him. At the beach, for example, I had to wait alone on shore while the rest of the family went for a swim, but as soon as Lee came out, he'd carry me out into the big waves. For hours we'd jump the waves and I loved every minute of it. Soon, however, I caught on to some of his wave tricks. In panic he'd say, "Oh look, here comes a big one! I don't know if we can make it over, hold tight, hold your nose, we may go under!" I'd close my eyes, bury my head in his shoulders, then at the last minute he'd jump up and we'd float over like two corks. It was all terrifying fun–and of course, he always acted like the big hero. After a while, however, I became a pretty good judge of both the waves and my brother, but this only made him beef up the drama. Turning toward shore he'd pretend like the undertow made it impossible to get back in, then he'd start frantically waving to the people on shore shouting "Help, help!" The first time he did this I screamed too. In time, however, I caught on to this one as well, yet to keep the show going I always played my part, not only because it ·was fun, but because I dearly loved being out in those waves . Sometimes it's hard to draw a line between teasing and just having fun, but Lee was good at both.

One time he started a neighborhood club and told me I could join if I went through his initiation ceremony. Sure, I wanted to join, but what would I have to do? "Eat cat's eyeballs", he replied. Well, I didn't want to belong that bad–and where was he going to get these eyeballs? He said it was a secret. I thought he might get them from the butcher shop–judged by some of the horrible things I had seen there. Once mom was trying to get me to eat some meat when Lee whispered in my ear, "Don't eat it, its snake's tongue!" Instantly I insisted mom take it off my plate. But if mom could buy snake's tongue in the market, why not cat's eyeballs? Anyway, if I couldn't join the club at least I could hang around and watch.

A dozen kids or so showed up and sat in a circle around the living room. After blindfolding them Lee brought in his plate of eyeballs–I swear they looked just like slimy eyeballs. The rule was they had to chew them and not swallow them whole, and if they spit them out they had to get out–leave. After these instructions he went around and dropped an eyeball in each open mouth. Several kids bolted before he got to them, but all the older ones passed the test. Afterwards, there were some eye-balls left on the plate, looking at them closely I asked if they were really eyeballs. Lee said "Oh no, they're just peeled grapes, here, have one." "No no!" I said, "You're just kidding me, they might really be eyeballs!" I had no reason to trust Lee, either way you never knew the truth. That's the way it always was with him. So early on, I learned never to believe anything he said–even when it was the truth.

To account for all Lee's teasing and tricks would take another book, it was a daily, endless affair. Despite this, however, he read to me every night, taught me all kinds of games, never excluded me from the gang, took me to movies, the amusement pier, in short, made mine an excep-tionally happy, exciting childhood.

I was too young to remember when I became aware of mom con-stantly saying to me things like "Now, be nice," "Be polite," "I expect you to be on your best behavior," "I hope you'll act like a little lady," "Don't frown," "Don't be bossy," her list of "be this, be that" or "don't be this or that" went on and on–for years. Because she said these things so caus-ally, it may have been more out of habit than anything, I don't know. All I know is that the older I got the more annoying it became. By the time I was two, it already bothered me, yet I didn't know why and didn't know what to say. I was not aware I was not good, not nice, that I was bossy or any of that; still, she wouldn't have said these things if she didn't think so. Obviously she wanted me to be other than I was, yet I didn't know what that could be, or "who" that could be. If you think you are being nice and someone tells you to be nice, it makes no sense; it can only mean you have a different view of what "nice" is. What mom meant by good, nice, sassy and so on, I didn't know. And anyway, how could I be all these things if I wasn't? How could I "put on" all she wanted me to be? Mom must have thought I had some switch inside myself I could just turn off and on. I didn't understand any of it, I only knew it annoyed me, yet I didn't know what to do about it or even how to express my annoyance.

Going out the door to play one day, mom said, "Remember what I told you, if you're too bossy nobody will like you!" Indignantly I replied, "I don't care if the whole world hates me!" and slammed the door behind me. Finally I had found my voice in this matter, but I knew it would not put an end to her constantly getting after me. I had to come up with something else, but what?

In the meantime, by the time I was three or so, I had memorized Popeye's tune I'd heard on the radio:

"I'm Popeye the sailor man,

I am what I am and that's all what I am,

I'm Popeye the sailor man–toot toot!"

I went around the house singing this, but paid no attention to the words. After a time, however, the words "I am what I am and that's all what I am" suddenly mystified me, I realized I did not understand them. He didn't say "I am **who** I am"–obviously he is Popeye–instead he said, "I am **what** I am"–so **what** was he? Now I knew what a sailor was–it's what Popeye did for a living–but what he did was not what he was. Something about those words "I am what I am" intrigued me and stuck in my mind, yet when I tried to think about them, figure out what they meant, I only drew a blank mind. Intuitively, however, I was certain they contained a great mystery and that the day I could crack this mystery, I'd be privy to some profound knowledge. I was as sure of this as the nose on my face. After I became aware of these mysterious words, I do not know how much time elapsed before the following incident occurred:

I was going out to play when mom started to utter one of her annoying caveats, "Now remember, be nice and don't ..." when suddenly, without thinking, I blurted out, "I am what I am and that's all what I am– I am myself!" Then I walked out and slammed the door. What I had said totally surprised me, yet the moment I said it, a light went on in my head. I stood on the back stairs a minute to realize what I'd said, it was the meaning I'd been searching for. Of course, "I am what I am" means I'm just myself! Basically I already knew this, I always had a strong sense of myself. What I realized at that moment, however, was that I now had the perfect weapon to defend myself against mother's endless caveats. I could hardly wait for the next opportunity to use this new weapon.

I didn't have to wait long, either that day or the next when mom started one of her complaints–like "Be nice." I looked her right in the eye and shot back,

Me: How can I be anybody but myself?

(Mom was taken back, for a moment she looked speechless).

Mom: Well of course you can't be anyone but yourself

Me: But you really don't like myself, otherwise you wouldn't always be telling me to be somebody I'm not.

Mom: I don't want you to be anybody else, when have I ever told you that?

Me: You wouldn't tell me to be nice or good if you thought I was. You only say that because you don't think I am nice or good.

Mom: I don't think you are bad, I've never said that. I just think sometimes you could be better, that's all.

Me: If you think I could be better than I am, that means you don't like the way I am now.

Mom: No, I just want you to be your best self

Me: So you don't think I am my best self

Mom: Not all the time.

Me: Name one.

If she gave an example of something I had said or did, I would explain to her why I said or acted as I did, which she really didn't want to hear. I told her that her disapproval was because it wasn't what she would have said or done, in other words, she disapproved because I wasn't her! I was just myself and she didn't like it. Once I accused her of not really liking me. Her response to this was on the order of "love the sinner, but hate the sin", meaning she loved me, but didn't love some of my behaviors. The next time mom told me to be such and such, I put it to her:

Me: Who do you want me to be, Shirley Temple? Or do you want me to be like yourself?

Mom: No, you can only be yourself, I just want you to be your best self

Me: Because you don't think myself is best, you're always telling me to be this way or that way. You really want me to be somebody I'm not.

Mom: Well, we can all be better.

Me: You don't like what I say or do because it's not what you would say or do. You just want me to be like you.

Mom: No, I just want you to be your own best self.

Me: What is my best self?

Mom: When you act the best you can—I think you know what I mean.

Me: No I don't. How am I not my best self? You don't think I'm my best self because I'm not your best self.

Now Mom was not one to argue, in fact, she avoided it like the plague. She couldn't stand it when we kids argued—which was all the time—and of course she never argued with dad, or he with her. When she'd had enough talk, she would end it with one of her pithy quotes from the Bible, some poet, or just a wise piece of common sense, and then walk away. I don't know what she said on this occasion, but it may well have been one of her favorites: "Oh the gift to see ourselves as others see us." I couldn't imagine what gift that could be. What matters is how we see our self, not how others see us—which is always according to their own self, their own biases.

The next time she got after me and I reminded her I was not herself, she said:

Mom: Everybody has a deeper self than the one others see, a self even deeper than the one we sometimes think we are. This deeper self is our true self, the source of goodness and virtue. To be our best self we have to tap into our deeper self–be it.

Me: That may be the way you work, but that's not me. You always think I should be like you.

Mom: Oh, I think that if you look deep enough, search within yourself, you'll find your deeper self.

Immediately I went to my room, knelt by my bed, put my face in my hands and looked inside myself. Though I searched and looked for a long time, I saw absolutely nothing. (In fact, it was kinda dark in there!) After that I ran back downstairs and told her:

Me: I've looked inside and there's no one else in there but me. There's no two selves, no deeper self, there's only me!

Mom: Well, keep looking!

For the next three or four years mom and I went back and forth about "myself." For my part, I neither liked nor dislike myself, I just wanted to be myself without mom always after me to be somebody I wasn't. Although she denied she wanted me to be anyone else, she obviously didn't like me the way I was. I decided the two selves she was referring to was a good self and a bad self. Since she seemed to agree with this, I went on to tell her that what she thought was bad behavior for herself, she also thought was bad behavior for everyone else. Yet everyone else was not herself, thus what she did not like in me was only what she would not like in herself. Besides, she was always telling me she never understood me–she'd say: "I can understand the others, I even understand your father, but I have never been able to understand you." If that was true, then all the more reason for her to stop getting after me when she didn't understand me at all.

Sometimes mom would say to me, "Oh, you're just like your dad!" I didn't like that either. I never wanted to be like dad, or like her, or like anyone else, I just wanted to be myself, and that's what mom could never understand. As for what myself was, I never had to think about it, it was just me–everything I was. Nobody else in the world was like me and I was like nobody else in the world. I experienced no divisions in myself, no confusion, it was Mom who was trying to create confusion and division in me–like her two-self theory. I wouldn't hear of it.

Her effort to divide me into a better and worse self was, in my view, an attempt to convict me, to make me feel bad about myself when I actually didn't. She wanted me to see myself as she saw me, and then have me reform myself according to her view. The only thing I knew about her view of me was that it obviously wasn't the best. What she thought of me, however, made no difference because I couldn't become what I wasn't.

She was trying to make me feel bad because I was what I was and not what she thought I should be. As said before, the idea of liking or disliking myself never entered the picture, yet even if it had, it wouldn't have mattered, either way, you are what you are, you're just yourself If anyone was going to convict me it would be myself, it would have to come from myself and not from anybody else.

It was not until I was seven, mom said something that not only momentarily disarmed me, but would be the last of these confrontations. The issue this day was over this two-self business: better-worse, higher-lower, true-false, deeper-shallower, whatever. In exasperation she pointed her finger at me, poked me in the chest and said emphatically, "You will never find your true self until you find God" (her exact words), and with that, she turned and went back to her work.

I didn't understand this at all. What did God have to do with it? Because I didn't know, I had no reply. It turns out this was mom's final word to me about myself It was the end of all those years of her getting after me, because she never again reminded me to act or be this way or that way. I don't know if she just gave up or merely changed her tactics. In her view, l was so bull-headed and stubborn that any insistence from her only made me more determined and stubborn. She used to say that to get her way with dad–who she also thought was stubborn–it was all a matter of timing, so maybe she thought she'd use this tactic on me too. All I know is that she never again tried to reform me. As it turned out, mom would never be wholly satisfied with me as long as she lived. It seems we have no choice but to take what we get and let go of what we wish we would have had.

As for what she said about finding God, I dismissed it because I already knew God. In fact, it was God who made me myself, and if He didn't like it, then He was the only one who could change it. Besides, by age seven I had already seen God in myself, and what I saw was definitely **not** myself! I never came upon anything mom called a "true self". As I saw it, my one single self was true, I didn't have one true self and one false self, which would have made two selves. Her making these divisions made no sense. My conclusion was that by "true self" she meant being true to yourself, that is, true and honest with yourself, with God and others, above all, not try to be somebody you're not. If this was the "true self", then I already knew it, and knew God too. It was mom who didn't know I knew, but then, by her own admission, she never understood me anyway.

In retrospect, I have to say, mom's final words–"You will never find your true self until you find God"–were not only profound and true, but prophetic. Years later, remembering her words, I realized what a truly mature, holy person she had been at the time–and probably had been from first we met.

Having to defend "myself" at an early age, however, was important to the development of my sense of personal integrity. I would never be shaped by others, their opinions and views of me. I had a strong determination to be just myself and was equally determined to be true to myself and to others. Because of this determination, I think I developed an automatic discernment between people who were authentic and those who were not–those who put on a self they were not or tried to be somebody they were not. And to think all this was sparked by Popeye's profound words, "I am what I am and that's all what I am"! For sure he had it right. Knowing "what" we are (our self) is a thousand times more important than merely knowing "who" we are (Popeye), or what we do in life (be a sailorman).

Age 5 or 6

AGES 5 & 6

Sometime after my fifth birthday, the family boat was finally launched. It had been in the making for at least a year, we watched it go up from scratch on a lot not far from our home. In those days there were no yacht factories or boat yards from which to pick and choose. Instead, you had to find a builder, have the plans drawn, and then watch it come to life. Dad named her the "Morning Star" after one of Our Lady's names in her Litany. Whenever we recited this Litany in Church, when we came to "Morning Star" we'd elbow each other.

When mom first saw the plans she was shocked it had no bathroom on board. Promptly she announced she'd never get on without one. For years afterwards, when one of us emerged from the bathroom on board, she'd say, "You can thank me for that!" Actually, mom was never gung-ho about the boat. She had never learned to swim, wasn't raised by the sea, and never enjoyed primitive accommodations–like camping out or even sleeping in a cabin. Her philosophy was: if you can't have all the conveniences and comforts of home, why go anywhere? To her, life without all the modern amenities was a return to the cave man era. But no doubt this is why we ended up with so many conveniences on board.

Every week-end we'd go down to the lot to see how the boat was coming, and every week, mom would say skeptically, "I tell you, it's not going to float!" Once the hull was completed, dad and Lee spent their Saturdays working along with the builder and his assistant. After many long months of anticipation there is no describing our excitement the day the boat was launched. It was hoisted on the back of a long truck bed. Dad was in the front seat while Marge and Lee sat on top the boat waving to mom and I as we drove behind. Slowly we drove from Venice to the Santa Monica pier where the boat was to be launched. Once on the pier, cables were wrapped around it and with dad standing on top holding on to the cables, the boat was slowly picked up, swung out over the pier and lowered into the water. When it landed gently in the water and the cables were undone, everyone watching clapped and cheered. I shouted with joy, "It floats! Mom, it floats!" Dad's big concern, however, had been the motor, but to his relief and joy, with the first turn of the key the boat came alive, she and dad were off

Apart from his boyhood experience of sailing a dingy, dad had no experience as a seaman, had never driven a yacht, and knew nothing about motors, all in all he was pretty gutsy, he just learned as he went along. Standing on the pier watching him drive the boat around to its mooring in the little harbor, was a moment of triumph, dad's dream come true. We were not only happy for him, but for ourselves. We eagerly awaited our first trip out to sea.

Sometimes we took day trips down the coast and anchored off shore for a swim. We also went out for evening spins around the gambling ship outside the harbor. Our usual destination, however, was Santa Catalina Island some 25 miles from the mainland where we'd anchor for weekends, or during the summer, for weeks at a time. We explored the island's shoreline, anchored in the coves, swam to shore, fished, played cards at night, in short, there was never a dull moment on board.

It would take too long to recount the next twelve years of adventures this little 30 ft. boat provided our family and friends. All the good times - as well as the suspenseful ones—the places we went, things we saw, I can only summarize by saying, until I was seventeen, the happiest days of my life were spent on this little boat. Although mom was a trooper, for her there would always be the inconveniences aboard; for dad, of course, there was the financial responsibilities of upkeep and moorage; for me, however, the boat was an unmitigated delight.

When summer was over I entered first grade. Though we were supposed to be 6, and I was not yet 5 1/2, dad insisted with the sisters I was bright enough to start—the same excuse he used for Marge. Before I could be accepted, however, the sisters wanted to meet me. So one Saturday morning dad took me to the convent of the Holy Name Sisters, along with several of my papers on which I'd written my ABC's. I took for granted I was going to be tested. While waiting for the sisters, he took me into their chapel and told me this was where, as an infant, the sisters had consecrated me to Mary, making me her special child. He had done this for all of us, thus we were all her special children.

It turned out there was no test, the sisters only wanted to size up my level of maturity. I must have said the right things because after that, every morning the three of us—Marge in sixth grade, Lee in the eighth—set out to walk the two miles or so to St. Clement's School. Though I liked school well enough, there is not much to report. One memorable event was the day sister wheeled in a chart, a large version of our first reader in the Dick and Jane series. Flipping over the large pages she pointed to the words below each picture and had us repeat them. After she'd turned a few pages I felt a certain "click" in my head, instantly I knew I could read, and not just this first reader, but, I was convinced, I could read anything. It was a memorable, delightful moment. I could hardly wait to get home and read to everyone.

As each one arrived home that day, I insisted on reading to them; everyone but Gert acted dutifully impressed. Because Gert was skeptical, after dinner she got out the first volume of the *Book House Series,* opened to a story and asked me to read. Fortunately it was one of my favorites. Putting my finger under each word I read it perfectly. Gert looked at me and said, "Why you've memorized it!" I couldn't believe this. Then she took out the last volume with adult print, flipped to the back and asked me to read something I'd never seen before. While I could read all the familiar words, there were a lot I could not read, so she showed me how to sound things out and pretty soon I caught on. As for the meaning of new words, Mom told me to just keep going because I'd gradually learn a word's meaning by way of its context, which proved to be true. Anyway, by the end of the first grade I could read anything, and with a house full of books, like everyone else in the family, I became an avid reader.

Realizing I could now read, one of my first tests was to get out the "C" volume of the Catholic Encyclopedia dad had marked for me years before. Lying on the floor I put the heavy tome in front of me and began to read about the Carthusians and the daily life of my Monk. It was such small print and slow going it took at least a week or more to get through the long article. The part I would periodically return to, however, was the daily life of the monk and austerity of the rule. After this I didn't have to wonder any more what the Monk did the rest of his day. Though I could not have given a reason for it, I found his austere way of life attractive and mysteriously intriguing. It left a lasting impression

The only other memorable event in the first grade occurred during religious instruction. The catechism answer to "Where is God?" is the simple answer: "God is Everywhere", and the moment I heard this, a light flashed in my head—which meant "I know it! It's true!" It was confirmation of what I already knew but didn't know I knew. Indeed, the phrase "God is Everywhere" perfectly expressed what the Monk and I saw and had known all along. To "contemplate" is just that, to see God Everywhere. Of myself I could never have thought of the word "everywhere," but that was the perfect word. You do not see God "here" or "there", but "Everywhere." The rest of the day I waited impatiently for school to get out so I could stand on the empty hillside next to school and just look "Everywhere" - see God. And so I did. For a long time I stood alone on the hill just looking, gazing at God. I could hardly contain my happiness. I was a bit older when Dad reminded me of something I did when I was five or so. In his own words: "One Saturday morning I was still in bed when I heard a commotion on the other side of the house. I got up to see what was going on. From Gert's window I saw a lot of people with dogs in our side yard I heard water running under the window, so I opened the window and looked down. You were pulling some dog up to the faucet. I said, "What's going on down there?" You looked up at me and said, "I'm baptizing the animals–they'll go to heaven won't they?" "Well", I said, "they will now!" Then I shut the window and went back to our bedroom and closed the door so no one would hear your mom and I laughing."

I recalled days before this event going from door to door around the neighborhood telling people to bring their animals Saturday morning to be baptized. To this day I'll never know why a dozen adults or so actually showed up. Did they really believe it, or were they just humoring me? There had been no snickering however. Everybody quietly waited their turn and then brought their animal to the faucet. After asking the dog's name, I put its head under the water and said, "I baptize you (Sparky, Bozo, or whatever) in the name of the Father, the Son and the Holy Ghost, amen." Evidently I had learned that only the baptized went to heaven and figured this meant the animals as well. For me, baptizing the animals was no game, I could not have been more serious, I really believed I was saving these animals for heaven.

After that, any time I'd spot a stray dog in the neighborhood, I'd shout to my friends, "Quick, get him!" Then we'd chase the dog all over the place until we cornered him, then pushing and pulling, drag him to the faucet to be baptized. If it was a big dog, sometimes it took four of us to get him to a faucet, and since we often had to follow the dog a long way from home, we had to use the closest faucet we could find. After the dog was baptized I always had a sense of relief, at least there'd be one more dog I'd see in heaven. The idea some dogs might not get there was too sad to think about. As for cats, well, they didn't take too well to the water, it seems they'd rather scratch you than go to heaven, so I figured they didn't need baptizing to get there. Like humans, however, dogs were special.

Dad said it was after this incident he took me to the Plaza Church (Our Lady of the Angels) for the annual blessing of the animals. I recalled the spectacular event, all kinds of animals blessed and sprinkled with holy water. Still, I didn't see any of them getting baptized. But no matter, I'd never believe animals didn't make it to heaven. Besides, when I had asked mom if they had peanut butter sandwiches in heaven and she said "Yes, in heaven you will have everything you ever wanted," I figured if they had peanut butter sandwiches, surely they had the animals too. And if I got everything I wanted in heaven, the first thing I'd want would be all the animals.

Speaking of my neighborhood friends, all were boys, five or six of them older and bigger than myself. Jimmy, who sometimes came around, was the only one my age and shorter, but he didn't fit in too well. He was a bundle of electric wires and the only one who ever gave me trouble. The policeman, who lived next door, told mom, "My wife and I get the biggest kick out of watching your youngster bossing those bigger boys around, but they just go along with her, whatever she says goes." Probably this is where mom got the idea I was bossy. The truth, however, is that no one else took the initiative to get things going. If I'd waited for them, we'd have stood around and never played anything. Besides, if they had come up with a good idea–or a better one–why wouldn't I have gone along with it? No, if they really thought I was bossy they wouldn't have played with me, and we wouldn't have had such good times together.

We played all kinds of games, marbles, hop-scotch, dodge ball, kick-the-can, cops and robbers–for this last one, we all had cap-guns. Sometimes I'd set up a schoolroom in the garage and play the part of teacher; or I'd organize a talent show in our outdoor shower with a big sheet for a curtain, costumes and all. We often played on the beach, taking our miniature cars to build roadways, bridges and the like. Altogether, our five years together was great fun, I can't imagine what my days would have been like without this neighborhood gang.

* * * * * * * * * * * *It was that time of year when the sea breeze grew into a chilly afternoon wind. From my bedroom window I could see my friends gathering for a game of cops and robbers, I called out the window and told them to wait for me. I hurried downstairs and was about to go out the front door when mom told me to put on a sweater. So I ran to the back door, grabbed my sweater off its hook and bounded down the back stairs. I turned left to run through the side garden and around to the front when, a few steps beyond the stairs, suddenly from somewhere within myself, I felt a powerful rush like the swift blowing up of a balloon, I seemed to be expanding in all directions. I stopped, looked at my arms and legs to see if I was actually growing, yet I saw nothing unusual. Still, this powerful air–or whatever it was–kept expanding in all directions. For a moment I was seized with fear and thought to myself "I'm gonna bust!" While I had no idea what would happen then, I suspected I might not be around to find out. Short of this happening, however, the expansion suddenly stopped. I waited in suspense, when, across my mind came the words, "You're too big for yourself!" after which the air diffused itself into a wild joy–wild because it was beyond me, uncontainable, not mine.

(It was as if this "air" had burst into laughter). After this, I felt it subside or draw back whence it had come–seemingly from somewhere in my body's mid-section.

The experience lasted only a minute or two. As soon as the Power (I never knew what else to call it) subsided, I noticed leaves swirling on the ground and remembered my friends waiting in front of the house. I ran through the garden and across the front lawn, leaping with excitement, "Guess what just happened to me?" I shouted, "I felt something powerful inside. It was like the energy of ten men, I thought I was gonna bust! Did you guys ever feel something like that?" Eagerly I looked from face to face and was struck by their stoical stance, they stood there mute, staring at me wide eyed–one of them with his mouth open. They reminded me of lifeless statues. I thought perhaps they hadn't heard me, so I asked again if they had ever experienced such a thing, but they didn't move a muscle. It was as if they were frozen to the spot. This struck me as odd. I thought, "I've got to put some life into these guys!" so I began assigning roles–who'd be cops, who'd be robbers–immediately they came to life and we were off.

Following this experience I was always aware of this Power, which seemed to have its own space within myself. Since prior to this experience I had not been aware of it at all, I took for granted that at the moment of the experience, it had blown into me and then never left. Though I did not realize it at the time, this experience was life changing, whatever my life would have been without it, I'll never know. A few years down the road I would refer to this experience as "The day I was born" because it was so pivotal to everything that followed, indeed, the experience opened up a whole new dimension in myself. I had always been aware of my own thoughts, feelings, emotions and energies, yet there was nothing mysterious or unknown about these. "What" I experienced this day, however, was totally different, a complete mystery. Finding out Its true nature would become the search of my life, a search that began on that day.

It was obvious my friends didn't know what I had experienced. I decided they were probably still too young and that their turn hadn't come yet. So I decided to ask the older kids in the neighborhood–ask if they'd ever had this experience. But the older kids didn't even let me get my question out, they didn't want to be bothered, just brushed me off. Then

I started on the adults, specifically, mom. After she heard me out, she said, "You know what I think? I think you have so much energy that at times you don't know what to do with it. What you felt was just a burst of good energy!" I thought this over and did not find it satisfying. For one thing, it could not account for this energy's sudden burst of wild joy–something I'd never experienced before. When I put it to mom, suddenly she seemed to understand, "Now I know what you are talking about. I used to have those same feelings when I was a little girl. I decided this happiness I felt was a sign that I was good, and once I realized this, I resolved always to be good so I could always feel this happiness–and I tell you, it works! Even now, if I look inside I can find this happiness, and from now on so can you, you only have to look inside."

I liked mom's answer, the only problem, I could not make a connection between my experience and having been good, in fact, I could not remember if I had been particularly good that day or not. But if I did not remember being bad, then I must have been good–well, anyway, there was no way I could find this same happiness just for looking inside, as mom was evidently able to do. Altogether I was not satisfied with her explanation. My experience had nothing to do with my being good, nor anything to do with my ordinary good energies. It was something else completely.

Next I went to my father. He was sitting after dinner in his big chair, the newspaper in front of his face. I said, "Dad?" From behind the paper he answered, "Hum?" "Did you ever feel there was something Great living in you, something Powerful?" Instantly he replied, "Sure!" Excitedly I ask, "Tell me, what is 'that'?" Peeking at me over the top of the paper he said, "It's myself!" and then burst out laughing. His answer was incomprehensible to me, I didn't see anything funny at all. I walked away feeling terribly disappointed. What I experienced in me was certainly not my dad!

After that I decided everybody must have had this experience when they were children, only they forgot about it when they got older. Since my parents had obviously forgotten, I thought there might be some adults who had not, so I decided to go door to door and ask the neighbors. Starting on the block across from Miss Farrow's house, I went down one side of the street and up the other.

At the first door I started out: "Could you please tell me if, when you were little, you felt some special power in you that could suddenly blow you up?" The lady said," No, and I'm glad of it!" At the next door I put it differently: "When you were little, did you feel something great in you, something right here"–pointing to my navel area. The lady said, "You mean did I ever have a stomach ache?" At the next house I tried putting it still another way, but when I was finished the lady asked, "You're the Roberts girl aren't you?" "Yes" I replied, "Well say hello to your mother for me," then shut the door. At the next house some man opened the door, looked at me, and without a word shut it again.

Half way up the next block a disheveled old lady came to the door and studied me suspiciously–frowning, squinting, kind of mean looking. She paid no attention to my question, but showered me with questions: "What's your name, where do you live, what school do you go to, is your mother home, what does your father do?" and so on. My impression was she thought. I was nuts and was thinking of making trouble for me. I got a little frightened and decided to give up, either it was impossible to make myself clear or else all these people had forgotten their younger experiences. I would never have success describing it to others, not for lack of descriptive words, but because "what" I experienced had no counterpart to anything I knew or had ever heard about.

Due to the failure to find a response from others, the inevitable question arose: could it be I was the only person in the world who ever had such an experience? I couldn't believe this for a minute. I figured that anything one person could experience, others could too. I did not like the idea of being the only one, a rare bird, an oddity. All I wanted was just to be one of the bunch.

Shortly after this neighborhood odyssey, sister at school was talking to us about Holy Communion and Christ's special presence in the Eucharist–it would be another year before we made our First Communion. At one point she said, "Although God is already present in you, yet when you receive Holy Communion, God will be Present in a special way." Whatever she said after that, I don't know, because the instant she said, "God is already present in you" I felt a sudden leap within–something like what a mother might feel when the babe in her womb suddenly kicks her.

Instantly I knew: "that's it! That's what I experienced, it was God!" I could hardly wait to get home to tell my father. The news that it was God, however, I took as the most natural, unspectacular thing in the world. For sure, everybody had this experience at some time or other, it had simply been my turn.

The way home was downhill along a dirt path. I stood for a moment on top of the empty hillside to feel the sea breeze and gaze at the blue sky with its drifting clouds. Though I already knew God was "Everywhere", yet God "inside"? If sister was correct, this was a totally different experience, but how could both experiences be God? I would have to ask dad about this.

Since we had dinner shortly after dad got home, I had to wait. Later, standing in front of his newspaper, I asked, "Dad, Sister said in school today that God was present in us." "That's right, sister's got it right!" he replied from behind the paper. "Well," I went on, "what I want to know is what does that Presence feel like?" He let the paper fall, the question seemed to surprise him. There was a long pause while he leaned back in his chair to think. The thought that I had stumped him made me feel very grown-up. Finally he leaned toward me, "I'll tell you what. Close your eyes and take a deep breath." I did that, but I must have gotten red in the face because he snapped, "Exhale for heaven's sake!" I did that. "There now," he said, "that is a much as you can experience of God in this life." I laughed, "You've got to be pulling my leg, I didn't feel a thing." Then almost angrily he asked, "Well, you feel life don't you? You feel alive?" I nodded. "Well that's it! God is your very life and breath, everything else you feel is only yourself!" Then he picked up his paper and went back to reading. For a moment I stood there surprised, disbelieving, disappointed. I experienced life and breath all the time, but that wasn't what I experienced! If he was correct, if ordinary life and breath is all one can experience of God, then what I experienced was nothing but myself. But if it was myself, where was it now, and why didn't I feel it all the time? No, he was wrong. But if it was not God and not myself, then what was it? Though I could not believe dad, he nevertheless cast a big doubt on my short lived certitude that what I'd experienced was God. After that I decided to search myself, watch everything within to see what I could see, above all, give this whole thing my best thought. At one point it occurred to me that what I experienced might be my future self or what I would experience when I grew up. But how could a five year old feel ahead of time what they would experience when they were 20 or 30? I couldn't even think about such a possibility—and besides, I might be dead by then. Then a question crossed my mind: what if other people honestly never had this experience, what if I was the only one? The idea of being the only one struck me as frightening. To be so alone, with no one to understand, to be regarded, perhaps, as a misfit, a freak or something. Then and there I determined to be sure I always fit in with the bunch, to never stick out in any way, above all, never talk about my experiences lest people think me odd. No, I just wanted to be ordinary like everybody else, even if meant making a concerted effort to be so. At this point I gave up looking to others for answers, gave up hoping they'd even understand my questions. Besides, anytime I was sure the mystery had been resolved, other people only cast doubt on it. No, from now on I'd keep things to myself.

But if I never asked dad again about my own experiences, I took every opportunity to bring up other people's experiences of God. Once dad remarked that Napoleon said the happiest day in his life had been the day of his First Communion. I said, "Well he must have experienced more than just his life and breath!" Dad said, "Sure, he felt happy to receive Christ"—meaning that feelings of happiness are not experiences of God; indeed, people can experience happiness and joy without God. Another time, after reading the story of Moses in my Bible History book at school, I brought up Moses' experience of God, but dad said this was God's universal revelation to all men, not just Moses' personal experience of God. Now I didn't understand this at all. Moses personally saw and heard God, if not, then all he saw and heard was himself. For at least four years Dad and I periodically went back and forth over this matter of experiencing God. At some point, referring to experiencing joy and love for God, he said, "In this life, that's as much as anyone can experience of God as He is in Himself." Now the qualification "as-God-is-in-Himself" I did not pick up on until much later in life. I never caught his distinction between

"God-as-He-is-in-Himself" and "God-as-He-is-in-ourself," thus my understanding was that while we could experience a love for God, this was not an experience of God. According to dad then, love of God was as much as we could experience of God–in this life at least. Although later, at age ten, I came upon a partial resolution to this dilemma, it was not until I was fifteen before this whole question was finally resolved.

Speaking of my Bible History Book–a children's version of the Bible–Marge and I came down with chicken pox at the same time and had to do our homework in bed. One of my assignments was reading another story from my Bible History book. When mom and dad were out one evening, I didn't feel good and put my book down on the floor face open, between our beds. A bit later I vomited all over it. Marge was fit to be tied, but managed to clean it up while I washed off the pages of my book. When we finally turned out the lights, however, the smell was so bad we couldn't sleep, so Marge got up, took a bottle of her perfume and poured it all on the nasty spot on the rug, which only made things more nauseating. (Despite mom's best efforts, years later we could still smell it at night). The very next day, however, I discovered the pages of my book were so puffed up, due to my having washed them, the book refused to close or stay shut. That, along with the fact the pages still smelled, prompted me to beg mom for a new book, but she said, "No" and made me use it the rest of the year. At first I tried to mask the smell by putting Marge's perfume on the pages, but it was hopeless. For the rest of the year, every day during Bible History at school, all the kids around me conspicuously held their noses. That book was a daily embarrassment.

In our home the usual form of punishment was being sent to our rooms. The only reason I was ever sent was for being sassy, talking back, being rude, especially to company which, it seems, was not too infrequent. Usually I blurted out something that unnerved dad and was abruptly dismissed. I honestly didn't mind being sent to my room, it was the only time I had a chance to look through Marge's drawers without her throwing a tantrum. I also enjoyed spreading my paper dolls around without her insisting I not cross some invisible line she invented to divide our spaces. Of course I could always read, do a puzzle, fool with the radio–there was always plenty to do.

On one occasion, however, things were different. I don't recall what I did to be sent to my room, but I was feeling very low and alone. I had the impression the whole family was down on me. They were sick and tired of me and glad to get me out of sight. I was also worried they might forget to call me for dinner—or might forget I even existed. I propped my arms up on the window sill and looked out. Where looking at nature had always uplifted me and dispelled my woes, this time it only seemed to share my gloom, everything looked as drab on the outside as it did on the inside. After a few minutes, however, from within myself came a strong leap, a burst of what could only be called "laughter"—felt something like a belly laugh. Though I did not laugh (there was nothing funny), yet it instantly swept away my gloom and problems as if they counted for nothing, as if they were even humorous. Not only was the gloom instantly dispelled, but in its stead was great joy. Indeed, life was beautiful! The message was clear and certain: It, the mysterious Power, was the only thing that mattered in my life, everything else didn't matter, wasn't worth the slightest concern. That's what It wanted me to know, to learn, to keep in mind. Compared to Itself, everything else in life was merely external and irrelevant.

Something else about this experience that can only be reported without comment, is that Its interior leap was accompanied by a spark of light over my head. Since my whole focus, however, was immediately drawn to the Power within, I never gave this flash of light another thought, had no idea about it. Perhaps what was most important about this experience was its being the first time I ever really looked within myself and saw something. I keep my eyes on this mysterious joy because I didn't want it to get away. Thus I watched intently as it gradually receded and became a quiet, but visible, place within myself. I had recognized the leap, and now I recognized Its place within, the same place where the first experience had bust forth. Though I might not know "what" this Power was, at least I knew where It was, and from then on could look at It, see It whenever I looked into myself. I might add, though what I experienced was comparable to laughter, yet like the air in the balloon, it was a mystery, what I experienced was not air and not laughter, I didn't know "what" It was, only "that" It was.

By the time. I was called down for dinner I had forgotten what I'd been sent away for. After saying grace, I picked up where I had left off, chatting happily about this or that, when suddenly I realized nobody else was talking. I looked around the table, everyone was staring at me. I thought. "Oh dear, what now?" Pretty soon, however, everyone began talking and things returned to normal. In the meantime, I was waiting to tell mom something. In the kitchen after dinner I said to her, "Remember you're always telling me that if I'm not nice nobody will like me?" "Yes", she replied. "Well, I just found out that God likes me even when I'm not nice"–referring to the joy I experienced despite having being ostracized. Mom was speechless. After a moment she said disgustedly, "Shame on you!" and walked away. Of course I felt no shame, on the contrary, I had the feeling that nothing in life could ever get me down again, never.

From this time on I looked upon life as a game that could never be taken seriously–to take it seriously only meant being caught in its gloom and unhappiness. If I was distressed or worried about something there would come a gentle laugh, and puff! my troubles vanished. It was sheer magic. It was as if this Power said to me, "If I don't care, why should you?" The lesson, of course, was not to make mountains out of mole hills, but to laugh at myself and forget about it. With few exceptions, this view of life was to color all its events and automatically separate what mattered from what did not. It was a view or attitude that stood me well over the long road ahead. Later, I would look back and realize that everything of importance I really knew about life and how to live it, I learned from this Power. It taught me everything I ever needed to know.

Although in the immediacy of my experiences I always thought this Power was God, yet there was no lasting certitude. God was in the very air I breathed, God was Everywhere, God was my loving Parent in heaven delete period and God was the silent One in the little white Host. That God could also be this personal friendly Power within, well, I'd never heard of such a thing and, evidently, neither had anyone else. People never talked of their experiences of God, instead, it was what they learned from books, the Bible, catechism, prayers and elsewhere. I was vaguely aware of this difference and sincerely looked for someone with whom to share my experiences, to talk about them and know they'd had them too.

I never had a specific name for "what" it was I experienced, my mind could never form a single image and there was nothing in the world I could compare it to. At the same time, however, I knew certain things about it. First and foremost I knew it was not me. It was totally independent of me, had a life of its own, was free to come and go, to expand or retract, I had no say whatsoever. Above all I knew it was powerful, a power unto itself; it was also a small light in myself- sometimes, a very bright light. Because of its continued presence and seeming interest in me, I regarded it as a friendly, good Power. Because it apparently wanted me to learn certain things, it was also a teacher. So although I did not know "what" It was, I actually knew quite a bit about It. At one point, I figured the way other people seemed to know God was from the outside, whereas I knew God from the inside, they were both God, yet different ways of knowing Him. This conviction, however, did not last.

At any rate, following this experience I knew the Power was always there, it went everywhere with me. Thus I looked upon its presence as a "Friend." From time to time I would experience its sudden and expected leap, and always it was something It wanted me to learn. This does not mean. however, I went around thinking about my Friend all the time, but whenever I remembered It, I would close my eyes and ask "Are you there?" and always there came a gentle leap and I'd go on my way, happy knowing it was still there. Sometimes I'd be playing with my friends or going someplace in the car, it could be any place, anytime, when I'd remember my interior Friend and ask, "Are you there?" My habit of asking for this assurance went on for perhaps a year before It evidently got tired of this game and let me know it.

This particular afternoon we were playing kick-the-can. I happened to find one of the best hiding places ever, a place so good, in fact, I was getting tired of waiting to be caught. I had squatted down in the middle of our neighbor's three tall garbage cans. To find me, one would have to look down over the top of the cans. Things got pretty boring down there. After a while I remembered my Friend and asked "Are you there?" but this time there was no response. For a moment I froze with anxiety–my friend was gone! Then I thought perhaps it had not heard me, so I closed my eyes, gazed intently within and urgently asked, "Are You there?" The response I got was rather explosive, like a hard punch in the stomach I was knocked off balance and sent sprawling amid the garbage cans. Hearing the noise of the cans I was immediately caught, but for me, the game was over, I had to go down to the beach and think this over. The Power's blow had been no laughing matter, it had meant business. I took it for a reprimand or warning of some kind.

Sitting on the beach, what I learned was that my Friend had no intention of being at my beck and call. My little game was over. I had no need to ask "Are you there?" because I already knew it was there, I had only to look inside to see It. So after this, I never asked again. Instead, whenever I remembered my Friend I simply looked within—a spot of light in the middle of myself. After a time, however, I realized I didn't even have to look inside to see it; somehow, I knew of its continued Presence without having to look at all. I don't know how I knew this, but I did. (In a way, I think I had a 'feel' for it). At any rate, this incident taught me that the Power could not only engender joy, it could also engender fear and knock me down. This incident instilled in me a respect I did not have before; this Presence was no lark, it meant business—but what business? In the weeks and months that followed I pondered its purpose in my life - why was it there and what did it expect of me?

* * * * * *

Although I was always sneaking cookies and apples to my friends, the nicest thing I ever did for them was say Mass. As far as I knew, none of them ever went to Church. I honestly felt sorry about this and wanted to provide them the opportunity. What may have sparked this decision was the discovery that two of my Philippino friends, Mackey Doodle and his little brother, were Catholic, but never went to Mass. I made a special trip to their home one evening to tell their father he should be taking them to Mass. The father said he was waiting until they were old enough to make their First Communion, and besides, he had to work Sunday mornings. I thought this a pretty lame excuse, but I genuinely felt sorry for the boys; they were eager to come to my Mass.

Any Saturday morning I was home, I held Mass in the upstairs hall at Our Lady's altar. About six or eight kids would be in attendance. None of them guessed all the planning, work and preparation that went into this project. First, a week ahead of time I'd go through the New Testament looking for the easiest passages to read for the Gospel. I paid no attention to the content, but only looked for the easiest thing l could read, which I then practiced reading every day. Next, I studied the progressive pictures of the Mass from my large Children's Mass book, which I propped on the altar in front of me so I'd know what to do next. With the help of mom's stole, crackers and grape juice, a little wine goblet, bell and other things, I became somewhat adept at this performance. I told everyone when to sit, stand or kneel, and permitted no nonsense when my back was turned. Naturally I skipped the sermon. With the exception of Jimmy, my friends had never been to Mass before—which is probably why they were so well behaved. For my part, of course, I thought I was doing them a favor.

On all the week-ends I said Mass there was only a single interruption, which was the time Lee came up the stairs, and seeing what was going on, faked a guilty face, scrunched over to make himself invisible, and tipped toed through our midst to get to his bedroom. I stopped everything to stare at him with a menacing frown until he disappeared into his room. Although he looked positively ridiculous, nobody even tittered. No one knew better than I how rude and disrespectful he could be. That he didn't mess up our Mass was a miracle.

The only problem I ever had was with Jimmy. Since he was the only other Catholic, I had no choice but to let him be the altar boy. After four or five Masses, however, he informed me it was time he took a turn being the Priest, and my turn to be the altar boy. The nerve of him! I couldn't believe my ears! He threatened to quit if I didn't let him. Suddenly I had an idea. I ran to my room and brought out a copy of the New Testament, flipped it open to any page and stuck it under his nose, "If you can read that, you can say Mass." Now I knew Jimmy couldn't read, he wasn't even in the first grade yet. When he admitted he couldn't do it, I snapped the book shut and said, "Nobody can be a Priest unless he can read the Gospels, so when you can do that, let me know and I'll see about it."

Well, Jimmy never came back, but for years I carried the scar he left behind. Not long after my refusal, a bunch of us were playing in an empty lot down the street when, for some reason, Jimmy and I got into a fight, a physical free-for-all. His sole tactic was to get a fist full of my hair and not let go - "dirty fighting" we called it. The hair he pulled out by the roots left a bald spot above my right ear the size of a nickel. Five or six years later, when mom was braiding my hair one morning, she said, "Oh, look, finally some hair is beginning to grow there!"

What brought our Masses to an end, however, was Stanley, my Jewish friend. One day he informed me his mom wouldn't let him come any more.

Me: How come?

Stanley: She said I could only attend my own (Jewish) services.

Me: Well, then you put on your own religious services and we'll all come.

Stanley: But where could I hold services?

Me: In your basement. I'll help you move things around and set it up.

Stanley: But I don't know if my mom will let me.

Me: Go ask her.

(He left and came back almost immediately).

Stanley: Mom said "No."

Me: Why not?

Stanley: She said that unlike your Church, where anybody can conduct services, in our Church only a specially trained person can conduct services.

Me: Well your mother has it wrong. In our Church not just anybody can say Mass, only a Priest can do that.

Stanley: But you do it.

Me: We're only playing. Does your mother honestly think I am saying Mass?

Stanley: You weren't?

As soon as he said this, I thought, "Was I just playing or wasn't I?" Without a doubt I was serious. I sincerely wanted my friends to know the Mass, and I wanted to do it as right as possible. Then came my own unanswerable question: "Where do you draw the line between play and the real thing?" I had to go down to the beach to think about this.

While I never thought I had or even could consecrate the crackers and juice, yet since all the words were right, what if unknowingly I had done so? On the one hand I knew this was impossible, still, I felt I probably should not be doing this—just in case. Had the whole thing been a lark, like our talent shows, maybe it would have been okay. But everyone—including Stanley's mom—took it as serious business, no different than going to a real Mass. Certainly I had no intention of duping anyone into believing something was true or real when it wasn't; on the other hand, I couldn't tell them it was nothing but a hoax! No, I decided that since I could not just play at it, I would never say Mass again. So that was the end of it. After that I wondered why my parents never objected to these goings on, where were they anyway?

Probably they were down in the living room holding their sides. Obviously they knew I was just playing. For my part, however, I never figured out where to draw the line between play and the real thing. It's a problem.

Two summers in a row my parents went to Hawaii and left us in the care of a nurse. We called her 'Aunt Claire' because she was an aunt of Dad's best friend, Bill Atwell. I had just turned six when they went off the first time, which was also the first time I'd been separated from my parents. The day they left, the Atwells drove them to the dock and I was allowed to go along. After visiting their stateroom decked with flowers, fruit and drinks, we toured the boat until it was time to leave. From shore I could see my parents waving at the rail. The orchestra began to play, there was a hail of confetti, deafening blasts from the smoke stack, and the *Lurline* inched away from her dock and moved into the lane headed for the harbor portal. The whole thing had been fascinating and exciting until I started back to the car—without my parents. That's when it hit me: no mom and dad.

The ride home was one of the saddest moments of my life; while Mr. and Mrs. Atwell tried to cheer me up, I couldn't say a word. It was dark out, I pressed my face to the small back window and thought to myself: "If you really love somebody, how can you ever leave them?" Mom and dad said they loved me, yet they left me, what kind of love is that? Who could be happy with that kind of love?" I decided love was just another word like so much hot air. After that I often pondered the nature of love and tended to doubt there was such a thing. Back home with my brother and sisters, however, my spirits lifted–lifted that is, until I encountered a big problem in the person of Aunt Claire. If she thought she was there especially for me–the others being grown–she was mistaken. She promised to make me pancakes the next morning, and I sincerely looked forward to them until I tasted one. It tasted like Clorox or whatever mom used in her washing machine, one bite and that was it. Aunt Claire was hurt, but since I didn't know how mom made her pancakes, I couldn't help her.

Next thing, Nurse Claire wanted to give me a bath–a perfect stranger give me a bath? I wouldn't hear of it. No one but mom and Gert ever bathed me. If they weren't around I'd just wait until they got home. Gert, of course, took on the job–with the nurse out of the bathroom at my insistence. Claire's next mistake was insisting I eat my vegetables, which mom had long given up doing. Things came to a head one night when, with some stinking Brussel sprouts in front of me, she said I'd have to sit at the table until I ate them. I probably sat there three hours before I fell asleep, my head on the table. The next thing I knew, Gert had come home from somewhere, and finding me asleep at the table was very angry. She picked me up and carried me upstairs to bed, stopping on her way past the living room to tell Aunt Claire, in her most authoritative voice, "From now on she's my responsibility!" I felt a warm glow come over me, from now on, I had it made. After that, Aunt Claire was out of my life forever. We never said another word to one another, I hardly knew she was around.

The only problem with this agreeable silence was that before mom left, she told me she had left money for me with Claire, for treats or whatever. So if I wanted anything, I was to ask her. Since I wasn't about to ask

Claire for anything, this left me penniless. Now my friends and I were spending our days at the beach building roads and tunnels in the sand for our miniature cars. I came to an impasse one day when I discovered I could not proceed with my construction without a dump truck and steam shovel, and I needed them right away. Since I could buy them at Miss Hollenbeck's shop on the beachfront, I ran home to ask Gert for the money. To my dismay no one was at home but Aunt Clair, whom I ignored. So I searched under the couch cushions, went through all the draws, but found nothing. Finally I spotted Marge's piggy bank on the kitchen shelf and figured she'd put money in there for future use and wouldn't need it right away. I was confident that when mom got home and realized the terrible mistake she'd made leaving my money with Clair, she'd be only too glad to pay Marge back. This, at least, is how I thought it would go. Since I had watched Marge slide out the .coins with a knife, I was delighted to find I could do it too, and once all the coins were out, I ran to the store and bought my new trucks.

Things went along happily until one day the silence of a quiet afternoon was broken by a blood curdling scream from the kitchen. We all ran to see what had happened. There stood Marge, holding her empty piggy bank, her face purple with rage. Claire and Gert sighed with relief and left the scene, but Lee stuck around to watch the fire. I told Marge right away I had taken the money and that mom would pay her back. But she needed the money now, this instant! She needed it to go to the movies with her friends. She told me to take the trucks down to the shop and get my money back–but they were so caked with mud and sand they were not returnable. Then she told me to sell my bag of beautiful marbles, but alas, the day before Lee had won them from me–by cheating, no less. (He always changed the rules to suit himself). Other than this, we couldn't think of anything I owned we could sell, everything I owned was a hand-me-down anyway. I honestly felt terrible for Marge, had I only known she needed the money I would not have taken it. I desperately wanted her to have it back.

While all this was going on, Lee kept putting in his theological two cents: "You've sinned," "you broke a commandment ... you stole... it's a mortal sin ...you're going to hell for this one!"–things like that. After we had exhausted the possibilities of my giving Marge anything of value to sell, Lee said to me,

Lee: Well, if you can't make restitution, then you'll just have to go to confession. (I had not yet made my first communion, but I had already gone to confession.)

Me: What good will that do? Marge needs the money now!

Lee: But you have to ask for forgiveness.

Me: What good is it if Father forgives me, but Marge doesn't?

Lee: Oh forget her, she may never forgive you as long as she lives, (a prophetic statement) what matters is that God forgives you.

Me: What does God care about fifty cents when he made the whole world?

Lee: But he does care, He said what you do to others you do to Him. He also said "thou shalt not steal."

Me: You're just saying that so I'll stay out of your drawers!

Lee: I didn't say it, God said it!

Me: But how can I offend God when I don't even know him?

Lee: Oh don't give me that! Of course you know Him, everybody knows God, you can't get out of it that easy."

After I blurted out "How can I offend God when I don't know him?" I don't remember anything else that was said because a light went on in my head, which meant I had come upon something true, something I needed to understand. So I left the scene and went off to think about it. In the meantime, Marge borrowed some money and went to the movies. After that, however, Lee periodically warned me of what was going to happen when mom and dad heard about this. I assured him I intended to tell them myself–how else could Marge get her money back? While I never experienced any guilt in the matter, I sincerely felt bad for Marge. After all, I too knew what it was to be penniless.

Sitting by the open window in my room I thought over what I had just learned. First, did I really know God, or did I just know about Him, know what others told me? Despite all my religious practices at home, school and Church, I had to acknowledge I really did not know God. Though I knew He was Everywhere present and that He knew me, yet that didn't mean I knew Him. But unless I really knew Him, how could I know when I was offending Him—or even pleasing Him? Would it always be up to other people to tell me? And who knows, they could be wrong. It made no sense that people—like Lee, for example—could tell me I had offended God when I didn't even know it or feel guilty. I saw no connection between offending my sister and offending Almighty God, surely God was beyond this petty stuff. No, I didn't see how God could be offended by someone who honestly didn't know him or know he had offended Him.

And how was it that everyone around me claimed to know God, even love God, but not me? Something was wrong here, surely I was not still "too little" or not old enough. After some thought, I came upon the only solution I could think of. From now on, every night when I said my prayers I would end with this prayer: "God, I don't know you and I don't feel any love for you, but I hope some day I will know and love you. Please make this possible." I was faithful to this resolution for many years. There was something about being honest with God that always brought satisfaction—and ultimately, results.

A few days later I got to thinking again delete space: if one did not know God, they could live guilt free and never know they had sinned, never know they had offended God. It struck me as odd that once you knew God you also knew sin, but if you didn't know God, then you really didn't know sin. With this thought a big question arose in my mind: "Would you rather know God and know sin, or not know God and not know sin?" With this question I suddenly felt trapped: on the one hand I wanted to know God, but on the other, I did not want to sin. Yet the choice was either I take them both (God and sin) or I take neither (no God and no sin). Having to choose between God or innocence struck me as a horrible, awful choice. But I was on the spot, I had to make a choice.

After thinking over the risk and consequences, I chose to know God and sin. For me, it was a momentous choice. While I could deliberately not want to know sin, I could not deliberately not want to know

God. Definitely I wanted to know God, even though it could mean I might end up without God–for having sinned, that is. Yet I would rather know God and lose heaven than not know God and win heaven because I never chose God. The connection between God and sin I would always find problematic. Down the road I would come up with different ideas, but this, at least, is when the quandary began.

I might add, I was incensed with the idea that the reason Jesus was put to death was because of my sins. How could he have died for my sins when I wasn't even born, hadn't had a chance to sin, and even now, was not a sinner? No, there was no way he could have died for my sins. Even if he knew ahead of time I'd take 50 cents from Marge's piggy back, to think he died over such a thing was ridiculous. The very idea of his dying for anybody's sins made no sense to me. He died because he was human, that's all. The way he died, of course, was terrible. I often wondered why God allowed such a thing.

When the day arrived for my parents to return we all went down to the dock to meet them. When mom spotted us from a distance she held out her arms. I ran toward her and just about reached her when suddenly, from out of nowhere, Lee stepped between us and quickly blurted out, "She stole all Marge's money!" I was so shocked and horrified I do not recall greeting mother. Instead, I chased Lee all over the dock, he had something coming to him and I was a good kicker! When dad finally hugged me, he said, "We'll talk about all that later"–referring to Lee's report of course.

The next day dad told me in no uncertain terms that my intention of returning Marge's money was not the issue. Nor was her being angry or needing the money the issue. The real issue was that I took what was not mine. This was wrong and I must never do it again. Unless I first asked permission, I must never take, use, or borrow anything not my own–did I understand? Yes, I understood.

When I went to mom and asked if she had repaid Marge for the money I took, she said Mom: No, I don't owe her anything. (I was devastated).

Me: But how can I pay her back?

Mom: You should have thought of that before you took it.

Me: But I thought you'd pay her from the money you left for me with Aunt Claire.

Mom: Well you thought wrong.

Me: What happened to that money?

(Mom shrugged her shoulders as if she didn't know).

Me: If Aunt Claire didn't give the money back and took it home, then she stole it from you, because you left it for me.

Mom: I'm sure Claire made good use of it around the house.

Me: But you said it was to be used for me. Can't you call her and ask for it back?

Mom: No!

Me: Well I hope you didn't pay her for taking care of me, because she didn't. Gert took care of me, Aunt Claire never did a thing for me.

Mom was exasperated but adamant. Because her refusal to pay Marge was not like her usual generous self, I was convinced dad told her not to give Marge a dime just to teach me a lesson. I could just hear him saying, "If we pay back the money she may do it again, expecting us to make it up for her." Because I could hardly believe mom's refusal, I periodically asked Marge if mom had secretly repaid or given her **any** money for whatever reason. But Marge always assured me mom never gave her a thing.

I had no intention, however, of giving up. I kept after my mom–did she even have fifty cents? Would she do it as a special favor for me? Why had she told me she left money for me when I never got it? Why didn't she leave it with Gert? I went on and on until finally, several weeks after their return, it was announced I was now old enough to get an allowance every week. Thus if I did chores around the house I could repay Marge with that money. So that settled it as far as my parents were concerned, but it opened a can of worms for me and Marge.

Marge never actually knew how much she had in the bank. Occasionally she'd put in pennies, dimes, a nickel, but kept no total. For my part, though I could count pennies one by one, I couldn't add up coins, didn't know what a dime plus a nickel was worth. After taking the money I had plunked it all down on Miss Hollenbacks' counter and asked for as many little cars as it would buy - I think I got three. Since the cars were ten cents each, I owed Marge thirty cents. But Marge insisted it was no less than 50 cents–some months later she calculated it had been 75 cents, and later, a dollar. This thing went on and on until I was eleven and she announced I owed her 5 years interest as well. By that time, however, we were already fighting over the broken watch she had sold me, but that's another story.

From the beginning, I thought my parents had made a mountain out of a molehill. For fifty cents the issue could have been resolved in a second, but instead, it went on and on, and made for a bit of bad blood. For the next year or so, if dad saw me with something–either new or belonging to others–he'd say, "Is that yours?" or "Did you get permission to take that?" This irked me, he not only wanted to keep the issue alive, but let me know he didn't trust me.

As for Lee, well, on the dock he had been despicable, yet he was the one who brought God into the picture, which at least got me thinking. Making a choice for God was the only good to come from this incident. As for my learning a lesson, the only thing I learned was never to rely on my parents to cover my tracks. I also learned that mom could never be counted on to help me or take my side if it meant countermanding dad's wishes.

* * * * *

My formal piano lessons began when I entered first grade. They were given as part of the school curriculum, not after school or on Saturdays. During the first year, however, I had to stay after school to practice in order to relieve the pile up at home, where we three girls had to get our practice in before dinner. Prior to these formal lessons, however, and thanks to Gert, I knew my way around the piano. Gert would pencil in the notes on a sheet of music so I could play some simple pieces, and occasionally, pieces that were not so simple.

A popular piece at that time was "The Umbrella Man", and at my insistence, Gert had written in all the notes and left me to it. One Saturday, Lee's best friend, Bill, came over to help him with garden chores. During their break, Lee asked me, "Why don't you play "The Umbrella Man" for Bill, he'd like to hear it." I was delighted, nobody else wanted to listen. In fact, if you didn't already know the tune, you probably wouldn't have recognized the music–I was no child prodigy. For me, it was an accomplishment just to make it through to the end of the piece. The two boys sat down behind me on the couch. Shortly into the piece I heard what sounded like snickering or suppressed laughter, but I couldn't believe they were laughing at me, so I went right on. Halfway through, however, there was an explosive outburst, and turning around I saw them slumped back on the couch holding their stomachs, literally crying tears of laughter. They didn't even notice when I jumped off the bench and announced indignantly, "I'll never play anything for you guys again!" and stomped out. Upstairs in my room I could still hear them laughing, so I turned on the radio to drown them out.

It was probably for the best that at my first music lesson with Sr. Cecelia, after proudly playing her some of my easier pieces, she abruptly dismissed them out of hand. There would be no pieces until I had mastered the eight scales and their accompanying major and minor chords and, with both hands, could do two octaves of scales with relative facility. This was a big order for little hands, but it was a challenge, and basically a good beginning. At that time the Order of Holy Name Sisters were renowned for their music instruction–they conducted a well-known College of Music in Northern California. Had I been able to stay with them, I'm convinced I might have done something in the field of music, which was a big part of my life–a big part of our family life.

By this time Gert (now sixteen) was not only a skilled pianist, but played the organ at Church. Mom always regretted Gert didn't take harp lessons as well, but it seems the only teacher was in downtown Los Angeles and not very convenient. Oddly enough, though Gert was the most musically talented in the family, she was the only one who couldn't carry a tune. For flawless sight reading, however, few people in the world could beat mom. Sight unseen, she could open to the most difficult classical piece–be it in 6 flats, 5 sharps, any key–and play it through without hesitation. I always wished I'd had that ability.

The day I discovered classical music was an important event in my life. Listening to the Lone Ranger one evening, I discovered I did not hear what was said because I was listening instead to the music. Without the music, the words and story were nothing. I went in search for more music like this and became an avid listener for life. My first discovery about listening was the absence of thought and the presence of some mysterious feelings, an automatic uplifting, a striving upward for some unreachable mystery, a longing for a glorious fulfillment that forever eluded me. Then again, I would feel the music had so inundated my whole being that I was part and parcel of the music itself I thought of music as the true nature of my soul, and like contact with nature, I needed it to survive. Just hearing the briefest excerpt and something in me automatically switch modes– from the mundane to the exalted, profane to the sacred, I wouldn't know how to put it. Following my initial introduction I lost all taste for popular music, could hardly tolerate it because it went against the very grain of my soul.

I did not need classical music, however, to come upon a blank mind. Even without listening to music I discovered I could go blank anytime I wanted. The choice to think or not to think, the ability to tune out anywhere, anytime, I regarded as my "mental secret." In these early years I came to recognize that all paths of knowledge invariably led to a blank wall in my mind, a wall beyond which I could not go. Thus whenever I tried to concentrate, especially on something abstract, my mind automatically drifted toward this wall. So whether I was listening to music, sitting by the sea, or trying to think about God, my mind would drift toward this wall and on touching it, there ensued a natural, mental silence. Though I was continually trying to get around this wall, penetrate it or at least understand it, my efforts only seemed to increase its thickness, resistance, impenetrability. Thus there was no idea, train of thought or mental image I could retain for long, before it bumped into this wall and dissolved into a pervasive silence, a blank mind.

I was certain that beyond this wall lay all the answers. There might even lie a different mind, a mind for which there were no mysteries. Coming up against this wall, however, always reminded me of my ignorance and incapacity. It seemed to limit, confine and restrict me because it locked me out of some knowledge or understanding I dearly wanted to have. At times the wall was even frightening, for I thought it was stunting my mental growth and intellectual development. For sure, this wall was a mystery, but one I just had to learn to live with–though not all my life.

* * * * * *

After mom and dad got back from their summer trip, we took the boat several times to Catalina Island. Out at sea my special place on board was sitting at the bow of the boat, bare feet dangling over the side. Surrounded by the open sea and sky, the sense of freedom and expansiveness was my idea of happiness. On one of our crossings to Catalina, instead of sitting at the bow, I lay on the deck, hands tucked under my head, gazing at the sky, my body in tune with the rhythmic roll of the sea. After a while it felt as if body and soul had dissolved into some ethereal weightless medium, a state of utter contentment and quiet joy. In this stillness the externals of life disappeared and left I don't know what–I could have been a little cork or piece of seaweed bobbing aimlessly and happily in a vast sea. Floating in this lightsome medium I could have been anything, yet the joy, peace and contentment was completely fulfilling. There was nothing wanting, I could have lived this way forever.

This experience lasted some time when suddenly, I heard my name called, and a hand with a hotdog was thrust out the porthole next to me. It was a rude awakening. Once more confronted with mundane existence, the world now seemed harsh and crude by comparison; ordinary life, contrived and unnatural. It was as if I had suddenly been pulled from a heavenly state and dropped into a crude world; it took some time to reorient myself. This experience was an eye-opener. Now I knew there was another dimension of life, a dimension so close you had only to sink into it. I knew, however, it would be impossible to live in this state and in the world at the same time, for despite their closeness, one precluded the other; in a way, they were worlds apart. I determined, however, to seek it out, do whatever I could to have the experience again.

To this end I put myself into situations conducive to having the experience–lying in the same spot on the boat, floating alone on the sea, lying silently on the beach, under a tree in the woods–I often spent hours waiting for the experience, yet no matter how I disposed myself to receive it, I could never make it happen. It seems that sinking into this dimension was something that could only be done to me, because on my own, I couldn't recapture it. Though I would have this experience a number of times, it always came as a surprise, out of the blue, always a gift. These later experiences, however, were never like the first; they were neither as prolonged nor as delightful. Also, instead of dissolving into some mysterious medium, I only seemed to become part of the scenery. I was convinced this was the delightful, contented, mysterious state in which all nature lived–rock, tree, ocean, everything. This is what they experienced, this is how they lived. Thus floating alone on the sea or lying under a tree, I was just part of the scenery, no more, no less.

Altogether this experience was a huge awakening, its relevance in my life was knowing this other dimension existed. Always it was before me as another possibility of life, a whole different existence. I was now on to a reality not of this world, yet somehow in this world. In this dimension it didn't matter who you were or what you were, simple existence was everything. The mystery, of course, was the true nature of its delightful "medium"–"what" was it I had dissolved into–air, space, or what? I was convinced this dimension somehow underlay all creation, and that only human beings lived in the harsh world of practical living–"reality", as it is called.

I was always struck by the difference between this experience and others I'd had–and would have. This experience dropped me into a dimension that had nothing to do with me or this world. It was totally impersonal–no me, no God, no world–instead, there was only a buoyant feeling of joy and utter contentment. By contrast, my other experiences involved myself and were totally in this world, the here and now. There would come a time, however, when floating impersonally in a mysterious sea of existence was no longer satisfying. As pleasant and mysterious as it was, the human dimension was wholly missing. By the time I realized this, however, I had already come upon something greater, a state or dimension neither in nor of this world, and having come upon something better, I would never again seek what was lesser.

AGES 7 &8

Two weeks before my seventh birthday I made my first Holy Communion. Though well prepared in school, mom and dad went out of their way to prepare me and plan a memorable day. I had read stories of this day in the lives of pious children and fully expected it to be a wonderful experience. I took for granted I'd be aware of God's special presence. In class we had been told that right after receiving communion, whatever we asked for–our deepest, dearest wish known only to God–it would be granted. I thought a long time about this and decided the only thing I really needed and wanted was to know God, and secondly, never to offend Him, so I asked for this.

When the great day came, however, I was a little disappointed that I experienced nothing at all–and was thankful nobody asked me if I did. But if the day was not memorable on that account, it was a genuine turning point in my life. Having attended Mass from birth–and not just on Sundays–and having been excluded from communion for seven long years, to finally be included as an adult and participate in the services, not only gave me a sense of being grown up, it was also the beginning of taking my faith seriously. Going to Mass I now had something to look forward to. For me, receiving communion would always be the center of Mass, so much so, if I could not have received communion I didn't see the point of going at all. After my first communion I wanted to go to Mass every day, so dad, instead of attending daily Mass downtown at the Old Plaza, as he usually did, took me to St. Clements every morning until school was out for the summer. ("Old Plaza" was our name for the founding California Mission in Los Angeles, otherwise known as Our Lady of the Angels Church).

One morning, because dad couldn't take me, I walked to Mass by myself. Across from Church was a low unmarked building from which I heard voices singing, but singing in a way I'd never heard before. It was so beautiful I sat on the steps to listen. After a bit, I grew curious and quietly tried the front door, but it was locked. I walked around to the side of the building, and discovering some opaque windows, climbed up on a ledge and put my nose to the window. In an otherwise bare room, I saw two lines of men facing one another, each holding a book, all of them dressed in black with white beanies and long fringed shawls. At the head of the two lines was a man with a book-stand in front of him. This unusual sight, along with the sound of their uplifting voices, impressed me deeply. Somehow I knew it was a religious service of some kind, but who were these men and what were they singing?

After inquiring around, someone identified the building as a Jewish Synagogue, and later I learned the singing was called "chanting." The next Sunday at Mass, singing our usual hymns, I was struck by the disparity between our Church hymns and the music I'd heard at the Synagogue. Our hymns had never uplifted me while the music across the street had swept me up by its sound alone. Prior to this I'd made no judgement about our Church music, but now I regarded it as impoverished and took a dislike to the hymns we had to sing. I dearly wished we could sing like they did in the Synagogue. As close as we ever got, however, was the occasional chanting of the Litany of the Saints. Later on, however, when I learned the Latin hymns and Masses, I came upon the only music in Church that uplifted my heart and soul to God.

Long before I was born, dad had signed up at the Old Plaza Church for an hour of adoration every third Thursday of the month from 2 to 3 A.M. I often heard him getting up in the middle of the night to drive downtown for his hour of adoration, and several times had asked to go with him. He said that after I made my First Communion I could go, so now I reminded him of his promise and he was good for it.

By this time I had already visited the Old Plaza many times. We not only went there for services and fiestas, but to visit the Claretian Priests who ran it, dad was not only a personal friend, but also their attorney. This old Spanish Church was the warmest, most homey Church I'd ever been in. Its dark interior was lit by candles and its statues of Christ, Mary and the saints, were dressed in real clothes. Equally noticeable was the devotion of the people coming and going to visit the Blessed Sacrament, some even approaching the altar on their knees. One had a sense this was not just the house of the Lord, but a house of the people as well. To the right of the main altar was a side chapel where there was Perpetual Adoration, or where the Eucharist was exposed in a monstrance year round. People signed up to watch an hour with Christ at various times of the day, weeks, and months of the year.

As dad promised, when the next third Thursday rolled around, he woke me from a sound sleep and we made the 45 minute drive through the dark empty streets. There was only one person in the chapel when we arrived, but shortly he left and we were alone. The altar was a blaze of candles and flowers, the radiant gold spikes of the large monstrance shimmered in the light, it was a beautiful, intimate setting. For a long time I knelt there just taking it all in. Though I had brought my rosary and prayer book, I never used them, but was utterly content to just sit, stare at the Eucharist, and listen to the silence. When receiving communion I had never experienced a thing, but here, focusing on the Eucharist, seeing It, I had a strong sense of God's presence. It came about imperceptibly, a kind of magnetic radiance that seemed to stream from the monstrance, spread throughout the chapel and even beyond. I could only sit there and marvel at it. I was sure if others had been present they would have experienced this powerful Presence as well. To verify this, on the way home I asked dad about this awesome phenomena, "Didn't you feel God's special Presence there?" "Of course," he answered casually. His matter of fact answer surprised me. To him it was nothing special, obviously he experienced that radiant Presence every time he went. Though I would return many times to this same setting, and always enjoyed it, I never again experienced that radiant Presence. Evidently dad had something going for him that I didn't.

Prior to this time I had no devotion to the Blessed Sacrament–or anything else for that matter. While I felt a special attraction to Mary and enjoyed saying the rosary, that's as far as it went. From this time forward, however, I had an affinity, almost a magnetic attraction to the Eucharist, one that would last a life time. This was no sentimental devotion, for me the Eucharist was indeed God's presence. In time I would come to know It as the divine, glorified Christ who had come again to be with us, only this time, not as the human man Jesus–who lived hundreds of years ago–but as the Christ Who is with us today. To me, the difference between the Eucharist and Jesus of the Gospels was the difference between the sacred and the profane, and why I thought this, or how I came by this division, stems from an incident that occurred about this same time.

Both at home and at school the name "Jesus" was rarely used, always it was "Christ." The name "Jesus" would never be familiar to my ears, never a term I used mentally or verbally. The only time "Jesus" was used was in sentimental hymns and prayers–like "Sweet Jesus", "Gentle Jesus", "Heart of Jesus", and so on. I had heard nothing but lovable things about this man, his special love for children, kindness to the sick, cures and miracles. In short, I knew the story of a lovable, gentle man who, for some mysterious reason, was hated enough to be crucified for doing absolutely nothing. Altogether, the impression was that of a mild mannered, kind person who loved everyone and wanted everyone to love one another. Despite all I had been taught in these early years, however, I never had any special feelings for him, 1 simply took him for granted without a thought. One Sunday, however, all this changed.

The Gospel that day depicted an angry Christ, whip in hand, throwing over tables and driving people out of the temple. I don't know if it was the violent scene itself or Fr. Patrick's dramatic reading–and his own frightening temperament–but I said to myself, "Sweet Jesus nothing!" Instantly, all those images of a gentle loving man went out the window. Given this frightening scene I realized I had been duped, never been given the truth about this man Jesus, never knew what he was really like. Since I obviously hadn't gotten it from others, I decided to read his life for myself. So then and there I determined as soon as I got home to read the four Gospels front to back. It was important to know the truth for myself

My brother and sisters had their own copies of the New Testament, so I took out Gert's, sat down in her quiet room and began to read. I didn't read the Gospels for the story line, which I knew already, but to focus on the kind of person he was–his temperament, character or personality–and form my own impression of him. I didn't have time to read the Gospels all at once, so during the week I read whenever I had time. In all, it took a week to finish.

The impression that emerged was of a powerful, dominating, demanding person who spent most his time arguing with the Pharisees and others either to prove or defend himself He didn't hesitate to put others down, call them names, and even condemned those who didn't believe him–literally threatened them with hell and damnation. In his reaction to others he said some frightening and insulting things. Without question, he was a tough minded, no nonsense, forbidding human being. No, I didn't care for him at all, and was glad I'd never known him or lived when he did. I would have keep my distance and never followed him. Though I had never experienced any sentiment for him anyway, now I was sure that all such sentiment was unwarranted and based on a false image of the man. It made me angry to think such a false image had been hoisted on me when none of it was true. Though I realized the man had not been a bad person and done some good things, yet he held no attraction for me. Altogether I found him frightening, even felt a certain aversion toward him.

When I was done reading, sitting with the closed book on my lap, while I had to admit I did not honestly like this man Jesus, I also felt caught in a bind. After all, everybody else seemed to love him. He was the center of my religion, so how come I didn't like him? What could he ever mean to me?   I couldn't think of a thing, my mind was a blank. Then suddenly the words popped into my head, "He's dead!", and with that, it felt like some burden had been lifted–a burden I never even knew I had. Instantly my negative view and feelings vanished. "Of course! Why hadn't I remembered that?" This man lived hundreds of years ago, he wasn't around anymore, he was in heaven now and totally changed–transfigured! Realizing the man in the stories was gone, resolved my dilemma. It didn't matter if I liked or disliked this figure of ancient history, it was irrelevant because I'd never have to deal with him anyway. I felt good about this. As far as I was concerned, the man Jesus was history, gone forever. Thus the kind of person he was didn't matter, it would never be a problem for me. From then on, I would always associate the word "Jesus" with sentimentality. All those sweet Jesus hymns, prayers and pictures, I now regarded as totally false. Any time I so much as heard or read anything sentimental, a switch turned off in me. I never developed a tolerance for the false image they portrayed.

I do not recall any particular time, age or moment when I learned the Eucharist (consecrated bread or host) was the living Christ, present with us here and now. I simply grew up with this belief   At this point, however, it dawned on me that the Eucharist was not, in fact, the historical man Jesus, the same as portrayed in the Gospels. Rather, the Eucharist is Christ now in heaven, or how he is right **now.** In the Eucharist there was no personality, no words, images or actions, there was just his silent mystery, a mystery that was the true Christ, the heavenly Christ, of this I would never have a doubt. At the time, however, I could not have realized the impact of this spontaneous conviction. That the Eucharist was the heavenly Christ was a reality that grew with me, became central to my life. So much so, that without the Eucharist I could never have been a Christian since the historical personality of the man Jesus played no part in my life.

Raised in a home where religious beliefs and practices were part and parcel of everyday life, in my early years I had taken much of it for granted or unquestioningly, but starting now (at seven) I can't think of a single thing regarding my beliefs, practices and religion, I did not question. I must have been born a skeptic because I questioned everything, if not aloud, at least in my own mind. I also spent a lot of time reading articles in the Catholic Encyclopedia (1917 edition) in search of answers and understanding. Trying to get it all together, make sense of the whole thing, would be the on-going challenge of my life. I never encountered anything so continuously challenging in my life as my Christian Faith. Without this challenge, it simply would not have been my life.

Ironically, though I did not like the man Jesus, I nevertheless continued to nod my head every time I heard the word "Jesus"–which we had been taught to do in school. Sometimes, when I knew his name was coming up, I'd try not to nod my head, but the autonomous habit had already stuck. There were other habits learned in school that also stuck. Thus every time we heard a siren in the distance, be it an ambulance or fire truck, the whole class stopped to say a silent prayer for whoever was injured, sick or in danger. This habit too, remained all my life. Something else we learned was a panoply of "ejaculations", short one line prayers, like "Jesus have mercy on me", etc. and a lot of these stuck. Needless to say, we picked up a lot of images, ideas and perspectives that tended to stick around even after we knew they might be flawed or even erroneous. Altogether, as a little one I picked up a lot of autonomous religious habits, knee-jerk reactions to things and events in life that later were not easy to overcome.   So too, after reading the Gospels for myself, the impressions I got of the man Jesus stuck with me forever. I never took on the images or feelings for him that other people seemed to display, and the fact I knew this, gave me a sense of being secretly different, not wholly one of the bunch.

* * * * *

One of dad's Jesuit friends, Fr. Lewis, had a spinster sister, Grace, who came to our home one afternoon for tea. I had never met her before, and was curious about mom's special preparations for the event. Though mom never had afternoon tea, she dressed me up, set out her best silver, baked her fanciest goodies, altogether put on a beautiful tea party for Grace. My parents had known Grace for some time, dad took care of her estate concerns; at the time I met her, she was going on 50. By any standard, Grace was an unforgettable character. She lived and talked with a flamboyant flair, was an animated none-stop talker with a deep, booming voice; she also spoke with a sophisticated dialect–possibly a combination of Bostonian British, or whatever. She was a large, tall woman, who wore flowing clothes and big brimmed hats with feathers and flowers. Besides a commanding presence, she was also quite rich, had been raised in luxury, traveled the world and lived in Europe where she mingled with the elite, even royalty. This day, when I first met her, I was both fascinated and suspicious. I thought there was something phony about her, that she put on airs and wanted to impress others. In time, however, I realized Grace was Grace, born to be the person she was, and that her demeanor merely reflected the social circle she had always moved in. Actually, Grace was a gracious lady, very devout and charitable, in short, a good woman.

At one point, after sipping her tea, Grace reached into her purse, took out a book and handed it to me. It was a picture-book of the life of St. Therese of Lisieux, the Little Flower, photographs of drawings made by Therese's sister, Celine. Grace made it sound as if the book was one of her most cherished possessions and said she hoped it would be as meaningful to me as it had been to her. While I was already well acquainted with story of Lourdes and St. Bernadette, I knew nothing of St. Therese and welcomed a book on my patron saint. I was fascinated by Therese's sweet and pious life, even though I could not relate to it. The next time Grace came for tea, she gave me a copy of St. Therese's autobiography, *The Story of a Soul,* which I read with interest. Needless to say, I could not identify with her family life or pious sentiments for Jesus, much less her own sweet and loving disposition. But I was interested in the monastic life she and her sisters had embraced. To find out more about this I went to the Catholic Encyclopedia. Since I had been through the disappointment of learning Carthusians were only for men, I wanted to find out if there was a comparable monastic life for women. Initially I made the mistake of looking under "Carmelite", but later, looking under "Discalced Carmelite" I found this was also an eremitical Order that, like the Carthusians, lived a solitary life of contemplation—an Order founded by a woman no less.

About six months later dad informed mom that Grace was going to become a Discalced Carmelite Nun—enter a monastery. Mom couldn't imagine it. Grace, born in luxury, joining one of the most austere Orders in the Church? "Why she's never even made her own bed!" mom exclaimed. Dad laughed, "But can you imagine her keeping their rule of silence?" Evidently my parents got a kick out of imagining Grace trying to adapt to such a life. Finally mom said, "I'll give her two months!" But dad replied, "You never know, if God has given her a true vocation, she'll get the grace." And indeed, Grace not only got the grace, but one day became superior of her community. Although, given her background, Grace would always regard her cloistered life as austere and sacrificial, yet, had it been easy, there would have been no heroics, and Grace thrived on that. In the coming years there would be talk of Grace's monastic life. As her attorney, dad had occasions to visit her and would come home with stories about her life, what she found hard, humorous or delightful. So between St. Therese and Grace I learned something about the monastic life, which, till then, I had only read about in the Encyclopedia.

* * * * * *

One summer evening at dinner, dad asked us kids what we would like to be when we were older. After everyone took their turn stating their ambitions, it was my turn, "I want to be a sailor when I grow up, I've known it all my life!" Everybody laughed. Lee said, "But girls can't be sailors!" What a shock! In the pit of my stomach it felt like a rug had been pulled out from under me, suddenly I had no future, nothing to do with my life, what would I be? I felt lost, also betrayed, somehow the sea had given me the wrong message. I was sure my attraction to it meant I was never to leave it, always live by it, or on it. Indeed, it was only because I loved the sea so much I wanted to be a sailor. I decided that after dinner I'd go down to the beach and see about this, figure out what had gone wrong.

Standing on the shore looking out to sea, I pleaded with it to give me some answers: what should I do with my life? What would I become? I asked, "What is it about you I love so much?" No sooner were my questions out then there came a swift rush or leap from within and a brilliant ball of light stood before my eyes–about a foot above my forehead–a light so brilliant I couldn't look at it directly. It identified itself as "love"–the word imprinted on my mind. Somehow I knew this ball of fire was the love I experienced for the sea, "It" was my connection to the sea, and "It" would be my life, my future. After that, it vanished. I looked inside to see if my Friend was still there because, initially, I thought it had leaped out of me and was Itself the brilliant Light. But no, when I looked within, It was there as usual, seemed not to have moved at all. I could not think about what I saw, I could only express my stunned reaction by running down the beach with everything in me crying out, "I love you, I love you!" I ran clear to the Ocean Park pier before dropping from sheer exhaustion.

Lying there, I tried to think about what I had seen and learned, but there was only a blank mind.

This experience was never far from my thoughts. Its mystery engendered many questions. While I could never put my finger on exactly "what" it was I loved, I knew it was both the mystery in the sea and the mystery in me, they were the same. Whenever I thought of the blinding ball of light, I wondered whence it came. While I felt the inner leap at the same instant I saw the ball of light, yet they were so different it was not possible to say one was the other. Had the Power actually leaped out and stood before me? Or was its leap a reaction to the brilliant light that suddenly appeared? Could the Power and Light be the same, or was the Light something else entirely? Was the only difference, perhaps, the Power's presence on the inside and how it might look on the outside? I also wondered if the coming together of the two–the mystery in the sea and the Power in me–had sparked the Light itself. Since I didn't know the answers I had to let it be. But of one thing I was certain: this Light would be the focus of my life, the love of my life, the connecting link between me, the sea, the Power within–everything.

I did not know what to do with this new knowledge. Always I was trying to fit my various experiences together: first, the Presence in the sea; then seeing God Everywhere; the indwelling Power, and now the brilliant Light, these were some of the pieces, yet my mind could not encompass them individually, much less put them together. To know the truth of them, however, became a driving force in my life. Nothing mattered so much as knowing and understanding my own experiences or "what", exactly, I experienced. In the immediacy of an experience I never doubted it was. God, either as cause or the experience itself; and yet the God I knew about didn't match any of my experiences. Besides, there is only One God, and my experiences were all so different, how could they all be God? Maybe one of my experiences was God, but certainly not all of them! Perhaps more than anything, it was the variety of different experiences that precluded any lasting certitude; no sooner would I be convinced I knew, then a different experience would come up. Perhaps if I'd known the Truth all along, my life would have been different, but since I didn't know; the search for Truth was an unavoidable life imperative. To know the truth of my experiences, the truth of God, the truth of myself, the truth of my beliefs and everything I learned, this is all I wanted to know, needed to know. (By age 10, for me, at least, the term "Truth" was synonymous with the word "God").

* * * * * *

For a number of summers, Marge attended Camp Teresita Pines, a Catholic camp located near Wrightwood in the Sierra Madre mountains. Marge was in her element at camp, the times she spent there were the happiest of her life. For some reason, mom thought I would also enjoy camp, but in this she sadly miscalculated. I wasn't there an hour before I came down with a terrible case of homesickness and carried on something awful, crying, demanding to go home **now.** In general, made everyone miserable. I had been away from my parents before, their summer trips to Hawaii, so perhaps I just missed being at home. By sheer luck; the next day Moony's parents came to visit her in camp. Moony was Marge's best friend who lived down the street from us. They called home and got permission to bring me home with them. When I got there, however, mom was obviously not happy to see me, she didn't greet me or even smile. For a moment this surprised me, it was not like her. But I was so relieved from feeling homesick, nothing could dampen my happiness at being home again. Immediately I took off for the beach. Later, after Marge came home from camp, the family took off for Catalina.

A major setback in my life occurred toward the end of the third grade, just after my seventh birthday. What precipitated this unhappy event was the day Fr. Patrick Pierce—our parish's Irish pastor—made one of his unexpected visits to our classroom. It was his habit to go around the school and barge into classrooms unannounced, any time, any day. I think it was in the middle of spelling when the door burst open and in comes Fr. Patrick, his long black cassock flapping behind him, looking like the devil himself Instantly he threw out his long black arm to point at some startled, unsuspecting child, which, this time, happened to be me. In a commanding voiced he roared, "You, the Roberts girl, where is your soul?" Now just the presence of this man was enough to make my mind go blank, but his question!? I couldn't even begin to think about it.

Though I dutifully stood up to answer, I didn't have an answer. For a second I glanced out the window from which I could see the ocean, and the image arose of my running down the beach crying "I love you", when suddenly Father shouted, "Well, where is it? Is it in your elbow?" The class tittered. Instantly I thought, Oh, he wants to know where in my body the soul is. Well, it would have to be in the center of myself, the same place where I experienced my interior Friend and with that in mind, I put my hand firmly over my navel area. Father shouted, "It's in your stomach?" Everyone laughed aloud. In utter disgust he hollered, "Sit down!" Then he called on a boy in the back of the class who stood up and gave the catechism answer: "A soul is a spirit that cannot be seen with bodily eyes." Instantly I knew this was wrong, the boy had answered the catechism question "What is a soul?", but Father had asked "Where is the soul?" For a moment Father paused, I was sure he'd caught his own mistaken question. But without another word he turned, motioned sister to follow him, and swept out the door. I was upset because I had not been allowed to defend myself by pointing out the difference between **what** something is and **where** something is. I decided to tell dad about this when he, got home that night

After school I walked home along the shore, wondering why Father's question had reminded me of my experience on the beach. After a bit it dawned on me, this Power or wonderful thing that resided in me, for sure, this was my soul! That's it! The mystery was solved, this Power within was my soul, everything else was merely my body. So my Friend had taught me correctly: namely, that only "it" mattered, and everything else outside of it counted for nothing. For a while I was at peace with this answer, but it didn't last. Without question, I knew that I myself was my own soul, it was because of my soul I could think and act independently, , do as I wished , yet I had absolutely no say over the Power within, While this Power might be inside my soul, it was **not** me, was not my soul. This Power was far greater than myself, it was beyond my control, a Power unto itself. But if it was not me and not God, what was it? Again I was back to square one. The interior Power did not accord with, anything I ever heard or learned of God; that God could be so close, so utterly obvious and totally known to me, and a constant teacher? No, I'd never heard of such a thing, God was beyond us. Though He knew our most secret thoughts, words and deeds, yet He was not so evident or conspicuous as the Power within. The most satisfying conclusion I could come up with was this: although the Power was not God Himself, it was nevertheless God's way of letting me know Him, of communicating with me, of teaching me. This conclusion I found satisfying–for a while at least.

That night I told dad what happened in the classroom and complained how unfair the question had been–Father's asking "where" instead of "what."

Dad: Well, you should have known that if what the soul is, is a spirit, something you can't see, then of course you can't point to where it is–you can't point to something you can't see!

Me: But since we always say the soul is **in** the body, then why can't we point inside the body? If it's not in the body, then where is it?"

Dad: Strictly speaking the soul is not inside the body. As the life of the body, it is everywhere in us, you can't point to any part of the body where the soul is not, or point to any part of the body and say where the soul is.

Me: But when we die the soul leaves the body, comes out of it, so if it can come out of the body when we die, it must be inside when we're alive.

Dad: To say the soul is **in** the body is just a way of speaking. Actually it's neither inside nor outside the body. We really don't understand how something physical like the body can be united to something non-physical like the soul. The soul is actually a mystery.

Me: So if it's not inside or outside, then it's no place?

Dad: Well it's no place you can point to. So the next time anybody asks you where your soul is, don't point anywhere.

Me: Then what should I answer–"I don't know"?

Dad: No. You should tell them the soul is a spirit that can't been seen with bodily eyes, that's the only answer that satisfies the question.

This was the end of the conversation. I got the point, yet was never satisfied that "what" answers the question "where"?   After this I was always careful to differentiate terms like "when, what, where, how" and so on—one cannot be cavalier with words! For the rest of my life this incident made me hyper-sensitive to word usage. Of course I would always think it was Fr. Patrick who blundered. Either he forgot his catechism (which asks **what** is a soul?), or else he deliberately asked a stupid question he knew had no answer–like **where** is your soul?

Not long after this incident we took our final exams for the year. Because we were finished by noon, we were allowed to go home early. When I got home mom told me sister had already informed her the school intended to keep me back a year–I would have to repeat the third grade!. I was incredulous, "You mean I didn't pass? I failed?" Mom said the only reason given was that I was a year younger than the rest of the class and they thought it best if I was in with my own age group. Immediately I rushed back to school to find out if I passed or not. Sister was alone in the classroom. She had just finished correcting our exams which were stacked on her desk in descending order from highest to lowest. I asked,

Me"   Did I pass?

Sr.:   Yes.

Me: Can I see my exams?

She pulled my papers from the middle of the stack. With the exception of reading, where I scored high, the other scores were average, neither high nor low. In other words, I rated in the middle of my class.

Me: If I passed, then why are you keeping me back?

Sr.:   Just being able to do the work and pass tests is not the only important thing in life.

Me: What do you mean?

Sr.: Your social maturity, fitting in with one's age group is just as important.

Me: How don't I fit in?

Sr.: We just think you'd fit in better with your own age group.

Me: But I don't know a single second grader, so how would I be better off in that group?

Sr.: Just think, you might be at the head of your class next year.

Me: My best friends are in this class, we've been together since first grade.

Sr.: You can still play with your friends, it's in your schoolwork you'd be ahead.

Me: I'd rather pass with a C and be with my friends than be head of a class I don't know, and repeat stuff I already know.

Sr.: You don't seem to understand and I'm not going to argue with you. I talked to the principal and she has agreed, so that's that.

Me: But it's not fair! If they are so concerned about my age, why didn't they keep me back last year instead?

Sr.: Please leave now, I have to go in a few minutes.

Right then and there I checked all Sisters off my list of authentic human beings—forever. Somehow I knew sister was obeying an order from Fr. Patrick, otherwise, based on my class work, my tests and social adjustment, there was no reason in the world to keep me back. That she had to obey an unfair, unjust and unreasonable superior or Pastor, was wrong and gutless of her. Sisters were nothing but puppets who cowtowed to authority and never dared stand on their own. If something was unjust or plain wrong, they wouldn't say a word, wouldn't lift a finger. What is more, they all put on similar faces to the public, which wasn't their true face at all. Because they were expected to be a certain way, their conformity made them all alike, there was something the matter with the whole Sister business. I never trusted any of them again, and never made a single friend among them.

Having to repeat a grade was a double blow in that I never knew the reason for it. To my mind it was forever unjust and unwarranted. Had I not been up with my class, perhaps I would have felt differently, but as it was, it left a scar that rankled me for years to come. When I pieced things together, I concluded that the sisters had always resented dad's insistence on taking me a year early. More recently, there had been some behind the scenes fuss about my not being old enough to make my First Communion with the class. There had been talk about the Pope's changing the required age and definition of the "use of reason." Dad made a special trip to talk to Fr. Patrick about this—dad insisting I be allowed to make my communion—so maybe there had been an argument, some bad feelings, I don't know. At any rate, it was always my opinion that his picking me out of the class that day was to see if he could justify my immaturity. Obviously, he had been satisfied.

Every year after school was out some of the sisters were transferred to other schools. Parents were invited to say their good byes in the auditorium after Sunday Mass. Since mom had known some of the sisters for years, she went to say good-bye while I played outside. When I came inside to see if she was ready to leave, suddenly mom appeared with my teacher in tow. Sister dutifully put her hand out for a good-bye shake, but I stood motionless and gave her the meanest, most insolent look I knew how, and walked away. After that I avoided all sisters whenever possible, I even changed my opinion of Sr. Cecelia, my piano teacher; where I had regarded her as an exceptionally talented, patient, good teacher, I now saw has an unsmiling, uncaring old spinster. Some prejudices die hard, but my dislike of Sisters never died at all—never.

Several years later, when Marge announced she would like to be a Maryknoll sister, I was fit to be tied. What had impressed her at that time—in fact, impressed the whole family—was our acquaintance with the life and work of Fr. Damian who had worked with lepers on the island of Molokai in Hawaii. At one point the Maryknoll sisters had joined him there, and it was through the Maryknoll priests, friends of dad's (who was also their attorney) we came to know all about Fr. Damien. On one occasion a Definitor General from Rome was passing through town on his way to Hawaii to collect data for Damian's possible canonization. He not only came to our home for dinner, but brought various relics of Fr. Damian–pieces of his clothing, splinters from his coffin, rosary and other items. We were all impressed with this saintly leper, and Marge especially. A life dedicated to working with lepers appealed to her. Once there was even talk of the whole family escorting Marge to the Maryknoll Novitiate at Terrytown on the Hudson River. That my sister might become one of "them" (a sister) was the worst thing I could think of. Since she was still in high school, however, there was always time to change her mind and I waited for this like a cat for a mouse. Every so often I'd ask her if she still wanted to join the Maryknoll Sisters, and when she said "Yes", I'd feel as sad as if she were about to die. Once, after several months had gone by and I had not heard any talk of her going, lying in bed one night I had to break the silence, "Marge–hey Marge! Do you still want to be a Maryknoll sister?" Half asleep she replied groggily, "I don't know." That's all I needed to hear. Immediately I jumped out of bed, burst into my parents' room to wake them up with the happy news, "Marge doesn't want to be a Maryknoll sister anymore!" After a few moments of silence, dad said rather grouchily, "Fine, just go back to bed!" I always liked to think I had something to do with Marge's change of mind, all my ranting against those ogres finally paid off. I didn't care what she did with her life so long as she didn't become one of "them." Whenever dad talked to us about the privileged grace of a religious vocation I shuddered with revulsion. Better, I thought, to die first.

* * * * * *

Sometime later, alone in Gert's room one day, I again experienced a sudden, powerful infusion of the interior Power. Though similar to the first experience–several years earlier–this time I had no impression of physically expanding. Instead, only the Power expanded, and to such an overwhelming extent, it seemed on the verge of taking me over completely. I froze with fear. Where earlier I had been afraid I'd bust–disappear or be no more–this time I was faced with the immediate prospect of the Power wholly possessing me, taking me over. If this happened, I'd be nothing but a shell, a mere appearance, a puppet with this Power running the show and leaving me with no mind or will of my own–and who knows what it might do in me? It would have been like being buried alive fully conscious of the fact I was being used, ignored, and utterly helpless; such a life would be a living hell. Without a doubt, this imminent threat was the most frightening moment of my life, there is no fear like it.

In these moments of suspense I could only wait in horror: would it take me over or not? To do so would have taken the smallest expansion of this Power and I'd be entombed forever. This was not the Power of a benign friend, but a terrifying threat, a stern, no-nonsense Almighty. After some tense moments it receded a bit or stepped back. Instantly I knew it was not going to take me over, not at this time at least. It took a while, maybe an hour, for the Power to gradually recede to its usual space in myself, and as it did so, my fear receded with it. What I learned was not only that this Power could take me over any time it pleased, but that It wanted me to know this; and also to know It was not going to do so—not now anyway. This experience couldn't help but change my relationship with this Power. After this, I was wary of it, determined to keep my distance, never get close, even ignore it if possible. It had its own space in me, and I didn't want it taking up any of my space. Where previously I enjoyed knowing it was there, from here on, I'd keep a cautious eye on it, never forgetting the fear it had engendered in me. From Its side, however, it gave no indication it ever respected my cautious distance. In fact, it let me know it was supremely independent and would do its own thing. The only positive note, is that despite my fear of its taking me over, it never happened, not in my whole life. I never possessed this Power, and It never possessed me.

Despite this frightening experience, I could not help but recall the benefits of its presence these last years. I figured it had always informed me of the truth, taught me the right attitude toward the ups and downs of life, opened up an inner dimension I wouldn't have known otherwise; it had been the source of knowledge and joy, even laughter; it had been a constant companion, and on account of its presence I would ponder the deeper things in life instead of what was merely passing and obvious. In short, it was actually teaching me, helping me grow up. While I decided it was really working on my behalf, I also determined to keep a respectful distance. After all, this was not an ordinary friend—I never talked to it, complained to it, never asked it for anything, and certainly never thought of it as a bosom pal or chum. No, this was not our kind of relationship.

* * * * * *

Sometime in 1939 my parents took us to the San Francisco World's Fair. All I recall is the impressive aquacade or swimming exhibition. After the Fair we spent several days in Yosemite Park where we took hikes and watched the fire-falls at night. This was my second or third trip to the park, the most memorable being the time grandpa went along and dad filmed him feeding the bears as they stood upright, towering above him. They took food right out of grandpa's hand. When there was no more food, however, they started banging our car around, so we had to leave.

Sometime after my ninth birthday, Gertrude was married and I inherited her bedroom. Though delighted to finally have a space of my own, I never felt it was my room. Whenever I entered I was reminded of Gert's absence, somehow it would always be her room. Had the decor been changed, perhaps I'd have felt differently, but apart from the scroll-top desk she took with her, everything was the same. In the alcove where her desk had been, Mom set up all my old doll stuff, even though I'd already lost interest in it. By the end of that year my stuff was given away and the alcove remained bare. It was shortly after I moved into this room, however, I came by a piece of knowledge I would ponder the rest of my life, a knowledge that completely changed both my views and rapport with God.

I was standing in the middle of the bedroom—not thinking or doing anything I recall—when as clear and forceful as if God were standing in front of me, I received a certain knowledge. This knowledge came from outside myself, seemingly from an indistinct light in front of me. It was not given with words or piece by piece, but instantly, all at once. It was almost like a blow to the head, because for a minute, at least, it felt as if my brain had frozen or become immovable. Since it was not conveyed with words—audible, interior or mental—nor imparted as an idea or concept, to convey this wordless knowledge it must be translated into words that can never do it justice. Although I would not call this an "experience," it was, nevertheless, mind-blowing. As best I can communicate this knowledge, its essence was this:

From the beginning God had a specific Plan for my life; an unalterable Plan that would be accomplished regardless of me, my desires, my plans, or anything going on in my life. I would not die until this Plan had been completed, and some day this Plan would even be known to others. God had a specific work to do in me and was going to do it come hell or high-water (if I may use the expression). This grand Plan was to accomplish something very specific, something God wanted to do or bring about. All my unusual experiences to this point had been part of this Plan, God's own doing. So too, from here on all such experiences—for the rest of my life in fact—would be God's doing and part of His grand Plan.

As soon as I could think about this, I did not regard it as good news. It was as if I'd just been notified I counted for nothing, would never be given a say in my life, God wasn't going to ask my consent for anything. Who I was and what I wanted was totally irrelevant, thus I—me, myself, Bernadette, a child no less—counted for nothing with God. To carry out His Plan he could have picked anybody, God didn't care "who" we were. It was as if God intended to "use" me for something—but what? That was the question! Perhaps if I had known 'for what', God's Plan might have been acceptable, I could have cooperated, gone along with it, but as it was, I didn't know, and to the end, would never know. There is no knowing this Plan ahead of time, it can only be known when it's over and done with. After this I would always think of myself as God's "experiment"—too little of this, redo that, not enough here, whoops! shouldn't have gone there ....so went the great Plan and my life with God.

This communication or piece of knowledge totally changed my view of God, and certainly my rapport with Him. From a caring, under-standing heavenly Parent, He went to a tough, no-nonsense task-master, so set in His ways that no recourse was possible. Trying to find something positive or good about this knowledge I thought to myself, "Well, at least I know I won't die until His Plan is finished"—thus I could play for time. But on second thought, since I didn't know what the Plan was, much less its finished product, it might be finished tomorrow—which meant I could drop dead anytime! No, there was nothing positive here. Even if one knows an event is God's doing, it doesn't help a bit, if anything, it makes matters worse because you know God is going to stick it to you come what may. Forget about asking for reprieves, it's not going to happen. All this may sound harsh, but it's the truth–my life in fact. What I would come to know as "love of God" was totally without any feelings of sentiment, almost emotionless, yet this love was tough, just as tough and determined as God Himself It was a kind of tit-for-tat relationship: if you get tough with somebody they're going to get tough with you–to survive, there's no other choice. I would never understand those who looked to God as a compassionate push-over. We all know He didn't blink an eye when Christ was crucified–why? Because it was all in "The Great Plan." Come what may, it will be done.

I don't know why I was ever given this piece of knowledge, it never proved helpful. While it is easy to see God's hand in good and positive experiences, it is hard to see His work in terrible or negative experiences– how or why would God do such a thing? Obviously, only He knows. I figured God had a special plan for everyone's life. If mine was different, it was only because I knew some unknown plan was at work, knew God was going to do it Himself, not me, but God–which was the part that bothered me. What counted wasn't me, rather, the big Plan was all that mattered, so long as it was carried out, it didn't matter who I was. As for my own desires, God didn't give a fig. He was going to do what he had to do and that was the end of it. Seeing the utter uselessness of ever asking God for anything, I resolved that for all my needs I'd only ask Mary, pray to her instead. Thus with few exceptions, I lived the rest of my life never praying to God for a thing, never. Mary would become the great provider in my life, so great in fact, I had to be careful what I asked of her, because I always got it. Thus I was ever careful not to abuse her endless generosity.

If at this time I did not try to forget about God, down the road there would be times when I tried my hardest to do so. Whenever I tried, however, I always got a divine "Hee-haw!" literally a sense of God's laughing. So much for trying to get rid of God, it won't happen–it can't.

* * * * * *

As for what was happening on the home front, I can only give a short sketch of some family activities. Every summer, of course, we vacationed on Catalina Island; at other times, we only took the boat out of the harbor for a day's trip to swim and picnic. On Sundays we frequently went for drives down the coast and had dinner at Victor Hugo's restaurant on the Laguna bluffs. We often went to Chinatown, its impressive Gateway erected by dad's law school chum, Mr. Hong, whose family we knew well. There were also trips to various Mission fiestas, to Dominguez seminary where we picnicked or had dinner with the Priests. Among our most fun times were the evening wiener bakes on the beach with the Atwell family whose dad, Bill, had gone to Loyola High with dad. They had five boys and a little girl, Betty, a year younger than I. By age seven I sometimes went alone on the bus to spend week-ends at their home in Santa Monica. Besides visits to the homes of friends and family, there were always people coming to our home to spend a day at the beach or at the amusement piers. If they stayed for dinner, afterwards we'd gather around mom at the piano and have a songfest. Of course there were the annual Parish events—plays, talent shows and dinners—not to mention some of the memorable birthday parties mom and dad put on for us. It's tempting to detail some of these family events, especially the more humorous incidents, but to do that would take another book.

In September I went back to the third grade again. If there is anything I did not learn the first time around, I never learned it the second time either. Everything was so repetitious it sparked no interest whatsoever, I could not recall learning anything new. As for my class standing—in the middle—that never changed either. At recess I continued to play with my old friends and never mingled with the new classmates. Altogether it was a complete waste of a school year. Because of this break in my academic momentum, I lost interest and never really caught up. Years later I would look back and have to admit that after the third grade—first time around—I had never learned a thing in school. If it hadn't been for what I learned at home, I'd have been a complete nincompoop.

The only good thing that happened in the classroom this year was listening to an hour of classical music on the radio. As long as we were quiet, sister didn't care what we did—write, draw, read or just listen. Always I put my head down on the desk, let my mind go blank and listened. I loved that hour and virtually lived week to week in anticipation of listening to the beautiful music. (I think this weekly program was specially geared for children.) Other than this there is nothing to report in the academic area; after New Year, however, school ceased to matter anyway, because the focus was to turn on my health and well-being.

Due in part to an inept doctor and circumstances beyond anyone's control, my childhood was destined to come to an early end. Sometime in February (1940), mother asked me, "I notice you are limping, did you hurt yourself or fall down?" "No", I replied, "I don't remember anything, I didn't even know I was limping." The only thing I could think of was that when I jumped on my left leg in hop-scotch, jump rope or whatever, I felt a dull pain in my left side, but I didn't think anything about it. When I was little and went to mom with some ache or pain she'd say, "Oh that's just growing pains," and since they soon disappeared, I took for granted any pain I felt today would be gone tomorrow. Until now, at least, this had always been the case, thus I didn't think anything about the dull pain I sometimes felt in my left side.

Before long, however, the sisters at school called mom to ask about my limping and she decided to take me to the family doctor. When he could find nothing wrong, he recommended we see an orthopedic specialist. Mom and dad inquired around and took the sisters' recommendation of Dr. Gallager who, they said, was regarded as one of best in Los Angeles—and a Catholic, of course. On the appointed day, mom took me to his office. He seemed nice enough, about dad's age, he had a limp due to polio when he was young. He took x-rays of my hips and legs, then had me lie on a table where he exercised my legs in various directions.

After seeing the x-rays, he told mom he could find nothing the matter, but if I continued limping to come back in a month or so, which we did. After the second visit mom said the doctor ordered me to wear special orthopedic shoes, but before we could get them we had to go to his office to get a prescription or something. I couldn't understand this, nor could anyone explain it to me—what good would corrective shoes do if the pain was in my upper leg? Right then I sensed something phony going on, they weren't telling me the truth, certainly there was nothing the matter with my feet. Over my objections, however, mom would only say, "It's the Doctor's orders, he thinks it will help you." Though she couldn't tell me how, she nevertheless went along with it, or at least she tried.

After mom picked up a specific description of the kind of shoes the doctor ordered, we went to a specialty store. The man brought out a pair of huge, black, stiff gunboats with heavy leaded toes. I pleaded for some kind of better looking shoes, but no, this is what the doctor ordered. They were so heavy I could hardly walk; I warned mom, "Don't buy them because I'll never wear them!" but she bought them anyway. Thus began the battle of the shoes.

Fortunately, it was a family habit to kick off our shoes when we came inside. There was never any rule about it, we could just as well have kept them on, but since we usually took them off, mom didn't fuss about my not wearing shoes in the house. She insisted, however, I wear them when I went out to play, but since the house had four exits, I simply avoided her, ran off and played where she couldn't see me from the house. School time, however, was another matter; every morning there was arguing and threats on both sides, until I devised a plan. I'd put on the gunboats and throw my school shoes out the window onto the side lawn. After I left the house I'd pick them up, change my shoes, and hide the gunboats under the 2x4 railroad ties in the car-barn –located the end of our back alley. On the way home, of course, I changed shoes and once in the house kicked them off again.

It was several weeks before mom caught on to this ruse and hid my school shoes so I couldn't find them. After that I threw my patent leather Sunday shoes out the window and things went on as usual. When she finally caught on to this, however, she called the doctor–told him, I surmise, his plan wasn't working. After that, she told me the doctor had ordered a different pair of shoes, so once again we went to the specialty store where I was in for a delightful surprise. The man brought out a perfectly ordinary pair of saddle shoes which, at that time, were the rage at school. While I knew they were not corrective shoes, I said nothing, after all, they were the neatest pair of shoes I ever had, and very expensive. On the way home I told mom I knew they were not corrective shoes, but she just shrugged her shoulders and said, "Evidently that's what the doctor ordered. I just wish they hadn't been so expensive." "Well if he told you they were corrective shoes, he's a liar!" Obviously the corrective shoes had been nothing but a cover up for the doctor's ineptitude. But if that was the end of the battle of the shoes, little did I suspect the terrible battles that lay ahead.

Years later mom told me how she discovered I wasn't wearing the corrective shoes at school. In order to see if I was just 'putting on' or faking a limp–the doctor's theory–she hid behind a telephone pole at recess to watch me. From a distance of the lower school yard, mom could only see a bevy of girls' legs in the upper yard, otherwise we all looked alike in our uniforms. She said by just watching legs, however, she could easily spot me because of the limp. Several times she spied on me like this, which is how she noticed I wasn't wearing those gunboats.

Perhaps matters would not have been so bad if my parents had not been annoyed at my limping. They were under pressure from others, however, especially the sisters at school, to find out what the matter was. Everybody asked, "Why is she limping? What's the matter? Has she been to a doctor?" and so on. For my part, I just wanted to be left alone. If the doctor couldn't find anything, then it couldn't be very bad. Although the pain got worse and the limp more obvious, I didn't think much of it. What annoyed me most was not the pain, but other people's constant concern about my limping.

One day I overheard my parents talking, dad's voice was angry, "Either the Doctor has to tell us what's the matter with her or there isn't anything the matter at all!" A few days later dad said he was taking me to see the doctor, which I found odd, because mom had always taken me. My impression was that dad intended to put the doctor on the stand, get to the bottom of this thing once and for all. Mom refused to go because she didn't want to be there for the show-down. What I did not suspect was that the show-down would not be between my father and the doctor, but between the doctor and myself.

First dad went in and talked to the doctor, then a nurse came and took me into a dressing room, told me to take off all my clothes and put on a white gown. I didn't understand this, even taking x-rays I never had to take off all my clothes. After the gown was on, I was ushered into the examining room where dad and the doctor were waiting. The doctor told me to take off the gown and walk up and down across the room so they could watch the movement of my left hip. Indignantly I said, "No!" Angrily dad said, "Do what the doctor told you!" I bust into tears but didn't move. Dad said, "If you don't, you're going to be severely punished!" The nurse untied the back of the gown and I stood there stark naked in front of two gawking men. "Just walk normally up and down the room", the doctor said. I walked to the window, turned around, and walked directly back into the dressing room. Despite the doctor's coaxing and dad's orders to return, I would have died first. I was humiliated, angry, frightened, and filled with hatred for the doctor.

After getting dressed I went back to the waiting room. When dad came out he wouldn't look at me, I knew he was upset. I was told to go into the doctor's office because he wanted to talk to me alone. I sat down in a big chair beside his desk determined to stare him down, not move or say a word. He greeted me nicely, offered me candy–which I ignored– then asked some yes or no questions: "Are you happy at home? Are your parents good to you? How do you like school? Do you have friends to play with? What are your favorite past times?" questions like that. I knew he was fishing for something (I didn't know what), but I didn't move, wouldn't even give him a nod or a head shake, I just stared at him with a look of sheer hatred. At first he tried to ignore this and avert his eyes, but finally he leaned forward and said, "You don't like me, do you?" There was no need to ask, it was perfectly obvious. I just continued to stare at him with a heart, mind and soul full of utter contempt. There was nothing for him to do but dismiss me. After that, dad went in alone and was there a long time. Though I wouldn't know until long after what was said, it didn't take long to figure out it was nothing good.

On the way home dad didn't say a word, even when I asked what the doctor had said, he made no reply. While I didn't feel he was angry with me, I knew he was upset and totally preoccupied. We drove in complete silence. I knew something was up, that some plan or plot had been hatched. What I didn't know is that the 'plan' would not begin until school was out for the summer, which was only a few weeks away. Though I recalled all my other birthdays, there was no recollection of my ninth birthday, it was just too clouded over with suspicion and foreboding.

AGE 9

The day school was out for summer I was told the doctor ordered me a long bed-rest. How long? As long as I limped, they said. It seems what bothered everyone was not my pain, but the sight of my limping. But to stay in bed all day every day, with no beach, no boat, no going outside? This was a blow. While I could believe the hateful doctor had ordered this, how could my parents go along with such a thing? I wasn't sick. Apart from pain when I walked, I felt perfectly fine. Were it not for the limp, no one would have suspected there was any problem at all, I never complained of pain, of course, lest they take me back to the doctor or tell me to go to bed, But here now, to be treated as if I were sick, galled me no end, yet all my protests and arguments were of no avail, I knew there was something going on behind my back, knew the doctor and my parents were being secretive and dishonest, yet I didn't know why, they wouldn't answer my questions, When I accused my parents of punishing me for limping, they denied it, "It was the doctor's orders," they said.

Me: But since the doctor doesn't even know what's the matter with me, what good will staying in bed do?

Mom: As long as you're in bed you won't feel any pain.

Me: Well there must be a reason for the pain, what does he say it is?

Dad: You tell us, the doctor can't find any reason for it.

(That was as far as any discussion ever went).

Later Mother told me that trying to keep me in bed nearly drove her to the brink. Although this "supposed" therapy lasted about six weeks, the only time I was actually in bed was when mom brought up my meals and played checkers or cards with me. For the first weeks, Lee went out of his way to move me around the house. He figured there was no difference if I sat in bed, sat at the dinner table, sat at the piano or on the front lawn, thus when he was home I was rarely in bed. After a few weeks, however, this abruptly ended. When I asked him one day to take me to the piano, he whispered, "Not until mom and dad are gone!" It seems my parents didn't want me any place but in my room, I was supposed to be "resting," they said, Rest when you're not sick or even tired? The whole thing was senseless and I told them so, But as said before, the worst part of this ordeal was not the physical pain, but the adult's refusal to tell me the truth, It was their conspiracy of silence that practically undid me.

Fortunately, because it was summer vacation, all my friends were home, Our house became an open door to the neighborhood gang treading its way in and out, going up and down the stairs to my room. We played marbles, had pillow fights, jumped on the beds, sometimes things got a bit rowdy, The constant traffic, mess and noise was hard on mom, she became exhausted, She said no matter what was wrong with me, she was in a far worse condition, As long as my parents were home I stayed in my room, but the moment they went out, I was not only downstairs, but if l knew they would be gone long enough, I'd go outside, One day a neighbor saw me playing down the street, Though not meaning to get me into trouble, she casually remarked to mom that she was glad to see I was getting better and could get out to play again, That did it! Mom must have called the doctor, because who should walk into my bedroom the next evening but the hated man himself, He had come to pronounce me well enough to get around in a wheelchair—no doubt mom's idea to get me and my friends out of the house, With a wheelchair I could be put out in the morning and taken in at night, which was fine with me, In response to the doctor's cheerful greeting and questions, I turned my face to the wall, wouldn't even look at him or say a word, Thanks to him I couldn't go to the beach, the boat, outside, or downstairs for dinner—all this punishment and he didn't even know what was the matter with me? I owed him nothing but contempt, Seeing my disdain, mom and dad were embarrassed and quickly ushered him out of the room, As mom closed the door behind her, she gave me a look of disgust to which I responded loud enough for the doctor to hear, "I tell you, he's nuts!"

The next day mom came home with a wheelchair, which was an instant neighborhood success. Kids lined up to take turns in it. Out of sight of the house, while my friends took turns going around the block, the rest of us would play games. It was especially fun going down the steeper hills with Lee. He'd put me on his lap and we'd careen down at top speed. If he lost control–which he usually did–we'd spin round and round and then topple over. Lee became adept at replacing screws and bolts, but after only a week we lost some of the strategic parts and the chair had to be replaced. Mom had no idea what was going on, she berated the man at the rental store for giving her a defective chair. Although the next one was brand new, it didn't last much longer. We went through three wheelchairs in a month, until mom finally caught on and our joy rides were over.

What was even more ridiculous, perhaps, was that after wheeling myself around all day, at night I would have to get out of the chair and haul it up the back stairs into the house by myself, Getting it down in the morning was easy, I only had to give it a shove and then hobble down the stairs after it, set it upright and get in, At the time I didn't find this a bit funny, I just thought the whole thing senseless, crazy.

After a month or so, when everyone was getting ready to return to school, out of the blue I was told the doctor thought I was so much better I could go back to school–was free to walk again, Though I was elated with the news, it was absurd, I hadn't even seen the doctor again, so what made him think I was any better? My parents, of course, weren't talking and I wasn't going to argue about going back to school, Although by this time the pain and limp were worse than ever, it was the deception going on behind my back that was worst of all.

If I was delighted to return to school, the sisters were not. Right off they called my parents and told them it was "Painful just to look at her"– watch me limping around, that is. They said walking in line I couldn't keep up, that I was painfully slow going up the two flights of stairs to my 4th grade classroom, that I often looked tired, pale and so on. I have to admit the two or three mile walk to school and back was difficult. Sometimes I felt so weak and breathless I had to stop many times along the way, which meant leaving home an hour early to get to school on time. Sometimes I sat down and cried, the pain was so exhausting. It was now 7 or 8 months since I first became aware of the limp. What had started out as a dull pain in my side was now producing such excruciating stabs of pain my whole body was momentarily immobilized. Though these spasms of pain would subside, they automatically cut back on my usual activity. Even during the night certain movements produced such stabs of pain, my sleep was constantly interrupted and fitful. I discovered it was only after a long time of lying perfectly still, with no movement at all, I could momentarily be free of pain, otherwise it was constant.

Despite this handicap, however, my friends didn't seem to mind. They never complained about waiting for me or excluded me from their games, In fact, they made numerous concessions and even changed the rules so I could play along, Since I had always been the boss or ring-leader, this change in positions was an eye opener, I never expressed my gratitude to these unquestioning friends, I doubt they even realized their own charity, yet they taught me much about genuine friendship and acceptance of others, a lesson not lost on me. For their part, however, the sisters at school totally ignored me, like everyone else they wanted to know what was the matter, what did the doctor say? I'll never know what my parents told the sisters, but since they were the ones who recommended the doctor in the first place, I'm sure my parents passed on what the doctor had told them, which meant they too regarded me as a lying fake, In their minds I must have been a mental case that didn't belong in their school, which is probably why, after a month or so, my parents told me the sisters didn't want me at school as long as I limped, They were told to get me a home tutor instead, The sisters may have suggested this ploy, along with the next tactic dad used, which I will get to shortly.

Not being allowed to go to school was a blow, Apart from a boring tutor who came several times a week to dish out 2nd grade work, I spent the day alone and confined, Lee, Marge, the whole neighborhood was gone, I played the piano so much it got on Mom's nerves and she limited my time, After I read all the books in the house, mom complained I was reading too much because she was getting tired of running back and forth to the library on my behalf, Because of the isolation, loneliness, and not knowing "what next", this was the worse month of the whole illness, Mom was busy with the house and other things while dad noticeably ignored me–acted as if he'd washed his hands of the whole affair, I don't think he said a word to me in all that time, Even at the dinner table there was not the usual family chatter, It seemed the home atmosphere had turned gloomy, I felt the whole situation sapping the spirit out of me, It was inevitable matters should come to a head, which it did one afternoon when dad said he wanted to talk to me in my room.

He started out calmly with a lecture on the sin of lying, reminding me it was against God, and that if l wasn't careful I might even lose my soul–go to hell, in other words, I could hardly believe my ears. For him to talk like this was so out of character I knew it was some kind of ruse or scare tactic. When he finished I said:

Me: But I know all that, so why are you telling me? Dad: I just wanted to be sure you knew.

Me: Are you telling me this because you think I'm lying about my pain?

Dad: What pain? Where is it? The doctor can't find anything the matter with you!

Me: Well you can't see the pain, but it's there just the same (pointing to my left side).

Dad: How do we know that?

Me: If there were no pain, how could I limp?

Dad: You could fake it.

Me: Why would I do that?

Dad: You tell me, we'd all like to know.

Me: Did the doctor tell you I was faking or is this your idea?

Dad: If the doctor can't find anything the matter, what else are we to think?

Me: If he said I was faking then he's the liar! He's just saying that because he's a rotten doctor and doesn't know a thing!

Dad: So you really feel pain?

Me: Yes! Why don't you believe me?

Dad: Because nobody can find a cause for it!

Me: You mean the doctor can't!

Dad: He ought to know, he's considered the best.

Me: Well he's not! Besides, since I'm the one who feels the pain, why should it bother you? I've never complained, never asked for your help.

Dad: We don't like seeing you limping around, that's all.

Me: Why does it bother you?

Dad: You look pathetic, everybody asks what's the matter. It's an attention getter, the doctor says there's no reason for you to be limping anyway, so you really don't have to. (Dad was angry now)

Me: But how can I help it?

Dad: You can if you want to! You might start to practice walking without a limp!

Me: But what if I can't?

Dad: (Angrily) Well until you can, I don't want you around me, I don't want to see you again until you have stopped limping, do you understand?"

Before he stomped out, he told me I was to go back to school as usual, How that came about I never knew and was not about to ask.

After he left I burst into tears. If he thought using the ruse of sin and hell would frighten me, he should have known better. I had no guilt or fear on that score, in fact, I hadn't yet decided if hell even existed. But if I had no fear of the Almighty, I was now frightened of my father. Since I could not stop limping, what might he do next–throw me out of the house, physically beat me? I had already been ostracized from family and friends, was the victim of a stupid doctor, surrounded by a conspiracy of silence, my parents refusing to believe me, and now dad didn't even want me around anymore, how could things get any worse? At least the truth had finally come out. Now I knew that the doctor and my parents thought I was faking the limp and lying about the pain, (Later I learned the doctor told them I faked the limp to "get attention"). That my parents believed the doctor and not me, meant they regarded me as a deliberate liar and fake who was out to embarrass, annoy or punish them, for what reason, I couldn't imagine; the whole thing made no sense. Realizing this was my parents view of me, gave me a feeling of being trapped and alone with no recourse to anyone in the world. Where I had always reveled in my independence, here now, I felt hemmed in by a choice-less dependency on two people who were against me, the situation seemed hopeless.

It was either that same day or shortly thereafter, standing in the middle of my room, I had an eerie sense of something hovering over my head. Looking up, I saw an ominous, foreboding gray cloud that gave me goose bumps. I knew that if it came down and enshrouded me, something terrible would happen, I didn't know what, only that it would be something awful. Though I knew I was not seeing this cloud with my visible eyes, it was as obvious as the picture on the wall. The next time I saw it—maybe a week or so later–the cloud was darker, thicker and lower down, I had a sense of some impending disaster about to descend on me, a powerful force from which there was no escape. My whole body shivered at the sight of it. The next time, the cloud was about a foot over my head, dark and heavy as if it were ready to burst and inundate me completely. The only reason this sight didn't freeze me with fear is that each time I saw the cloud, my eyes immediately turned to my interior Friend, that steady light within, I was sure Its power alone was holding the cloud in abeyance and would never permit it to engulf me, Though the interior Power was awesome and mysterious in its own right, I had good reason to trust it with my life, During our last four years together It not only taught and informed me of what was important in life, it was the instigator of my most joyous and uplifting experiences, I knew its Power alone was holding this threatening cloud aloft, and in so doing, it was holding my fear in abeyance, For me, the ominous cloud was merely a threat, one that would never be carried out.

Just knowing I had this powerful adversary with me, made me feel so secure I didn't see how anything could bring me down. During this ordeal, when I felt abandoned by my parents and falsely accused, I became completely dependent on Its friendly presence. Whenever I was feeling miserable I'd fix my gaze on it and know everything would be okay. Thus over these trying months I developed a grateful dependency on this Power, it was my main-stay; Its presence, the only happiness I had. So despite all the pain and conspiracies, it was my interior Friend that kept my spirits up and going.

In the meantime, I had to figure out a way to live in the same house with dad without his ever seeing me walk–limp, Since I couldn't just fade into the walls, I had to have some strategy of avoidance, come up with some plan, During the week when he was at work, I could manage, I'd get to the dinner table first and leave last, then sneak up to my room, but week-ends presented a problem, Since I wasn't going to stay in my room all day, there was no choice but to leave the house early and stay away all day, Just to get in and out of the house I'd have to peek around corners, listen for his voice, anticipate his whereabouts, literally sneak around the house, Once I accidentally met him in the hall and froze in place to let him by, but he shoved me hard against the wall–a push of disdain like "Get out of my sight!" Some days later he stormed into my room again, threatened me with hell and damnation, shouting so angrily I thought he'd gone mad, I was not allowed to say a word and told never to speak to him again. Without a doubt I was afraid of him. If he wanted to avoid me, I wanted to avoid him even more,

Early on Saturdays I'd make a peanut butter sandwich and leave the house, I couldn't play with my friends for fear dad would either come out or see me from a window, so I had to stay at a distance where I rarely saw anyone I knew, While I liked being on the beach, the knowledge I had no other choice made for a long day, I looked forward to going home and sneaking some food up to my room. Because mom never asked about my sneaking around or why I was gone all day, I took for granted she knew dad didn't want me there. Since mom never countered dad's discipline or orders, she obviously went along with this.

Throughout this ordeal mom and dad never gave any indication of being divided on what to do or how to treat me, Mom's attitude, though calm and non-threatening, was also disconcerting, She insisted on acting as if nothing was going on, that everything was normal and as usual, she wouldn't permit me to criticize dad or listen to my complaints about his behaviors, she didn't even want to talk about my problem, never even asked how I felt. Although later mom would say that throughout this ordeal she had "never believed the doctor and never thought I was lying", by that time it was too late, she never lifted a finger on my behalf, So whatever her protestations behind the scenes, it was of no consequence to me, For all intents and purposes, it was obvious she went along with the whole thing.

When Sunday came around I didn't see how I could go to Mass with mom and dad without there being another explosive scene, so my plan was to tell mom I didn't feel good, stay in bed, and then leave the house after they had gone, As it turned out I didn't have to say anything, When mom came to see if I was dressed, seeing me still in bed, she said, "Good, just stay in bed, we'll have a nice breakfast when I get home." When she got home, however, I was gone, This plan worked for two week-ends, It was on the third week-end, however, an incident took place that broke my spirit and brought everything to a head.

On a nice day the ocean front is crowded with people out for a Sunday stroll. On this Sunday I was in the midst of this crowd when, suddenly, I spotted my parents coming toward me from the other direction. Hoping they wouldn't see me, I aligned myself on the other side of a tall man and tried to keep in step with him. But it didn't work, without a word my father rushed over, put both hands on my shoulders and pushed me backwards. Though my fall was checked by a passerby, I landed on my bottom and was not hurt, not physically at least. The people around stopped to help me up and then looked back, questioningly, at the man who had done this. I too stood and looked after them, hoping mom would look back to see if I was okay, or, at least acknowledge me in some way. But she never did. My parents continued their walk as if nothing happened. Watching mom disappear in the crowd, her back to me, was like a knife in my heart–physically I felt a pang in my heart. Somehow I had thought her neutral. While she had never overtly taken my side or uttered a word of sympathy, she never seemed to be against me, But now I realized she was just as against me as dad, Seeing her disappear in the crowd, my last hope for a bit of human understanding disappeared with her.

Immediately I went down to the sea and sat on the shore, how could I ever go home again? How long could this go on–how much more could I take? I had already learned that if I sat by the sea long enough, it had a way of drawing me into its mystery and washing away my worries and concerns, So I sat there–sometimes lying down, listening to the waves– until well after sun down. I would have been glad to stay there the rest of my life; I couldn't bear the thought of going home, The sea often had a way of imparting some message to me, something I must learn or keep in mind, If there was any message this day, it was that I needed a miracle. Only God could help me now, only He could resolve my predicament, I thought that if my parents could only believe me or find out what was the matter, that would be the miracle. While I couldn't imagine how God would do this, knowing He could do anything, I determined to beg for His help, I decided that before bed that evening I'd pour out my heart, storm heaven, plead God for His special help, With this resolve the thought of going home was not so bad, now I had a reason–I was going home to pray, With this in mind, I got up and hobbled home.

Before going inside, I peeked in the dining room windows to be sure dinner and the dishes were over, Taking off my shoes I quietly went in the back door, took some bread from the breadbox and headed for the stairs, Although the stairs could be seen from the living room, I thought that even if l was seen, at least I wouldn't be heard, From the corner of my eye I could see my parents quietly reading and do not know if they saw me or not. If they did, I appreciated their silence, nothing said be-tween us could have made anything better or worse than they were.

Since it had become too painful to kneel, I sat on the floor beside the bed to say my prayers. Over the years I had come to look forward every night to making an Examination of Conscience. It was the only time in the day I attempted to truly know myself, look deep inside to question myself, question not only my thoughts, words and deeds, but above all, question what I honestly believed and thought about things. The central issue, of course, was truth and honesty. While I knew I could never fool God, and was always aware when I deliberately fooled others, yet my real quandary was whether or not I might be fooling myself without knowing it. Did I honestly believe or agree with things I had heard, learned, read or done? Sometimes I posed questions that only drew a blank mind, which I learned to get around with the excuse that at least I couldn't be responsible for what I didn't know, Then I'd say, "God, if I need to know, you will have to give me the answer." I had decided that since God was the only one who really knew me, the only One who knew what he had created here, if I was to know anything more about myself, then God would have to let me know what that was. Without question, this nightly habit of examining my conscience was one of the most valuable practices in my life, I only mention it here because on the night in question, I skipped it completely.

Sitting beside my bed I poured my heart out to God, complaining I couldn't take it anymore, couldn't go on like this, I was a helpless child with no one to turn to, only He could rescue me now, I told Him He should not allow such injustice to go on, it was wrong and only He could make it right, All He had to do was let them find out what was the matter with me, certainly this was little to ask, While I never expected anything immediate to happen, I did expect some sense of assurance God at least heard me. I would even have settled for a sense of satisfaction for having prayed at all, at least prayed so hard, But after sending my prayers heavenward I never felt my pleas went beyond the ceiling of my room, With no place or image on which to focus my mind and heart, it seemed my prayers went nowhere, I'd never had an image of God in mind, knowing He was "pure spirit" and "everywhere" precludes having an image to focus on—after all, you cannot focus on someone you've never seen (or can't see), much less focus on someone who is "everywhere", I was totally aware I'd never had any personal one to one contact with God, no face to face encounter, but without this, how could I ever focus on God or even say I knew Him? While my desire and intention was on target, this was obviously not enough, it engendered no satisfaction or assurance God heard my prayers, much less that He cared enough to answer them.

Since I had to admit I neither knew nor loved God, I realized my presumption in asking for His special help, I only asked because I'd hit bottom, was down and out, and He was my last resort, Such a last minute ditch, however, obviously warranted no concessions or special attention. Seeing the futility of my pleas, left me more desperate than before, with this last hope gone, there was only one thing left in my shattered life–the ever present Power within. Until now, the thought of appealing to it never crossed my mind, Praying or appealing to it was not the type of rapport or relationship we had, This Power was a teacher, a tough, no-nonsense teacher, never a savior or comforter, It had never catered to the changing scenes in my life, my ups and downs; in fact, it was never concerned with my external life at all, if anything, it poo-pooed it as irrelevant and could sweep it away as a pesky fly, If this Power tried to teach me anything, it was never to get involved and caught up on all this business, and until now, at least, I don't think I ever did.

Another reason for not appealing to this Power was the fact it was helping me already. It alone was holding up the ominous cloud, and I had no reason to think it would not continue to do so, More than anything, however, I was reluctant to appeal to it because I never wanted to get too close–one automatically learns to stay away from fire lest they be burnt, or even consumed by it, This was an awesome, totally independent Power, there was no second guessing what it might do, All in all, It was just not something you pray to, Besides, It had some work to do in me and would do it come what may, thus no appeal would alter this in any way, Despite this, however, I figured I could at least pose a question to It, I decided on the simple question, "What'll I do now?."

So kneeling on my one good knee beside the bed, I buried my face in my hands and looked inward. To my surprise, Its space within was burning brightly–I couldn't recall ever seeing it so bright–it looked like a little star, a diamond glittering in the sunlight, In my surprise I forgot the question–never got it out–because no sooner had I seen the brilliant diamond than It seemed to be retracting, retreating or moving backwards. I watched incredulously as it gradually became smaller and dimmer, a mere pin-point of light, then abruptly, It disappeared! I could not believe my eyes. To test my sight, I deliberately lifted my head and looked around the room, I could see perfectly, so I closed them again and looked within.

This time, however, what I saw was the most horrifying sight of my life, Where the Light had been, there was a huge black bottomless hole–I say "huge" because it seemed to take up all the space within me, not merely the discrete space the Light had always occupied. On seeing this, there arose from that black space a pain such as I'd never experienced before, not a physical or emotional pain, but pain of another dimension entirely, Later in life I would compare this pain to what a child might feel in the throes of an irrational tantrum, or what an adult might experience when his will is suddenly thwarted, Since mom affirmed I never had tantrums, I cannot be sure of this, I only know it's not something you bring on yourself or can even control; in some respects, this pain is out of control and absolutely unendurable, It absorbed me completely.

This pain may have lasted 15 minutes or several hours, I don't know. The next thing I knew I was lying flat on the floor, my head toward the window, feet toward the bed, feeling so physically frozen that the slightest movement caused excruciating pain. It was as if every bone and joint had been frozen stiff. All I knew is that I had to get warm, get into bed, since it was impossible to get up, I painfully rolled over on my stomach, squirmed my body around to face the bed and slowly dragged my way toward it. Getting hold of the side-board, I finally managed to pull myself into bed. Altogether this took maybe an hour.

I lay there waiting to defrost, not only my body but my mind, for it too was frozen. At first it felt like my brain had been locked in a vise, but after a while, it felt like I had no brain at all, my head was just an empty skull. In this condition sleep was impossible, so I just lay there, my senses seemingly unimpaired, yet not able to think at all. I knew where I was, knew something awful had happened, and knew the slightest movement was painful, and that's about all. Though I never did experience any warmth, my body must have adjusted, because after a while the lack of warmth didn't bother me–probably because I couldn't think about it.

When mom came in the next morning, she looked shocked, said nothing and walked out–obviously I wouldn't be going to school that day. Later she brought some food and urged me to eat, Although I could see her and hear her asking me what the matter was, or how I felt, I could not respond, my mind could not generate a single word or thought, I could only stare at her, Later she returned and spooned chicken broth into my mouth–and later, other stuff as well. Apart from this I just lay there. Whether my eyes were open or closed made no difference, I didn't sleep a wink, (Later mom told me, "You lay there for two whole days because nobody could budge you, that's when I made a doctor's appointment– over dad's protests.")

It was late in the afternoon of the third day when I caught sight of a patch of light flickering on the wall about 4 or 5 feet from my bed, it must have been the reflection of afternoon sunlight playing on the wall. I stared at its flickering movements for quite a while, then of a sudden I felt a physical crack–click or snap–in my brain, at which moment I recognized what I was looking at, it was a picture of waves breaking on shore. As I continued to watch, the picture seemed to imprint a message on my mind–"Get to the sea!" I understood, somehow I had to get to the sea. After that the light on the wall broke up and faded away. Because something in me had relaxed or defrosted, I may have fallen asleep, I don't know. The next time I opened my eyes I was surprised to find it was morning. I knew what I had to do.

Getting out of bed was so painful, that under any other circumstances I would not have tried. I'll never know what kept me going, I experienced no determination or will-power, It was as if the body mechanically knew what it had to do and did it. It must have taken an hour to get dressed in my school uniform. After that I slowly made my way down the stairs and out the back door. Mother caught sight of me from the kitchen and came after me, "You can't go to school, you're too sick, go back to bed, we are going to see a new doctor in a few days, it's too late for school anyway", on and on she went, sounding very alarmed. Almost like a zombie I kept walking straight ahead and never said a word. Finally, halfway down the alley, she stood in front of me and pleaded, "At least wait a minute while I fix you some lunch, you've hardly eaten anything in days." So I stood still, my back to the house, and waited until she returned with a bag–my usual peanut butter sandwich and apple. After that I continued on my way. When I got to the trolley-bam I turned toward the ocean, crossed the tracks and went down an alley to the beach. At the first sight of the sea I felt a certain relief. I hadn't the slightest idea or expectation of what would happen there, I only knew I had to be there, be where I knew I belonged.

It was a foggy, chilly morning. There wasn't another soul on the beach. I went down to the water line and sat down. When one of the waves splashed around my feet I took off my shoes and socks. The next time it splashed around my feet, I was amazed to find the water as warm as toast. I'd never known the sea could get so warm, I scooted down closer to feel it again. On one of its surges, it came up higher and swirled around my ankles and legs. Because of its warmth I could wiggle my toes and move my ankles without pain, so I scooted down even more. The next wave swirled clear around me, and since my clothes were now wet, I got up and walked into the water. As I waded in, any part of me immersed in the warm water was immediately freed of pain, so I kept going, walking into the sea, clothes and all. When the water was up to my chest, seeing a wave coming, instead of jumping over it, I decided to go under. The instant my head went under my mind cleared–defrosted or returned–and everything in me cried out "I'm myself! I'm myself again!" The surprise, the joy and jubilation was overwhelming. It was an unrepeatable experience that would forever be etched in the depths of my being. My beloved sea had done this for me, its inscrutable, magnetic mystery had been there for me! I never doubted God had worked this miracle, but not the God I didn't know or the one I had prayed to, no, it was God whose mystery is the sea, or sea whose mystery is God, This is the God who worked the miracle for me.

I decided to swim out beyond the waves so I could float on my back, be in tune with the rhythm of the sea, I had already been convinced that the happiness and contentment I experienced was the sea's own experience it was sharing with me, a kind of shared secret between us, After a while, however, I began nodding off, about to fall asleep. Something told me I'd better get to shore while I still had the energy, So I turned over, swam a ways and let one of the waves carry me onto shore, Before I lay down, however, I felt extremely hungry, so I took the food from my bag, Never before or after has any food in the world tasted as good as that sandwich and apple, When I finished, I flopped back on the sand and instantly fell asleep.

When I awoke, I could tell by the position of the sun it was late afternoon, time when all the kids would be home from school. Lying there free of pain, I wondered if the pain in my leg was also gone–dare I hope for this miracle as well? The only way to find out, of course, was to get up and walk. Before I did, however, I posed the question to myself: what if the pain is still there, would I be disappointed, would it lessen my joy and gratitude? No, nothing could be more important than just being myself. Without this, I couldn't function even if my leg had been cured. Besides, the pain had never been the real problem, it was the treatment I received from the conspiracy of silence hatched by the doctor and my parents. No, physical pain was the least of my worries.

With no expectations I got up and put my full weight on both legs and carefully stepped out. For the first few steps I felt nothing, no pain, but as I walked down the beach it was obvious the pain was still there, only instead of the usual 11 on a scale of 10, the pain was only a 3 or 4 which, comparatively speaking, was easy to live with, After I had started walking, however, I noticed something else, I felt taller and was sure I had grown several inches, I decided the first thing I'd do when I got home, was look in the mirror to check this out.

On the way home I became aware that not only in height, but in other ways I was somehow different, I had changed, yet couldn't put my finger on "how", Although I had returned to myself, yet it was not the same self For one thing I felt new, or as if my life was starting new from this point on, I also felt invulnerable, as if nothing could ever get me down again, I had a strong sense of self-sufficiency and independence, and that to the very depths of myself–a depth where nothing and no one could ever touch me–I was my own master, Also, it seemed the past was dead, all I'd been through the last months were gone, wiped out, none of it mattered any more. There would be no continuation of the past because everything now was new, it was the beginning of a whole new life. Though I had never lacked any sense of self, yet by comparison this new self was huge, strong, with a certain sense of dignity and uprightness never experienced before. It was as if instead of running from challenges–from people, situations or whatever–from now on I'd be waiting for them, not out of defiance, but as a test to this new self, Though I did not think of it at the time, with the emergence of this new self, my childhood was over, finished, I couldn't go back, The one who walked into the sea was no more, and the one who emerged was a new person.

When I got home I went straight to the long mirror in my bedroom to see if I had grown, Though I couldn't tell if l was actually taller, I did notice my uniform was at the top of my knees instead of at the bottom– as the school required, I made a note to tell mom so she should let the hem down, After changing my clothes I went down stairs and resumed life as if the past eight months hadn't happened, It never occurred to me to avoid dad, and as far as I could tell, he'd forgotten all about it, There was no talk about the last few days, much less the last weeks or months, If my parents were surprised at my new behavior, they didn't say a word. I asked mom if she had called school to get my homework assignments, and then tried to catch up on anything I'd missed the last few days.

Over the years it had become my habit before falling asleep each night to check on the Power within, sometimes I'd go all day without remembering its presence, but once in bed, I'd look within to be sure it was still there, On this particular night, however, I knew it was not there and had no reason to look within, When I thought about its abandoning me in my hour of greatest need, this struck me as so heartless and uncaring, I determined that if it should ever reappear I would have nothing to do with it, wouldn't give it the time of day, For sure, I could never trust it again, if it dumped me once, it could dump me again, no, I'd never give it that chance, At first I felt angry over its disappearance and wished it would return long enough for me to vent my anger on it, but as it stood, I couldn't be angry at something that wasn't there, something that no longer existed, Realizing there was nothing on which to project my anger, it (the anger) abruptly disappeared.

I'm convinced that had my Friend disappeared anytime earlier in life, I would not have gone to pieces; I would have wondered about it, but never collapsed. It was its timing that was so cruel and inexplicable, When, at the lowest point in my life, I turned to it for help, that it chose that minute and that scenario to dump me–knowing full well what a blow this would be–was unforgivable, never understandable, If this was God's do-ing, He made a big mistake.

After my Friend's disappearance I never had any reason to look within myself, For one thing, there was nothing to see anymore; for an-other, I didn't want to risk seeing that terrible black hole again! Despite this, however, once in a while a sudden wave of nostalgia would sweep over me, a feeling of emptiness in the pit of my stomach, an unthought, unwilled longing for my old Friend. At these unsolicited moments I had to admit I dearly missed its Presence, and for a moment my heart sof-tened. After all, our years together had been happy ones, its Presence had been part of my childhood, a happy childhood, now gone forever. Still, I would not have wanted It back, Whatever It was meant to be in my life it was no good, even if it had been God Himself I would not have wanted to see or experience its Presence again. Perhaps the most important thing I learned from its disappearance was that whatever this Power had been, it could not have been God–as I sometimes thought it might be–because God is not something that comes and goes, rather, God is "that" which is always here–indeed, Everywhere, This is the God I wanted to know, not a God Who is here today and gone tomorrow.

The next day, or so mom informed me, we were going to see an-other doctor, She had read in the newspaper where Louis B. Meyer–of Metro Goldwin Meyer Studios–had fallen off his horse, broken some bones and been treated by a Dr. Wilson, an orthopedic specialist, Mom said, "I thought, any doctor good enough for that man, is good enough for my little girl, so I got hold of his office and made an appointment." "Why bother?" I asked, "If he doesn't find anything the matter, what are you going to do, take me to another doctor?" All she'd say was, "We'll just have to wait and see."

On the day of the appointment, the three of us set out in the car. We traveled in silence until I leaned over the front seat and said, "What do you expect this doctor to find? If the other doctor didn't find anything, what makes you think this one will?" In a voice of determined finality, mom shot back, "God will hear a mother's prayers!" After that nobody said a word, we didn't want to interrupt her prayers.

The large waiting room was crowded. It must have been an hour before we were ushered into a small examining room where we waited another hour. Once again, silence was golden. Mom sat with her eyes closed saying her rosary; Dad sat with his arms folded, lost in his private thoughts; I sat with my elbows on the window sill watching the people on the street below. At one point we heard an envelope dropped into the slot attached to the door. Later we heard someone take it out, and another few minutes the doctor walked in. After introducing himself, he said, "I understand she's been having some pain in her left hip area." After my parents "Yes", he looked at me and patted the table to climb up. With eyes closed as if in deep concentration, he gently exercised both legs. He took my right leg, bent it at the knee and moved it slowly to the left and then to the right. He did the same with my left leg, which he couldn't move without noticing a spasm of pain. With that, he lowered my leg, opened the door and said to someone in the hall, "I want a picture of both hip joints in an open position"–something like that. I followed the technician who took the x-rays and then returned to the room where there was another long wait. At some point we heard a file dropped in the door slot, I was sure it was the x-rays.

About a half hour later we heard the file taken out and a minute later the doctor walked in with two x-rays in his hand. He went straight to the window and motioned my parents to stand on either side of him. Holding up one x-ray he said, "See, this is her right hip joint, notice the ball and socket configuration and the rounded end of the femur, her leg bone. This is a normal healthy bone." Then he held up the other x-ray, "This is her left hip joint, you can see that instead of a rounded femur, it's flat, it has degenerated, this is her problem. It's called Paget's disease, not unknown in children her age." Then he put down the x-rays, turned and looked squarely at my parents, "What I don't understand, is why you waited so long in coming. Her case is far advanced, didn't she ever complain of pain?" Perhaps my parents were too shocked to answer, they didn't say a word, so he turned to me and asked, "You've had a lot of pain haven't you?" I didn't answer either, though I did nod my head, It had just dawned on me that I had never once complained of pain; had I done so I'd either have been taken back to the hated doctor or sent to bed, and besides, they didn't believe me anyway, No, despite the pain I had never complained, it would only have made matters worse.

The doctor went on, "We don't know the cause or the cure, but in the majority of cases, when the bone reaches a certain level of degeneration, it rebuilds itself. For now, all you can do is get her a pair of crutches and have her keep her weight off her leg. Bring her back in three months and we'll take another x-ray. You can rent or buy crutches downstairs, just tell the manager what I told you, he'll know what to do. If you have any questions or want to discuss this further, you'll have to make an appointment, right now I have a full schedule." After nodding good-bye, he turned and left the room. Altogether he'd spent no more than 10 or 15 minutes with us. Almost nine months of hell cleared up in 15 minutes! Really, what had it all been about?

On the first floor of the doctor's office was a medical supply store. I was carefully outfitted with the right size crutches and given instructions - where to put my weight, how best to keep the foot up and so on. The man said because I'd be growing we should come back every 5 or 6 months to be refitted, which we did; in the next 18 months I went through three different sizes, On the way home I could not resist voicing a bit of vindication, leaning over the front seat I said, "See, I told you something was the matter, I wasn't lying, but you didn't believe me!" After a moment, mother again uttered one of her definitive statements, "God has answered my prayers, that's all that matters now!" After that we rode home the same as we had come, in silence. For myself, I sat there wondering how come God answered her prayers but not mine? I concluded: one first had to be a mother.

As soon as we got out of the car I set off to test my crutches, see what I could do with them, or what they could do for me. Just like the wheelchair, they were an instant success with the neighbor gang. Everybody tried them out, even the shorter kids who could barely manage. By the end of the day I was taking two, sometimes three stairs at a time and literally running around the neighborhood. In a game of tag I never had to be IT because with my three foot extension, I could tag others with a bop! before they could get away, I also discovered I could use the crutches as a weapon, No need to chase Lee for a kick in the shins anymore, with my wooden arm I could just reach out and whack him, which I did—many times in fact, So I quickly mastered the crutches and found there was no activity they restricted, Though in the first months I still had a dull pain when getting around, after that, unless I suddenly twisted my leg, I got around with no pain.

When the sisters at school found out I had a bone disease and would have to be on crutches, they flat out told dad I didn't belong there—too many stairs they said. But who could believe that? I had no problem with stairs, nor was it necessary for them to make the slightest concession on my behalf. I was convinced they were afraid I might have a communicable disease. When I probed my parents for the real reason, they said they didn't understand it themselves, and repeated what the principal told them, namely, that I'd be better off in a school for crippled children where the facility and curriculum were geared for children like me. That the sisters regarded me as a "cripple" galled me, but I couldn't stand them anyway, So now my four plus years at St. Clement's school came to an abrupt end, While I would never miss the sisters, I did in fact miss school, the kids, even my lessons, As it turned out, after I left I never learned another thing in school, never.

Since it was only a few weeks until the start of Christmas vacation, it was decided I would begin the new school after the first of the year, Mom brought home my school books and dad made daily assignments so I could stay up with my class, I agreed with my parents, I didn't want to repeat the fourth grade, thus I took my studies seriously, That dad helped me with my math, not only this year, but for all my school years, was a boon, Besides being an attorney he was also a CPA, had worked his way through law school (supporting a young family) working for the IRS, He knew his math and taught me a lot of short cuts—of which my later teachers disapproved.

While I didn't look forward to going to a new school, I figured it was better than being alone all day, Mom's busy presence around the house couldn't compensate for school, Most of the time, I spent reading, I had no idea what to expect at school, apart from facilitating people with crutches and wheelchairs, I thought it would be an ordinary public school, "The School for Crippled Children" as it was called, was located near downtown Los Angeles, a good distance from our home. It had a bus service, however, that picked up and dropped off each child at their door step, which made it a slow ride across town every day. It also meant leaving early and coming home late. There is nothing positive to say about spending three hours on a bus every day. This factor, however, was the least of the problems the school held for me.

On my first day, Dad drove me to the school and went in to fill out some papers, By the time he finished, the first period class was nearly over, I was told to wait in the hall where someone would take me to my classroom, I was standing in the hall when the bell rang, All the doors on the long hall swung open and out poured human beings I never knew existed, had never seen before, people I could not have imagined in this world, Twisted deformed bodies, withered limbs, dragging feet, contorted faces, some were hunched over, spastic, made twitching movements, others felt their way along the wall, not a normal face or body among them, and all of this accompanied by the noisy click and clatter of canes and metal braces, guttural sounds and unintelligible speech.

I could not have been more horrified had it been a vision of hell; in fact, that's just what I thought it was. Never having seen people like this, much less a sea of them together, was the shock of a lifetime. I had no idea such people existed or that such deformity and illness was possible. The sight alone was frightening. But when I realized they were all coming down the hall toward me and that in another minute I'd be engulfed by them, I experienced a moment of sheer panic. I ran back into the office looking for dad, he must come and see I didn't belong here. I was not one of them, not like them at all. I was sure he'd see what an awful mistake he'd made and take me home.

Dad, however, was not in the office, the lady at the desk said he'd already left. I rushed out to the parking lot and when I saw the empty space where his car had been, my stomach fell. I doubled over with a sense of hopeless despair. After a minute, however, I stood upright and looked overhead, "God", I said, "You've never helped me before, but I beg you to help me now!" Somehow I had a sense my plea went straight to God, that he had, in fact, heard me.

But then I thought, "What can He do right now? Right now I've got to help myself." I couldn't go back inside, I didn't want to get near those kids. I felt neither contempt nor compassion, I was simply afraid of them, didn't want to get near them. These kids had never lived a normal life and never would, that's why they were here. But since this was not my case, why should I be put in with them? What did we have in common? I was convinced mom and dad had no idea about this school. It was definitely not the place for someone who merely had a broken leg or a temporary limp, as I did. When they knew the truth, surely they wouldn't send me back.

I decided to sit down on a curb in the parking lot and wait until the buses arrived after school. I was there an hour or more when a lady from the office saw me and nicely insisted I come to the office with her. I asked if I could call my mother to come and get me, she readily agreed. Mom must have gone out, because she didn't answer, I asked if I could wait and call again. The lady said that would be fine, but to remember, everyone would be leaving the office for lunch before long. I called again when the office people were about to leave, but still mom was not home. Going out the door, the principal (I think it was her) said cheerfully, "Come on and get some lunch with me in the cafeteria." Now mom had given me money to buy my lunch, I had even looked forward to it, but when she opened the cafeteria door and I saw all those kids, I told her I was not hungry. When she offered to treat me, I told her I had the money, but didn't feel hungry–which was true, "Well", she said, "your teacher always brings her lunch and eats in the classroom, come on, let's go down and you can meet her." So I followed her down the empty hall to a large, sunlit, airy room. Behind the desk sat a short frail woman, both legs in braces (from Polio) who greeted me cheerfully.

After a bit she handed me some tests to ascertain my placement level. I told her I was only there for the day, but would do the tests anyway, which were extremely easy. After lunch 6 or 7 kids came back to class, two of whom looked perfectly normal. I discovered, however, that the children were highly asocial and difficult to talk to. This was made worse by the fact instruction was individualized, everyone going at their own pace, which cut out the possibility of working together and getting to know one another. With no group instruction the class just never jelled, it evinced no spirit individually or as a group. I never saw a smile or once heard the sound of laughter. It seemed as if each child was absorbed in his own little world and the school made no effort to bring him out. Physical care was all this school was about, as a place of learning it was a complete sham. I was angry at the existence of such a school, convinced that these kids would have been better off surrounded by healthy kids in an ordinary classroom. Without such a contrast, these kids had no way of being aware of other possibilities, other behaviors, interests, or way of life.

Going home on the bus that day, I was careful not to sit next to anyone that didn't look normal, If they didn't look normal I couldn't trust their behaviors, didn't know what they might do—put their hands on me, pull me, maybe drool on me? Besides, some of them didn't speak right, I couldn't understand them, and we had nothing in common to talk about anyway.

When I got home I told my parents about the maimed children, kids they had never seen; if they came to see for themselves they'd know the school was the wrong place for me. I was met with various arguments: I'd only be there a short time, there was no other school I could go to, they didn't want me to miss a whole year and repeat the fourth grade, my staying home every day, even with a tutor, had not been a good experience, and on and on, When I realized they intended to make me go back to that school, I broke down and cried, I begged and pleaded with them not to send me there, I reminded them I had never appealed to them for anything before in my life, so wouldn't they please do this one thing for me?

Though my parents were honestly sympathetic, they were also between a rock and a hard place, what else could be done? When I told them I'd never get on the bus the next morning, dad said he'd not only take me to school every morning, but escort me to my classroom to make sure I didn't encounter a lot of kids in the hall, Although he did this, matters didn't improve, The kids were not friendly, nobody played together,

I was alone all the time–for lunch, recess, even in the classroom; what's more, the place always had a sickening antiseptic smell; in short, the whole place was downright depressing.

Every day I carried on, demanding, pleading, arguing with my parents. At one point dad assured me, "I promise you, after you've finished this grade you will never go back to that school again!" I didn't bother to ask "How come?" I couldn't think that far ahead. I wanted out NOW, not later! I told dad to go to the local public school and see if l could get in there, instantly he replied, "I'll do it tomorrow!" Of course the local school told him that if I'd been in their school, they'd have sent me to the Cripple School anyway, They said the school had been built because the local schools had neither the facility nor staff to care for these types of cases, To be lumped in with these "cases" at the Cripple school, simply unnerved me.

Still, every night brought on another round of pleading and arguing, and every night more disappointment. After a week or two mother told me in no uncertain terms, "I don't want to hear another word about it! There's nothing we can do, you'll just have to be patient and make the best of it, that's all!" After this, if l even started to complain, she'd throw up her hands and walk away. In time I not only felt exhausted, but something in me gave up, the fight had simply gone out of me. I became unable to care about anything or take an interest in anything, it seemed there were no good times left for me. Later my parents said that my despondency worried them more than my illness. One night after mom had abruptly cut me off, dad motioned me to follow him into his office, "You can tell me, what's going on with you and the school now?" I poured out all the misery of heart and soul I could verbalize. He was touched, "Mom and I don't like this arrangement any more than you do, but if you left now you'd have to repeat the grade, and for your own sake we want to avoid that. But I did have a thought, maybe they'd let you take your final tests early so you could get out early." When I asked, "How soon will you know?" he said, "I'll talk to them tomorrow."

The next day when I inquired about the outcome, dad said the school had left it up to the doctor, so now he'd have to make an appointment to see him. While I couldn't imagine what the doctor had to do with this, if that's what it would take, so be it. Dad had already had one consultation with the doctor, mainly about the disease and its prognosis, now he made an appointment to discuss my "despondency," as he later put it.

The first time dad talked to the doctor he naturally asked why the previous doctor had not caught the disease, Doctor Wilson told him, "It takes an expert to detect it in the early stages; also, the x-rays have to be taken with the bones in a certain position"–so much for that previous inept so and so of a doctor! Doctor Wilson also said that from the looks of my x-ray, the bone had been deteriorating for over nine months and that in another six months they'd know more about the outcome. When dad asked what to expect if the bone did not rebuild itself, he was told I could be crippled for life. Although he said doctors had tried operating– to get blood circulating in the bone or something like that–it had not been successful. I don't know what else they discussed, but unlike myself, dad always kept the negative possibility in the back of his mind. For my part, I never had the slightest doubt the bone would rebuild itself. In my view, the bone had little to do with the whole ordeal, an ordeal I was sure had another cause and purpose in my life. What I had learned during these months probably could not have been learned any other way. No, my hip bone had just played its part, a small part, and now its part was over,

The second time dad went to consult the doctor it was to tell him he thought I'd had a "personality change"–dad's own words. Initially dad was concerned about all my ranting and raving about the school, I'd never behaved that way before. Right now, however, I acted despondent and disinterested, which was also not like me. The doctor told him that considering all I'd been through, he was not surprised; he regarded this as a perfectly normal reaction. At the same time he told dad to look into other possibilities for me, because, he said, "Everyone has a point at which enough is enough." After that dad began to listen to me and think of new possibilities. For one thing, the doctor told dad that being in water was the best physical therapy I could have, thus two or three evenings a week dad took me to the indoor Venice plunge down the street. This not only gave me something to look forward to during the day, it was my sole enjoyment during the months I had to spend at that school.

Another possibility dad thought up was that since the other children at school were so unhappy and unsmiling, I might try to do something about it, go out of my way to think of ways of making them a little happier. But this was impossible. I was just as unhappy and unsmiling as they were, and since I couldn't help myself, how could I possibly help them? Later, however, I thought this over and decided I might challenge myself a bit, So the next day, I grit my teeth, held my breath, and walked down the hall with the others, When I made it to my classroom, I not only had a sense of relief, but a sense of triumph "I did it!" After a few times, I lost my fear of the kids and the horror of being one of the bunch. While this brought pleasure to no one else, I knew I had to start with myself, and this, at least, was a beginning.

Unfortunately, I didn't get much further with dad's possibilities, My attempts to engage other kids in talk or conversation was met with no response, While my class may have consisted of ten children, no more than 6 or 7 were in the room at any one time, there was a lot of going in and out for medication, therapy, special classes and whatever, Also, our desks were scattered all over the large room, there was no contact unless one got up and went over to another's desk, which nobody did, With no interaction possible, and because I completed my day's assignments quickly, I took Nancy Drew books to school to relieve the sheer boredom. The teacher didn't mind at all.

It was probably mid-February when dad sat me down and said the doctor had suggested taking me on a trip. The school told him that as long as I passed my final exams and the doctor thought I needed it, my absence didn't matter, Dad said his friends, Mr. and Mrs. Drudis, had offered to drive us (in their big Cadillac) to Mexico City where we'd visit the Shrine of Our Lady of Guadeloupe, Initially all I wanted to know was how soon we could leave, how soon I could get out of that school? He said it would take three or four weeks to finish up some of his legal work, and this would give me time to prepare for my exams, He had already picked up the exam requirements and said he'd help me, which he did.

Although the expectation of getting out of school early and taking a trip was helpful, nothing overcame the daily sadness I experienced in school, While I lost my fear of the kids, they were obviously not a happy lot, The best off were the blind and those with heart problems, but the others seemed debilitated in spirit as well as body, Unless you had never known any other life, such an atmosphere could only drag you down.

The only thing that bothered me about the proposed trip was its primary destination–the Shrine of Our Lady of Guadeloupe, To me shrines meant primarily one thing: places where people went for cures, places of pilgrimage for the sick, dying, and the hopeless, Right now I regarded these as depressing places to visit, I honestly did not want to go, Though I had a sincere devotion to Our Lady, and knew dad did too, I was suspicious of his desire to take me there at this particular time, After all, there were a lot of other places we could go, One day I asked him,

Me: You're not going there to pray for me are you?

Dad: Do you think we'd go there and not pray for you?

Me: God already answered mom's prayers, so what's there to pray for?

Dad: Don't forget, there's always the chance the bone might not re-build itself

Me: But I know it will! Why can't you believe me?

Dad: Despite your assurance I, for one, cannot presume on God or nature to restore your hip, so checking in with Our Lady might be a wise thing to do–kind of like insurance. Besides, there are more important graces than physical well-being, graces we need in order to lead a holy life.

Me: Well, you can pray as you please, but I'll never say a single prayer for myself (I never did).

Dad: Don't worry, we'll only be at the shrine nine days (for a novena) out of the six or eight weeks we'll be traveling in Mexico. So there is going to be a lot of other places to see and things to do. You'll see, it will be a trip to remember!

The very idea of people praying some kind of cure or miracle for me was absolutely appalling. Perhaps if I had not known the bone would heal itself, this would not have bothered me so much, But as it was, I knew others were praying for what was already a fait accompli, thus their prayers were for nothing, a complete waste of time. I also had no tolerance for anyone who tried to treat me as if I were sick or in need of sympathy, much less in need of prayers or special consideration. If I detected any such attitude I'd abruptly walk away in disgust. It had been bad enough to endure physical and psychological insults, but going to the shrine struck me as worse–it was a spiritual insult. There just seemed to be no end to this whole thing.

For the next five weeks I studied hard and passed my tests without a problem, I stopped complaining about school and, for their part, my parents never mentioned the shrine business again, Mom was already packing when dad suddenly announced we would not be able to leave for another three weeks because the Drudis' couldn't get away until then– some problem either with Jose's car or his wife. The disappointment was keen, because it meant another three weeks of school. Since I had already passed my tests I argued there was no need to go back, but dad explained I was only allowed to go on this trip because the doctor had prescribed it, otherwise I had no excuse to be absent, so back I went.

In the months I'd been at school I only made one friend, a little blind boy on the bus going home. We sat together every day. He showed me the basics of reading Braille, and assured me although he could not see with his eyes–he was born blind–he saw everything in his mind and didn't miss a thing. I asked him if he saw me in his mind, he said he could if he could put his hands on my face and hair, to which I responded, "Never!" He chuckled and said, "Well, then I'll picture you the prettiest girl I know." That touched my heart. Something else that touched me was the homecoming he received every day. His pretty mother would meet him at the door of the bus and swoop him into her arms as if he'd been gone for months. She was the only parent who came out to meet the bus every day, and every day I looked forward to this happy reunion. For a few seconds I felt their happiness, but afterwards, there was nothing but sadness all around.

The morning we left for Mexico, mom was all upset about leaving Marge and Lee behind–ages 15 and 18 respectively, Although Gert would be looking in on them, they'd be mostly on their own, Mom especially hated to miss Marge's 16th birthday, the age at which she and dad had thrown wonderful parties for Gert and Lee, The last thing I saw dad do, as he came out the back door, was give Lee the keys to the boat, he and Marge planned to take some friends to Catalina on the boat, I thought it wonderful of dad's trusting them to go alone, As we drove down the alley listening to mom going on about her poor children left behind, I looked out the back window, and there were the two of them in their bathrobes, literally dancing in the alley, jumping up and down as if shouting hooray and whoopee! I didn't tell mom what I saw. Either it would have hurt her feelings or given her more cause for worry.

We left sometime in mid-April intending to arrive in Mexico City just before May 1st, Our Lady's day, to begin the traditional nine day novena at the Cathedral. It was a leisurely trip, never driving more than four hours a day; we stopped in every little town, and by three in the afternoon were in a hotel for the evening. Now the Drudises—Jose and Amelia—were truly an odd couple. We always thought theirs' had been either an arranged marriage, or at least one of mutual convenience, Amelia was at least 10 years older than Jose. She had gout in her feet so bad she could hardly walk, but she had also inherited a lot of money and property from her family—the Dominguez family, one of the early Spanish settlers in Southern California. Jose, on the other hand, was a poor Castilian artist born in Spain and as distinguished looking as a chivalrous knight or matador. Where Amelia was frumpy, chunky, easy going and mindless, Jose was elegant, fastidious, had a mind for detail and the eye of an artist. His unflagging care for Amelia, however, would have been the envy of any woman. He did everything for her but light her cigarettes—she was a chainsmoker. He did not permit her to smoke in his new luxurious Cadillac however—which is why we had to stop at every little town and oasis so Amelia could light up,

As we approached Mexico City, around every curve we watched for our first glimpse of the Cathedral, When it finally came into view, Jose pulled off the road and parked so we could look down on the City with its impressive Shrine, We had arrived in time to begin our Novena on the first day of May, the month of Our Lady.

We signed in at the Reforma Hotel for a ten or twelve night stay, Before daylight the next morning, my parents and I took a taxi to the Cathedral for the May Day opening of the novena–the Drudises did not get up so early, The huge plaza in front the Cathedral was crowded with people waiting for the doors to open at the stroke of five when they would process into Church, The only ones allowed in ahead of time were the ill or crippled who could not make it in the procession, Because I was on crutches, dad got us in, a fact I did not approve of, we could just as well have come in with the others, Nevertheless, on this occasion I was probably able to take in more as an observer than a participant, and besides, I had nothing in particular to pray for anyway.

At the appointed time the Cathedral bells rang out, the organ boomed, the large doors swung open and thousands of people, most on their knees, moved slowly up the aisle, everyone carrying flowers or a lighted candle, everyone singing the catching, repetitive refrain, "Oh, Maria, Madre Mia." One would have had to be a rock not to be effected by such a scene. Without effort or even intention, one is automatically swept up beyond themselves in an overwhelming movement of oneness wherein the individual is lost in the glory and mystery of a Oneness beyond himself, I felt like a piece of driftwood suddenly inundated and buoyed up by this sea of faith and devotion, a power only God and Our Lady could generate. The procession went on for well over an hour, By the time everyone was in, the flowers along the altar rail were piled so high, it was impossible to see the altar, A bevy of altar boys then appeared and quickly removed the flowers so Mass could begin.

The Shrine was a homey, warm, busy place, its dark interior aglow with candles and the lingering fragrance of incense, People freely milled about leaving candles and flowers, knelt on the cobblestone floors with arms outstretched in prayer or traversed the main aisle on their knees, Masses were going on around the clock at its many side altars–visiting priests from around the world lined up to say Mass at the Shrine, There were alcoves with mementos of cures lining the walls from ceiling to floor and, of course, there was the center piece of it all, the framed mantilla with our Lady's image above the high altar, There was a sense this was indeed our Lady's house, built by her children who freely came and went, a home always open and welcoming to one and all.

I was relieved to find the atmosphere of the Cathedral not so much one of petition and supplication as an out-pouring of faith and love wherein individual needs were secondary to the welfare of all. I found here a largeness of spirit that precluded the continuous harping on private concerns, a spirit focused more on the other than on one's self. Although I had already resolved not to pray for myself, I now found it would have been impossible anyway. I felt this was a place of spiritual, not physical, miracles. Remembering the children at the school for cripples, I did not pray for their physical cure, but prayed that somehow they would become happier people.

When we came out after Mass the plaza was filled with stalls selling food, religious articles and native art. Dad said that every day I could pick out one thing to take home, and then bought me a colorful Indian basket to keep them in. I loved the tiny rosaries in their silver cases, the miniature altar, the tiny pottery tea set, and much, much more. The basket was my treasure chest, truly a child's delight. Afterwards, we went back to the hotel for a late breakfast and then off to see the City sites and historical places. We made trips outside the City to visit a number of beautiful abandoned Churches, some with attached monasteries or convents. It seems while the people were free to practice their religion, the clergy and religious were not. Their schools, convents and monasteries had been closed by a government edict, religious were not even allowed to wear religious garb on the street -which explained the many women we saw dressed in black and wearing black veils, Many religious communities had left the country, which left the religious education of the people to their own devices, or what they could learn at Sunday Mass.

In the afternoons we returned to the Shrine for Benediction and other services, it seems there was always something going on. Every day at noon lines formed to pass behind the altar beneath the miraculous mantilla of Don Jose on which was imprinted the picture of Our Lady of Guadeloupe. My father bribed the sacristan to allow us to stand in front of the altar (literally on the altar) to get a better perspective of the picture at close range. He also bribed the curators of the Church museum to let us in before the crowds made it impossible to see anything. It seemed dad was continually busy around the Shrine, serving Mass or finding something new for us to see, During the days of the novena my father was in a kind of euphoric state, one of intense joy, utterly absorbed in his spiritual life, his devotions and the goings-on at the Shrine, I had never seen him this way before, and would never see him like this again, so completely in his element, so totally immersed in his faith and love for Our Lady and the Church.

For myself, I was just content to watch the people around me, ever amazed at the unselfconscious way they prayed aloud and expressed their devotion in public, sometimes their demonstrativeness gave them an ecstatic appearance, I didn't know quite what to make of this, but there was an air of freedom about the place that gave it the feeling of home, Absolutely, I felt utterly at home in Our Lady's house, more at home than any place on earth, For me, at least, the focus in the Cathedral was not on the miraculous image, but on the pervasive presence of Mary that seemed to fill the cathedral itself, There was no focal point of this presence, it was just "there."

Although it bothered me to think my parents were praying for me–the first on their list at least–it made me think of what I would ask of Mary during the Novena, I had to think about this, think over what I honestly wanted most in life, I could come up with nothing more important or meaningful than my sincere desire to see God, Not see God in heaven some day or maybe when I was older, I wanted to see God now, or as soon as possible, So this is the favor I asked of Mary, if she could get this for me from God, I would be eternally grateful, indeed, I could ask for nothing more in life, Now I didn't know if the favor would be granted or not, Mary might not ask God, and even if she did, God might not grant it, All I could do was ask, and so I did.

On one of the final days of the Novena–possibly the last day–I noticed smoke from the candles had formed a hazy cloud near the ceiling of the church, Several thousand candles of every size had been deposited everywhere in the Cathedral, people even stuck them on the stone floor, Since they were going night and day it was not surprising their smoke formed a hazy cloud in the upper regions of the church, I was sitting there watching this cloud when it seemed to condense into a scene of Our Lady moving slowly from the upper right side of the church to the left. On her right, someone was taking down notes as Our Lady spoke to him (or her). Behind them was a retinue of people or angels I could not see distinctly because the cloud seemed to trail beyond the walls of the shrine, Both Our Lady and her secretary were looking down on everyone, If the secretary pointed to someone, Our Lady would say something which was then noted in the book, Sometimes she would point to someone and say something to be written down, The whole scene was very business-like, obviously Our Lady was granting requests and seeing to individual needs, I observed all this with much the same detachment I had looked out the window at the doctor's office watching people in the street below, Nothing about the scene surprised me, I took for granted Our Lady was taking care of business.

After ten minutes or more of watching this, suddenly the secretary directly pointed at me, as if asking Mary "What about that one?" This unexpected gesture was a jolt that roused me from a detached spectator to an embarrassed focal point, It was disconcerting, I felt caught off guard, Mary glanced in my direction and then gestured to her secretary with a casual wave of hand, as if to say, "Oh, she's already been taken care of," then continued on her way, Where to someone else Mary's gesture might have been taken as a dismissal of sorts, I understood it perfectly, It meant my prayer, my deepest wish had already been granted–I would see God!

Now I only needed to know "When? How soon?" But Mary had gone on her way, I watched for some time until her figure grew distant and eventually dissolved in the candle smoke. When I realized I was once more looking at a cloud of smoke I questioned myself: "Did I really see Mary or could I have just imagined it?" But as soon as I asked the question, I knew the answer didn't matter, I had the sure knowledge my request was to be fulfilled, that's what mattered; how I came by this knowledge was totally irrelevant. It was this promise from Mary I carried away from the Shrine, from the novena, from the whole trip in fact. This promise had a settling effect on me. I felt at peace with my problem with God, at peace with my life and everyone in it. I recognized this as a grace and was now glad I had come to the Shrine.

From that moment on, I lived each day in a state of expectancy, thinking any minute I might suddenly see God, After some weeks, however, I became resigned it might not be that day or even that week, Though life went on as usual, Mary's promise was never far from my mind, Even after months went by, her promise was still as bright as the moment I knew it had been granted.

As the novena drew to a close I became concerned lest my father was still holding out hope for a miracle on the last day. I didn't want him to be disappointed when he discovered that after all his prayers, the pain, the limp and the crutches, were still very much in place. Continually I told him to expect nothing, assured him I didn't need a miracle, didn't want one, and if offered one, I'd even turn it down, On the final day, however, something else happened, something that could not have been more embarrassing than if there had actually been a miracle.

On the last day we were no sooner out of the Cathedral then a group of about 20 women dressed in black—religious sisters I later found out—emerged from nowhere and formed a wide circle around me. Whether this was a spontaneous movement, a Mexican custom, or a conspiracy, I didn't know, but I suddenly found myself in the middle of a circle where all eyes were focused on me, At first I looked frantically around for my parents, but didn't see them. When I tried to walk through their circle, one of the ladies took me by the shoulders and turned me around to face everyone. After this another woman—evidently designated for the task—stepped forward, hugged me warmly, kissed me on both cheeks, and said in Spanish "May the Mother of God cure you!" I could not respond because I didn't know what she had said, I just stood there feeling miserable, so embarrassed my hands broke into a cold sweat, Some man outside the circle must have ascertained my predicament and fairly shouted a translation of what the lady had said, When I heard it, I was angry – everybody standing around waiting for a miracle! Finally I caught sight of my father in the crowd, he was grinning from ear to ear and gesticulating wildly, Finally I understood, everybody was waiting for me to say "thank you" to the kind lady who had embraced me, So I walked up to her and extended our American hand-shake, and with an embarrassed smile said, "Thank you." At this, all the women broke into grins and applause, everyone went "Ah!" After this the ladies turned and walked away.

No doubt this display of love and concern was well intended, but for me, it was a traumatic ordeal, When I reached my parents I began to vent my feelings, "That was the worst thing that ever happened to me, It was terrible, awful, I'd rather have died." But dad was beaming, so tickled pink he could hardly say a word. Finally he blurted out enthusiastically,

Dad: "But that was the miracle!"

Me: What miracle? There hasn't been any!

Dad: Yes there has been–you smiled!

This took me by surprise, I didn't understand, He went on, "You don't realize it, but no one has seen you smile in months, not at home or school, anywhere. You haven't been able to see yourself, but you should have seen yourself just now!" Suddenly it occurred to me this whole incident had been set up ahead of time, so I asked dad, "Did you bribe those ladies to do that just now?" He laughed so hard tears rolled down his cheeks, Mother, however, assured me that what had happened was as much a surprise to them as it had been for me, She also affirmed the truth of my unsmiling face these last months. The news of my serious countenance was unbelievable, I never accepted it, My parents, after all, couldn't have watched me playing most afternoons with the neighborhood gang, surely something humorous must have happened. At any rate, dad put his arm around me, "I told you", he said, "The greatest miracles are always spiritual. The only miracle I asked for you was for you to be happy, and when I saw you just now, I was sure of it!"

Well, he was right in a way. Still, I would rather have died than been trapped in that embarrassing situation–all those ladies expecting some immediate cure or something. It was a nightmare, just thinking about it got me hot under the collar. At any rate, that was it, that was the miracle of Our Lady of Guadeloupe–I smiled! While this was true, my real happiness was hidden from all who looked for external signs, a happiness born of a promise and locked in my heart, a promise known only to Our Lady.

The only mistake the adults made on this trip was taking me to a bullfight. I'd never heard of them and had no idea what to expect. Initially I enjoyed the music and colorful opening parade, but when the bull started butting the skinny horses around the ring–they looked like depressed old nags–and several of them collapsed, I was heart-broken, this was terrible, shocking! A bit later, however, they stuck stilettos in the bull, and after that, a wicked looking knife! There is no verbalizing the disgust and anguish I felt, It literally made me sick to my stomach–heart sick as well, Such deliberate cruelty I had never thought possible, While everyone around me was standing and cheering I sat with eyes closed, a tiny rosary clenched in my hands, After a while dad poked me and said, "What are you doing?" I said, "I'm saying nine Our Fathers and nine Hail Mary's for each bull", He didn't say anything, A bit later, however, Jose complained to dad that my disapproving posture was offensive to the people around us, so dad whispered in my ear, "Remember what I told you about 'When in Rome do as the Romans do'," but I didn't give a fig about the Romans, I was praying for the bulls, The very idea of faking enjoyment was out of the question. To the very end–through the slaughter of 7 or 9 bulls–I sat with my eyes tightly closed praying as hard as I could for each of those poor bulls and tortured horses, Obviously I should never have been there, Later in our hotel room we heard people shouting and cheering from the street below, Looking out the window we saw thousands of people crowding the street carrying on their shoulders none other than the matador himself! I learned out the window and started to shout "BOO" when mom grabbed the back of my sweater and pulled me in with a reprimand–something about being disrespectful in other people's country. I was struck by the utter incongruity between the people at the bullfight and those at the Shrine, I was never able to make any connection.

After we left Mexico City we traveled south for another week stopping at Cuernavaca … and other places whose names I do not remember. While dad's sole interest had been the Shrine, Jose had other places he wanted to see, in fact, much of the time we spent in Church, Jose was visiting museums and art galleries. He especially wanted to visit some ancient ruins in southern Mexico. One destination was spending several nights at a well-known hotel or resort situated on a hill renowned for its beauty and other amenities. When we got there, however, it was closed and so we stayed at a unique, but smaller place down the hill.

This was an open air villa with beautiful tiled porticos, verandas and patios, the feet of the tame goats clicked along the corridors and exotic birds squawked in their large cages—there were other animals as well. I thought it the most unique homiest place we stayed during the whole trip. The second day there, I had my tenth birthday, After dinner the proprietor walked in with a colorfully decorated cake and candles while he and the help sang happy birthday in Spanish. After I had blown out the candles the proprietor solemnly announced: "Now you are one-tenth Mexican!" and everyone applauded. For myself, I believed him, besides having the same Mother, I loved everything about this Country, its beauty, people, music, indeed it had an indefinable spirit I identified with completely— except the bullfights of course. I was sure this birthday portended a good year ahead. As it turned out, it was just that, a year to remember.

From beginning to end, my ninth year had been one long ordeal, whenever I remembered this period of my life, however, the bone disease never came to mind, rather, it was the tragic event of the interior Power suddenly disappearing, After four years of companionship, the lessons it taught me, the joy and love it revealed, its sudden defection was a blow so terrible it took a miracle to bring me back to myself, back to health and normalcy.

With this recovery I discovered I could go it alone, had a certain sense of wholeness, because now there was no mystery in me, no space within that was not myself. What remained after its departure was only me, the real me, all of me. Though this new self would sometimes totter on the brink of its own weakness and helplessness, yet it retained some inherent facility for rising to every challenge and picking itself up by the boot straps. There was something deep in myself that seemed invulnerable and incapable of destruction, something that could never be localized as a space or a power, its essence, however, never seen or truly known. Though I now had a strong sense of myself and my own independence, there would be times when I knew there was still something wanting.

* * * * *

We arrived home a week before school was out for summer. Though I was not expected back at school, mother suggested I might like to go back and show my class the pictures and articles I had collected in my basket, I liked the idea; so with the aid of a map, postcards, and my basket of treasures, mom helped me organize a talk, My teacher happily consented to my sharing the trip with the class, One by one I took out my small mementos–little Mexican dolls, jumping beans, a picture of Our Lady of Guadeloupe, whose story I told the kids, As the articles were passed around, I talked about each one and explained the religious mementos as well. I ended my talk singing the procession hymn I'd learned at the Shrine, The kids' responses were heart-warming, it was a kind of ice breaker, a shared interest that got us all talking, Evidently the talk was a success because the teacher asked if I would take my basket to some of the other classrooms as well, In fact, she lined it up with the other teachers to have me come at certain periods of the day for the rest of the week.

This was a whole new experience for me, an unforgettable week. I went from classroom to classroom sharing my basket of stuff, telling the story of the Shrine, the horrors of the Bullfight, the beauty of the Sunken Gardens, always I was amazed at the keen interest the kids took in all this. When I finished they thanked me profusely and clapped, it was quite overwhelming. After those talks all the kids knew me, greeted me in the hallway, I even ate lunch with them in the cafeteria. What I learned, of course, was that these kids were no different than myself. We couldn't stand other people's pity or being treated as if we were sick; since we were as normal and intelligent as everyone else, we only wanted to be accepted as such, to be just one of the bunch.

By the end of the week my delight and sense of satisfaction was high. I was amazed to find everyone so happy and smiling and wondered what miracle had taken place while I was away. When the last day was over and we were saying good-bye I wondered how I could ever have been so afraid of them. I remembered how I used to look cautiously out the classroom door before venturing into the corridors; of how I refused to eat with them, the fear of sitting beside them on the bus. But now, all this fear and avoidance had given way to feelings of friendship, even iden-tification, for I had finally come to recognize myself as one of them , We shared much the same tragedy in our lives and yet, despite it all, we had not succumbed, We had, in fact, overcome.

As we crowded in the main hallway saying good-bye, I recalled my initial view of this very same scene- a vision of hell I'd thought, But here I was now, standing in their midst and feeling sad I would never see them again, I would often ponder the radical change between my first and last days at school, In itself the change seemed like a little miracle, yet, it had only been due to a little basket of Mexican souvenirs.

Postscript

Later in life, whenever the subject of my illness came up, I'd berate my parents for not having believed me, Though I always thought dad should have apologized for the way he treated me, he never did, He never even admitted he had made a mistake in believing the doctor instead of me, He'd only shrug his shoulders and excuse himself, "I believed the doctor because he was the specialist, I trusted he knew his business," was all he ever said. I put this down as sheer pride—what else? On the other hand, if what mom said was true—namely, that she never believed the doc-tor and always believed me—if I asked her "Why didn't you tell me that?" she never answered, instead she'd say, "Don't forget, I was the one who found Dr. Wilson and insisted we take you to see him." So in the end she was the heroine! Her behaviors, however, belied her conviction. In every way she went right along with dad and the doctor, if this was not against her conscience, it was certainly against her child. It seems it never crossed my parents' minds to admit they had been wrong, much less offer any regret or apology for not believing me and for what they put me through by going along with that charlatan. Perhaps they honestly never knew what I went through or what they put me through. All I can say is that I had more respect for dad's honest, though terrible mistake in believing the doctor, than I did for mom's cowardice when she didn't believe him, As things turned out, the issue was rarely brought up because I'd just get hot under the collar and nothing, after all, could be done about the past.

AGE 10

What I had to face next was a major family move. Unknown to me and prior to our trip, the family had anticipated a move to Hollywood where dad had built an apartment complex. The news of moving away from the beach was bleak indeed. Having to leave the sea, my friend and greatest inspiration, struck me as an unnatural withdrawal of my life's support, a wrenching I didn't see how I could survive. Some of the best moments of my life had been spent on its shores. I decided to go there and ask for its help once again. Gazing out to sea I knew that mere physical distance could not separate us, the mystery of our bond was something I would carry with me wherever I went, its mystery was in me, part of me. Also, I noticed the sea had a certain air of detachment and independence that was never caught up in people's comings and goings. When all of us were long gone, the sea would still be there, unchanged, relentlessly doing what it was created to do—to be. I wanted to emulate this detachment and independence, be able to walk through thick and thin in its same change-less state. With this determination I took courage and made ready to move.

Dad had built a U-shaped apartment complex, with our home spanning the back of 8 units on both sides. He also moved his law office from downtown Los Angeles to the corner of Hollywood Blvd., a block from home. Since the new house had all new furniture, linens and dishes, there wasn't a lot of moving to be done. One day I'd come home from the beach and all the pictures on the walls had been transferred to the new house; another day our books were gone; still another, mom had taken most the clothes from my closet; and so things kept disappearing until the final day arrived and we kids only had a box or two of personal junk to put in the car.

Lee and I were the last to leave. If we shared anything deeply it was our love for this home and our life at the beach. We lingered until late afternoon, wandering around the house joking about this or that and recalling happy times. We were near tears when we finally got in his car to leave. At the last minute I said, "Just a minute, I want to go back and kiss every room goodbye." So he waited while I made the rounds, kissing the wall where the monk had been, where the altar had been, and lingered in my room with its happy and tragic memories. It was two sad hearts that drove down the alley that day, life would never be the same for either of us. Lee wouldn't last in Hollywood more than four months, and I would never live in another house I ever regarded as "home."

The only familiar objects in the new house were a few pieces of art tastefully displayed around the rooms. Although the altar was gone, dad had built a special niche in the upstairs hall for Our Lady's statue. After inspecting the rooms, I noticed the monk was missing and asked mom what happened to him. She didn't know and told me to ask dad. There were some anxious moments waiting for dad to come home. When I asked him he said he wasn't sure, "He could be in one of the boxes out in the garage, let's go see." Standing on a tall ladder, he handed down several boxes. Anxiously I went through familiar pictures and portfolios until, finally, I found him! Utterly relieved, I hugged him to me. Dad said, "If there is anything else you want here, take it now because mom intends to get rid of these things." Indignantly I asked "How could she ever get rid of the monk?" "We didn't know you were so attached to him, but from here on, he's yours." I was delighted and took him to my room to be installed on the wall. Unfortunately, Marge and I were back to the old battle of sharing a room, there was no way she was going to have that monk on the wall. We made a deal, she could have the top of the vanity for her stuff and I'd put my stuff on top the dresser, which is where I propped up the monk. The only problem, he kept falling over, so after a time I put him safely in my top drawer to await better times.

It was a long, hot, boring summer. Lee had a summer job, so I rarely saw him, and Mom was busy managing the apartments. Apart from reading and playing the piano, I had nothing to do, no one to play with, nowhere to go. The street out front was busy day and night—no possibility of ever hearing silence again—and out the back door was a line of concrete garages. There was no private garden, no place to be alone either indoors or out of doors. The sounds of the ocean had been replaced with the noise of city traffic. To top it off, was the terrible heat. Twenty miles inland from the ocean there were no overcast mornings or afternoon breezes. Instead, there was a relentless stuffy, muggy, sticky heat that all but sapped the soul's energy. This unaccustomed heat magnified the boredom of the long summer, how to fill time was a major occupation. When dad installed an air conditioner at the top of the stairs, I spent a lot of time reading in the wake of its artificial breeze—something to do at least.

Altogether I had a feeling of being hemmed in, a kind of spiritual claustrophobia. The lack of a natural open environment with no visible horizon was a matter of great sensory and spiritual deprivation. No, this was not really a home, it was just another cramped city apartment. I felt boxed in, not only between four walls, but by the apartments on either side—and beyond that, apartments all around us. The one uplifting element were the giant Deodar trees that lined the street behind us. Because I could see them from my bedroom window, I moved my bed next to the window sill so I could lay on my pillow and look at them. Had I never known anything better, perhaps city life would have had something to offer. But as it was, my first impression would be my last: city life is the worst possible environment a human being can live in.

Among the books I inherited from Gert were a series of Elsie Dinsmore books, the story of a motherless little rich girl abandoned by her father and mistreated by the relatives she lived with. Poor Elsie had only two sources of comfort, her Mammy and her little book, The Imitation of Christ, a book of short pious sayings. Whenever Elsie felt down and out she found comfort in reading from this little book, excerpts from the Gospels, Augustine and others. In short form, it presented the proper Christian view of life and its events and how to respond to them, all of it based, of course, on Christ's earthly life as the model for imitation. I was so impressed, I got out dad's copy of the Imitation and read it front to back. Somehow this reading lit a spark of religious fervor in me. I determined to start there and then on this path to a good life. To be able to live this way was the challenge I now set for myself.

While there was nothing I could do about the externals of my life, I could work on my interior life, those matters of mind and heart. I needed to shape up my life and not depend on favorable events or people. In short, I had to get things right on the inside regardless of things on the outside. So I mapped out my day. I would start by going to Mass with dad every morning, say the rosary every day, read the lives of the saints, take time at night for a deep examination of conscience, and try to spend some time alone to think, pray, or just lie on my bed and look at the Deodar trees. I pretty much stuck to this regimen for a year before my fervor waned. During this time, however, I learned a great deal about myself, what I could or could not do, and what I still needed to know. It was the first time I had ever examined my interior life or deliberately focused on myself to take note of my interior reactions. Dad commented one evening at the dinner table, "All the great philosophers say the highest wisdom is "Know Thyself", a saying that struck me as curious because how could you not know yourself? Then I recalled mom's earlier words, "You'll never find your true self until you find God." So I began searching myself and came to a few conclusions of my own.

For the first time in nine months I was able to look within myself and not immediately see either my old friend or its absence. Basically, everything I saw was just myself, seemingly different levels of myself, and the deeper I went the more nebulous or unknown things became. There didn't seem to be anything to call a "bottom", instead, everything seemed to converge on a small dark center, a mysterious center I could never see into. I took for granted this dark center was my deepest self or as far as I could go, if mom was right, it was probably my "true self." But what exactly was that? I gave this a lot of thought and concluded: I do not really know what I am, only God knows what I am because only God knows what He created. I was convinced this was true of all creation. Thus all we could know of ourselves and the world was really superficial. At bottom then, what we really are, what everything really is, is a mystery known only to God. Carrying this a bit further I concluded that just as we do not know "what" God is, so too we do not know "what" we are, and in this respect we are truly images of God. Thus as God's image, we are as unknown or unknowable as God Himself. Satisfied with this conclusion I was convinced that the philosophers' quest to "Know Thyself" could only lead to a dead end, lead to a mystery beyond human knowing, a mystery known only to God. After this I dismissed the philosophers' quest as a fruitless waste of time and never thought about it again.

Some of the things I learned and habits I developed during this time would stay with me forever. For one thing, I took on dad's habit of making a thanksgiving after communion—that is, remaining after Mass instead of leaving right away. Dad told me theologians believed Christ in the Eucharist remained present in us until the bread had been completely assimilated into our bodies, which they figure took about 10 to 15 minutes—depending, of course, on the type of bread and our physical condition. So this was the time to focus on Christ's Presence, be with Him and ponder His mystery. It wasn't long after I started going to daily Mass I noticed a subtle change in myself. I could never figure out what had actually changed. I only knew that when leaving Church I had a subtle sense of what I might call "purity", as if I was somehow new, as new as a newborn babe. Interiorly I felt quiet, satisfied, happy. But once I got home and became involved in the daily routine, that whole aura left and I was back to my old self. Whatever the change had been, it didn't last, and since I didn't know how it came about in the first place, there was nothing I could do to get it back. The next morning after Mass, however, there came the same subtle state, and an hour later, it was gone again. This subtle phenomenon of change would always intrigue me. Indeed, I would notice it the rest of my life.

At one point I wondered how long this state or condition would last if I had nothing to distract me, or if, say, I remained alone in my room or maybe stayed longer in Church. When I tested this out, however, I found that while it could be prolonged, it didn't last. It seems that even if I had no external distractions my mind created them anyway. One day, however, I tried my old trick of letting my mind go blank, and while this worked to clear my brain, in time the distractions drifted back. Then I decided I needed to practice going blank, and so I did. What I discovered is that I could, in fact, stay for longer periods without distractions. On several occasions, however, I stayed blank so long a fear arose I might get stuck in this silent blank state forever. When this happened, I immediately reverted to my thinking mind and was glad I could do so. As long as going blank was my choice and I had control over it, there was nothing to fear. Over the long haul the ability to "go blank" served me well. As a little one, I had thought this mental ability odd and put no value on it, but here now, I valued it as a way to prolong a mysterious state, stay in a sacred place.

Because dad's office was just up the block, he was home a good deal of the time. Where, at the beach, he had been gone before we got up and only returned before dinner, now he left about nine o'clock, came home for lunch and was back before five. Mom said adjusting her day to dad's schedule was the hardest part of the move. For me, however, it was a boon. Here began years of talking and discussing things with him—we talked about everything—and I can't think of anything of value or importance in life I didn't learn from him. Since I never learned a thing in school, without this free flow between us, I could never have regarded myself as remotely educated. But if I picked up a great deal, respected his learning and views, this does not mean I agreed, or even believed it all. Far from it. The great benefit of our talks was the challenge it presented me, thus after giving his view on something, he'd ask, "Well, what's your idea, how would you resolve it, do you have a better answer?" and so on. Whether deliberately or not, he challenged me to think for myself.

One evening he told me the story of Socrates, his favorite philosopher. He went over Socrates' theory of learning, of arriving at truth through intense debate and dialoguing, which he described as two people seriously engaged in argument as to the truth of something; if they just kept at it long enough, suddenly they would come upon the truth. Now I could identify with this method. Sometimes when arguing I suddenly blurted out something profound that surprised me, something I had not known or even thought of. Sometimes it was as if a spark of light in the mind alerted me to some truth or something meaningful that I must pay attention to, or think about. Because of this, I tended to believe truth was stored in some unknowable level of the mind, a level, however, not available to its rational functions. Thus it was only when you got to the end of all reasoning and thinking (through arguing perhaps) that truth could be uncovered.

Dad also went over Plato's analogy of the man-in-the-cave, or appearance versus reality. He told me other stories and sayings of the Greek philosophers who I decided to read for myself. Four or five blocks from our house was the Pickwick bookstore on Hollywood Blvd. that sold new and used books. I often went there and spent hours browsing, sometimes mom or dad gave me money to buy a used book. The first book I bought was Lives of the Greek Philosophers, followed by Plato's works. (His Republic was so shocking it left me with a life-long prejudice against Plato's thought processes). At any rate, I gradually became acquainted with the various schools of ancient Greece, which doesn't mean I fathomed all I read. It was merely the beginning of a life-long love of philosophy. More than any other subject I was at home in a philosophical milieu.

Once I did not have enough money to buy a certain book, so I decided to wait for the right moment to ask my parents. The next morning at breakfast, Lee and Marge presented dad with a barrage of needed permissions–go here or there, do this or that–when suddenly he banged his fist on the table, "You can do anything you want! You are free, free to do anything–anything but sin!" Dad always smiled when he said this (we'd heard it before), but seeing my opportunity, I asked, "But how can we be free to do what we want if we need money to do it?" He shot back, "How much do you need?" "Two dollars," I said. "Alright!" He stood up and searched his pockets, pulled them inside out. Besides his keys, he had 25 cents. Giving mom a helpless look, "Mother, don't we have some money to give this girl?" So I got the money–and the book.

This was the only time I asked dad for money because we all knew he rarely had any on him. Some mornings after he left for work, mom would run after him, "Mark, do have some money on you?" Then she'd hand him some bills. Mother was the family banker and bookkeeper, she paid the bills and, with few exceptions, bought everything for home and family. She often told us, "Your father never once questioned anything I bought, not once." For the most part mom had to buy dad's clothes as well. To get him into a store to buy a suit, however, she said she had to start working on him a year ahead of time. As for shoes, he would only shop for them when he was walking in his socks–with his shoes on. There was something about dad reminiscent of an "absent minded professor", high on the theoretical, low on the practical.

Sometime in July my parents got word their friend, Grace Lewis, now known as Sr. Mary Magdalene, was going to make her first profession as a Carmelite Nun and would be allowed visitors for a few days. Although, as her attorney, dad could visit whenever necessary, mom wanted to see her and asked me if I wanted to go along. Of course! I was curious to learn about her monastic life and looked forward to hearing about it.

We drove to Alhambra, east of Los Angeles, and parked in front of a red brick monastery. We were warmly greeted by two elderly sisters, Ignatius and Aloysius, who were in charge of the convent's external affairs and old friends of dad's–they knew him before he was married or just after the community had arrived in Los Angeles from Baltimore, Maryland. They said they had known me since I was born. It seems as each child came into the world dad brought us for a visit and, according to the sisters, brought us at least once a year to see them. Although they said they had not seen me for several years, I did not recall ever meeting them before or having visited the monastery. Their claim might have been true, however, dad took us to visit so many different convents, seminaries, rectories, Churches and Chapels that, as little kids, we never really knew where we were.

They also said that at the beginning of my illness dad had called the community to ask for their prayers. They had made several novenas for my recovery and expressed joy their prayers had been answered–the answer they referred to was that after returning from our trip to Mexico the x-rays revealed the first sign of the hip bone starting to rebuild itself. Naturally Dad interpreted this as a sign from heaven, while I knew it was just the expected course of the disease. I believed in miracles, but this was not one of them.

After a bit we were ushered into the parlor where, from behind the black grate, we heard Grace's booming voice greeting us. She pulled back the curtain on her side and there she was, her large face beaming beneath a white veil and crown of flowers. As was customary, she was accompanied by another sister who, this time, happened to be the Prioress, Mother Therese, superior of the community. While Grace and mom chatted about mutual friends and other things, Mother Therese told me to move to another seat so she could raise the black veil she wore over her face and we could talk face to face through the grate. (The Sisters didn't have to wear a veil over their face when visiting family or children.)

Immediately I took a liking to Mother Therese, I felt completely at home with this out-going, seemingly fun-loving Nun. At one point I asked her to go over the Carmelite day, I was curious about life behind the black grills and high wall. As she went through the details and routine of their daily life, I couldn't help but compare it to my present life. That each sister had her own cell was my idea of paradise–having to share a room with my sister was, well, something next to hell. That the sisters fasted and never ate meat, was also perfect–I'd be free from mom's constant nagging me about food, especially meat, which I detested.

When she told me about their grounds, some of it wild and uncultivated, that each sister was assigned a part to care for, I thought this ideal–where I lived there was only a common formal apartment garden.

That the sisters observed silence most the day was wonderful–I loved silence, I had listened for it all my life. Where I lived, however, there was no silence possible.

There were two hours of recreation each day when the sisters sewed, embroidered or knit as they chatted. I could do that, I knew how to sew. And after the recent move, mom had sent me to a lady to learn how to knit.

As for Mass every morning, I already did that. About the two hours of silent prayer every day, well, I was trying at least.

When Reverend Mother finished going over the monastic day, she said,

R.M.:   There now, you know what we do in here, you know the schedule.

Me: But tell me, what's hard about this life?

R.M: (She laughed) That's just it, it's not really hard–although many people think it is. (After a pause) To those who love God, all things are easy.

When she said this, my stomach fell–"To those who love God", but I was not one of those. No, I did not honestly love God, never experienced any love for Him. This is why I asked Our Lady to let me see God. I was sure no one could see God and not love him. For a moment I almost told Reverend Mother the truth–that I didn't love God–but for some reason I held back. Maybe I was ashamed, or thought it would shock her, so I put it to her as delicately as possible:

Me: Don't you think someone could live this life even if they didn't love God?

RM: (Throwing up her hands) Why would anybody want to do that?

Me: Because it's a good life!

I went on to tell her why life "out here" in the world was not a good life, and why I was convinced that if more people knew about their life, they'd all want to come and live here. She laughed and said that my view of their life was not shared by many people.

R.M: After a few months of the "good life", when the newness wears off and the routine of community life sets in, they'd leave. Living in a community is not easy sometimes. When things get tough they'd just leave–why not? Why put up with things or people that may rub you the wrong way? (She paused a few moments and went on). Anyone who comes here solely for their own sake, expecting some advantage for themselves, wouldn't last two months. Our Carmelite vocation is to pray for the world; we leave the world, sacrifice our own pleasure in it, to pray God's grace and help for others.

What she said went deep. Living this life for the good of others and not yourself was the highest ideal I could imagine, but since only the love of God made this possible, how could I ever do it? Then I remembered

Mary's promise—to see God—which I never doubted she'd keep. Relying on this, I asked:

Me: Do you have any vacancies?

RM: (She thought a moment) Yes, I think we have two vacant cells.

Me: Could you save one for me?

RM.:   Of course! If you have a vocation there will always be a place here for you.

Me: But in a couple of years those cells might be taken.

RM: I assure you, when you are ready there will be a cell for you.

Me: Is that a promise?

RM.:   (She leaned forward and with great deliberation said). Before God, I give you my word, I promise that whenever you want to come, there will be a cell here for you.

The moment she said this, it was as if a gavel had fallen in my favor—my whole life settled with a single stroke! Prior to this I hadn't given a thought about the future or what I'd do when I was older, but now it was decided. I knew what I wanted to do, knew exactly where to go, and had the assurance I'd be able to do it. Without any mind-rending decision, without any expectation of holiness, even without any love of God, the decision had been made. I was as happy and content as a pigeon come home to roost. Now I had a life to look forward to, to get ready for, to plan on.

Before we left, the sisters showered me with religious mementos: a relic of St. Therese, a beautiful rosary chaplet, scapular, medals, holy cards, I don't know what else. As we went out the door, the Extern Sisters told me to be sure and come back to see them. I assured them "I'll be back!" Going down the stairs of the monastery I was overtaken by a sense of exhilaration, a joy that spread through my whole being and reminded me of my experience at the Shrine. Once more a decision had been made on my behalf, and once more I recognized a mysterious inscrutable Plan at work.

Following this decision I had a new sense of freedom, I no longer felt hemmed in and trapped by circumstances. Even city life would now be easier because I knew it was only temporary and for a short time. In the years ahead I often had a sense of waiting, a feeling of doing time in this world. Sometimes I'd be caught unawares by a great longing to leave this worldly life, a longing that stemmed not so much from love of the cloistered life–which I had never lived–but a longing to transcend all the irrelevancies and make-believe that made up so much of the adult world. After my glimpse of a good life, so simple, direct, and devoid of wasted time, I now had a measure of contrast between it and life in the world, a standard of judgement that could cut through and discern the unauthentic from the false.

At home I didn't tell my parents what had conspired or my life's decision, but then, they never believed anything I said anyway. At dinner they talked about Grace and what she said about her life in Carmel. At some point mom shook her head and said, "I just don't understand why anyone would want to live that kind of life, it's not natural." "Of course it's not natural", dad said, "it's supernatural, you have to have a special grace to live it." When the subject of the Little Flower came up, mom said, "If it hadn't been for her doting older sisters, we would never have heard of her." Now I had read Therese's Story of a Soul, it said nothing to me, her spirituality was too sentimental to suit my temperament. When I told dad I really didn't care for her, he said, "Well, when you're older you can read the life of the Great St. Teresa of Avila, she's the one who founded the Order (of Discalced Carmelites). You might like her." Now any time dad referred to reading a book and said, "When you get older", I knew I had to read it immediately. So after dinner I looked in his library and took out her autobiography.

Although St. Teresa's experiences of God were in the form of visions, voices, raptures and other phenomena I could not relate to, still, her experiences were certainly more than the feeling of life and breath–which years before, dad said was all we could truly experience of God in this life. So I picked out some passages describing her experiences and took them to dad, "See? Read here. You said we really couldn't experience God, but St. Teresa had experiences of God–and she's not talking about just living and breathing!" With a gesture of casual dismissal he said, "Oh that," referring to her experience, "that was just to increase her faith!" I didn't know what to say to that. If he was right, however, he just dismissed all the Saints' reported experiences of God as no more than an increase in faith. Obviously, the Saints were people low on faith! Later I got to thinking about this. Without their extraordinary experiences, the Saints might have had no faith and not served God at all –they might even have become devils! On the one hand, this certainly gave me a new perspective on the Saints, and on the other hand, I knew I would never need such experiences because I already had a strong faith in God.

Reading St. Teresa, I was also somewhat shocked when she said she was a sinner. I believed her absolutely. Since God called so many sinners to be saints, I wondered if people who had never sinned could be one. I pondered this, because I never thought of myself as a sinner. The notion of original sin–everyone born a sinner–made no sense to me. No use blaming sin on our inheritance instead of our own perverse selves. I was sure mom also never believed in original sin–many times she emphasized that everyone was born good and that we came from the hand of God utterly pure and innocent. It seemed to me that between original sin and the devil ("he made me do it"), people could always find a way to excuse themselves, slough off their own responsibility. On the other hand, according to dad, who adamantly believed in original sin, unless one knew what they were doing was a sin, knew it to be an offense against God, then there was no sin. If he was right, then certainly, ignorance was bliss!

Anyway, from here on, whenever I read of saints and mystics who had visions, revelations and all the rest, I referred to this as "cheap spirituality." While their experiences may have increased their faith, I thought them irrelevant and self-serving. I came to look upon all such phenomena as extrinsic, without true depth, experiences that smacked more of the psychological than the supernatural. From here on I could not stomach reading the lives of anyone–be it saint, mystic, or holy person–who had "extraordinary" experiences. Far from being impressed, I had a positive aversion to the stuff, never saw any truth in it at all. I also had no patience with anything that smacked of the sentimental. One day, however, I came across the lives of the early Desert Fathers, whose ascetic antics I found utterly bizarre. Mom was fixing dinner in the kitchen so I took the book, sat in the breakfast nook and read her excerpts. The two of us just laughed. Mom shook her head and said, "I've never understood what any of that has to do with God or leading a holy life." I didn't either.

Several times during these years I would again discuss with dad the experience of God's presence in ourselves. He said that in essence, man's faculties were inadequate to experience God as He-is-in-Himself. The disparity between the nature of man and the nature of God precludes such a possibility. Through grace, however, which was God's medium to man, our faculties could be touched and informed by God, informed as to his existence, his love and goodness, etc., yet a direct confrontation was out of the question. After all "No man can see God and live", life in the flesh was not meant for such a vision. According to him, God was present in us only by his sustaining power that gave us natural life, and also by grace, a gratuitous gift that gave us eternal life (not merely natural life).

I asked him how it was that some of the Saints claimed to see God and experience the certitude of His presence. He said that the important thing here—regarding the Saints' experiences—was the grace involved, not their experiences, which were purely individual reactions to grace. God was the cause of the experience, but the effects or experience itself was their own. Thus whatever description the saints gave, were only descriptions of their own reactions, while God, of course, remained forever indescribable. He said that experiences themselves do not inform us of truth, at best they can only affirm it, because truth, like God, is beyond mere experience. Instead of experience, dad laid full emphasis on enlightened, non-experiential faith, which he regarded as the greatest of all God's gifts. For dad, however, faith was not primarily an intellectual assent to belief, but rather a strong will to love God and do His will.

At that time I did not fully understand all this, but it gave me something to think about. Though what he said did not resolve my quandaries or unravel the mystery of my own experiences, yet what I learned from him was far greater and more important than anything I ever learned elsewhere in life. Though his answers struck me as strangely arid, his perspective gave me a point of reference with which to evaluate my experiences, know what in them was important and what was not. Because of this, I was always trying to figure out what, in my experiences, belonged to God and what belonged to me. I had no problem with God being unknowable in Himself, indeed, if he were knowable there'd always be some people who wouldn't like Him. Better God keep His mystery to Himself. Still, this didn't mean we couldn't know and experience Him. Despite all I learned from dad, I was never convinced people were totally incapable of experiencing the one true God.

Another problem I had with dad's view had to do with grace. While God gives grace without our experiencing it—thus we receive the sacraments and experience nothing out of the ordinary—yet is the grace of experiencing God the same grace given in the sacraments, or is it a different one? It seemed to me everything depended on what was meant by "grace", if grace was not God, then how could it make us holy or more perfect? And besides, who would want anything that is not God? Who would want to experience only themselves—for heaven sakes!

If grace is not God's sharing His own life with us, then we are no better off than, say, He had given us a car. While man's experience of God is certainly not God's experience (who knows if God even has any?), nevertheless, God must have made man such that he could truly experience God. Then too, if the human Jesus could experience God, then so could we. Why not? My conclusion was that those who never had such experiences would naturally downgrade them. Thus I figured that while dad knew his theology, he may not have known the experience.

* * * * * *

At the beginning of summer, dad said we wouldn't be taking the boat out until the apartments were rented and his legal affairs in order. He hoped everything would be in order by August so we could go to Catalina for a week. It seems things went well because in August we packed up and headed for the boat, now moored at the Wilmington Yacht Club in Los Angeles harbor. It was our habit to go down to the club in the late afternoon, get the boat ready, load our stuff on board, eat dinner in the club, sleep on the boat, and then leave the harbor at the crack of dawn when the water was smoothest. Sometimes I'd only wake up after dad was underway.

On this summer day, however, after dinner dad decided to take a ride around the harbor. Finding the waters at the port entry so calm, he decided to keep going and make the trip over that evening. Halfway across, however, we were not only engulfed in a dense fog, but it got rough, the roughest waters we'd ever been in. For the first time I saw mom scared. Because dad had to navigate solely by compass, she was afraid that if it was off the tiniest bit, we'd miss the island completely. After uttering her "Never again!" she and Gert–who was expecting her first child–commenced saying their rosaries. Dad, however, showed no great concern, he was even cheerful, said he'd give a dollar to the first one to see the beacon in Avalon bay. When we spotted it, however, we were all relieved for mom.

After a week or so, when about to set out for home, although the sea was like glass, someone hoisted a storm warning flag on the pier–which did it for mom! She insisted the two of us (she and I) return on the big steamer. Her concern was clearly unwarranted. What angered me, however, was her trying to use me and my crutches as an excuse when we all knew it was simply her own fear. I made a big fuss about it. Dad finally took me aside and asked me to go with her just "to keep her company, make her happy." With genuine sadness–and a bit of resentment–I watched them sail away without me. An hour later mom and I boarded the steamer where I took up my position at the rail to watch for our boat. When we got close, dad went off course to come as close as he dared alongside the steamer where I looked down on everyone waving and cheering. I could only wave back through tears and watch as they faded into the distance behind the steamer. The ocean, of course, was like glass. It turns out I never saw mother until it was time to disembark.

Before school started we made another trip to Catalina, this time with Aunt Mabel and Uncle Joe (dad's brother), a comic team who had never been on a small boat before. For sheer humor and laughs, this was the funniest trip I ever made. It was also the only time I fell overboard–slipped on a wet deck. (At one time or another, everyone but mom had fallen overboard). I was insulted, however, when Uncle Joe jumped in to save me–since I was the better swimmer. He swore he had only jumped in to save my crutches from floating away. After I got out I remarked how glad I was I didn't have my watch on. Marge had just sold me her old watch for 10 cents a week, and mom had had it repaired. After dressing, when putting on the watch, I noticed it was not running, so I gave it a shake that sent its insides across the cabin into the bilge—that murky water under the engine. Of course it never ran again. Since I couldn't see the logic of paying for something that no longer existed, I stopped paying Marge. This fuss over the watch, however, only opened the old wound of the piggy bank money she had never recouped—and to which she had added 5 years of interest. Any lull at the dinner table and Marge would take the opportunity to remind me of my debts, which at that time she calculated to be at least $50.00! This is all it took to start an argument.

Mom never liked us kids arguing. She took it for a sign we disliked one another, which wasn't true, we merely disagreed with one another. Our arguing, however, never bothered dad, whether by temperament or profession, he liked a good argument. On one occasion when mom tried to stop us, he quoted her something from Chesterton on the difference between arguing and quarreling, the former being a way of learning, the latter, not. To discern the difference he went over the logic of right thinking and the ten major fallacies of wrong thinking—like ad hominem, non sequitur, vicious circle, equivocation, and so on. Employing these fallacies was quarreling, wrong thinking, and often mean spirited, whereas avoiding these fallacies was right thinking and true argument, an intellectual challenge wherein we might learn something about the issue at hand. Dad was especially fond of syllogistic logic and often used examples to challenge my thinking. I have to say, I took to this like a duck to water. I loved to argue, yet I rarely found anyone else who did—it seems most people cannot distinguish it from quarreling. From the time dad first pointed out logical fallacies, I became aware of them for the rest of my life. What I learned was that these fallacies were a matter of common usage employed in almost everyone's ordinary speech and conversation. My recognition of these fallacies, however, became a means of discerning who I could talk to with profit and enjoyment, and those with whom discussion was bound to go nowhere and be a waste of time. Without question, Dad's lessons in logic served me well.

One pleasantry before school started was mom's taking me to the Hollywood Bowl for an out-of-door production of the opera Carmen. This was the first opera I had seen. I was so impressed that in the next few years I probably saw a dozen or more, sometimes going by myself to the Shrine Auditorium when the opera company was in town. Several times that summer–and every summer thereafter–Marge and I went to the Bowl for evenings of classical music "under the stars." While mom always got box seats up front, I preferred the highest (furthest away) seats, because few people were up there, I could lie down on the bench and look at the stars while listening to the music. This was a delightful experience, one I repeated whenever possible.

I looked forward to the start of school. Although as a new student I wondered how the kids would take to a classmate on crutches, yet anything was better than being cooped up in an apartment. As it turned out, nothing could have been easier than matriculating into the fifth grade at Blessed Sacrament School. Because it was a large class we were divided into two sections, and whether the kids in our section had been deliberately chosen or not, we ended up with all the uninhibited, unstudious trouble makers, probably the ideal class for me. There were only two or three quiet loners, the rest seemed to share a restless, humorous, daring wild streak of some kind. For four years this was my group, and while I don't think we learned anything–I know I didn't–I doubt any of us would deny we had a good time, got away with murder, and came away with some unforgettable memories.

Something I did learn at school, however, were the traditional Latin hymns and Masses. From the fifth grade on, all the girls were expected to be in the Church choir. We not only sang every Sunday at the children's Mass, but frequently sang High Mass on Holy days and special feasts. We also sang the Mass of the Dead (my favorite) at funerals. There was also a young boys' choir conducted by Mrs. Biggs, wife of the Church organist. I was amazed to discover that the most despicable boy in our class–Stanley–had the voice of an angel; it struck me as utterly incongruous. Once he put a tack on my desk seat and the brawl that ensued was never actually resolved. Besides our school choir, the Church also had a paid professional choir conducted by Mrs. Biggs. Because they sang the high Mass at noon every Sunday, after our family attended the children's Mass at nine o'clock, we'd go home, eat, then mom and I would go back for the noon Mass, which was always magnificent, sometimes a bit heavenly. So there were good things going on in Blessed Sacrament Church, even if there was no learning going on in its school.

On the first day of school everybody gathered round to take turns on my crutches and ask what my problem was. On that same day I met Sally, the closest friend I would ever have. The end of the first week she walked me home from school, and after that we were only separable if it couldn't be helped–or on occasion we had a fight and didn't speak for a day. We couldn't have been closer if we were sisters. Mom used to say she could have raised Sally as her own, but then, everybody loved Sally, in every way she was a lovable person. Sally and I were together on Dec. 8th when we heard on the radio that Pearl Harbor had been bombed. We immediately went outside to watch for Japanese planes overhead. Within the next six months or so, Lee joined the Coast Guard and spent his active duty in the Pacific on a mine-sweeper.

With the onset of the Pacific War, one of dad's immediate concerns was the government's confiscation of property belonging to the Japanese-American citizens in the Los Angeles area. As attorney for the Maryknoll Fathers who had a Japanese parish downtown, dad already had Japanese friends and clients who now needed his help, but alas, help he could not give them. Their homes, farms, properties, businesses, bank accounts, everything was taken or frozen by the government. Dad said over and over it was unconstitutional and that some day the government would have to pay for it; he even said the act would go down as an ignominious blight on the country's history.

When the local Japanese-Americans were taken to the internment camp of Manzanar in the Mojave Desert, the Maryknoll Fathers went with them. Dad made a number of trips to see his friends in camp, he did what he could to keep them informed of the condition of their confiscated property. I know dad did everything he could legally do for them, which wasn't much. On several occasions we went along with dad to visit the camp, the first time being the Easter of 1942.

The closest town to the internment camp was Lone Pine, a one-horse town where we stayed at what was probably its only hotel. We arrived on Holy Saturday and the next day, accompanied by one of the priests, we went to the camp, heard Mass and had breakfast with its Catholic community. It was either on this or the next visit, the children in the camp made their First Communion, all of them beautifully dressed in white as if they had never left home. Despite the cramped living conditions—families separated only by curtains in a single Quonset hut—I was surprised to find the people so cheerful. Later, Father took us for a tour of the camp and pointed out a lone man walking one of its deserted streets. He told us it was Dr. X, a professor at UCLA, highly respected everywhere, but so depressed by what had happened that Father's congregation had a perpetual novena going for him.

After celebrating Easter in camp, on Easter Monday my parents planned a drive up Mt. Whitney for a picnic. At that time Mt. Whitney was the tallest mountain in the U.S. Its eastern face looked down on the desert and the internment camp, even from the hotel window I could see its snowcapped peak. Driving up the mountain there was still a lot of snow on the road. We could only go as far as the snow plow made it, at which point, however, we found a picnic spot to the side of the road. An overgrown path led to a rushing stream, so after lunch, while the rest of the family hiked upstream, on my crutches I was able to follow the path downstream a ways.

The path came to an end at the edge of the stream, and though I could see the path continued on the other side, there was no way of getting across, the spring run-off was in full force, virtually a roaring torrent. I spotted a tall boulder by the stream, circled it to find the easiest way up, and discarding my crutches, scrambled to the top. It was an ideal perch from which to survey the surrounding forest, so beautiful and untouched. I let my mind go blank, the better to relish it. I had already learned from the sea the secret of how to simply "be there", be part of the scenery, devoid of worldly cares and mundane concerns.

I had probably been sitting on the rock less than a half hour when there occurred what, for me at least, was one of the most momentous events in my life. It was not so much a personal experience as an objective "seeing" or "knowing", but since what I saw and knew was not through the senses or intellect, I have no idea how I saw and knew. Though I tried on a number of occasions to describe this event, no description was satisfying. If anything, my words only seemed to fictionalize it. All I could do was give my impressions after the fact, such as they are. First, the whole thing took a matter of seconds, it was so quick I always referred to it as "God's passing by–as if I'd caught sight of God when he wasn't looking.

Though I had no impression God saw me, I was certain God deliberately wanted me to see Him, that He had in fact, lined this up. This seeing was so definitive and pivotal to my life that without it, my life would not be my life. I also regarded it as the most spectacular or sublime of my experiences because it left me a knowledge of God's utter transcendence, magnificence, glory and brilliance. I would always refer to this as seeing "God Passing By" or "God in the Woods," which was my expression for God's utter transcendence. After this sighting, if anyone had ever asked me, "Have you ever seen God?" My answer would be a resounding "Yes, absolutely!" Any other answer would only be a lie.

There were two parts to this experience. First I saw an immense brilliant light that momentarily cast its shadow over the entire forest. I'm not sure how these two impressions, light and dark, fit together, perhaps it was a case of "now you see it, now you don't." I only know the light was so brilliant I couldn't see the forest. Either way, however, I know this light stunned my brain, stopped it completely. The second part is more easily describable: an instant after seeing the light, from within myself came an explosion of uncontainable joy, in one respect it reminded me of the balloon experience five years before, only this time I understood it as a grace from God, a taste, as it were, of His own glory. What I noticed about this explosion, however, was its delayed reaction, it did not happen when I first saw the light, but the instant after–a fact I always found curious.

It took two full weeks to return to my usual self–two weeks before life could resume where it had left off. My mind–my whole being–was in such a state of disinterestedness I could only go through the motions of ordinary living. For two weeks I lived in the afterglow of this "seeing", which only gradually wore off. I was even aware of the moment when its last vestige disappeared. If I learned anything at all it was this: see God and you will never be happy in this world again, never even be deeply interested in it. One glimpse of God will ruin your life forever. You will never again be able to put you heart, mind and soul into anything in this world. Such is the enduring effect of such a sighting: It leaves Its imprint on the soul forever.

Later, when dad quoted the saying "See God and die", I could understand it, but only if the vision were permanent, in which case It would blind you to the world forever, so of course you'd be gone– dead to the world. But a passing glimpse of God? No, you wouldn't die. If that were case I wouldn't be here. Now I never had to guess how or why I came by this experience. Simply put, Mary had kept her promise. I could never image what my life would have been without this gift.

I had been on the rock at least an hour before I heard the others calling. At first I thought I couldn't move, yet I was able to climb down and make it back to the family. I wasn't in the car five or ten minutes, however, when I became aware that my old friend, the interior Power, had quietly returned. There it was, a light within, acting as if it were right at home and nothing had ever happened. After a 16 month absence, after abandoning me in a time of crisis and leaving a frightening black hole in its wake, after the horrible days following its disappearance, to think it had the gall to return was beyond my comprehension. I was not happy about this, but since I was now absorbed with something far beyond it, I paid no attention to its return. Besides, it could disappear any second, and I hoped it would. Weeks later, however, when the afterglow had faded away, I deliberately set my mind to live as if this interior Power did not exist. I not only didn't trust it, but since I had now seen God, I knew for sure this Power was not God. Absolutely, I would give it no space in my life.

Not long after our trip to Mt. Whitney, my parents had some special guests for Sunday dinner. Mom had arranged a beautiful table with her best silver and crystal, it was all very formal and elegant. In the middle of dinner, however, I experienced a forceful thrust or "leap" from within. Instantly I knew God was passing by. Immediately I left the table, rushed outside and looked upward. Though I only saw Its afterglow–comparable perhaps to seeing the tail of a comet–all other interests dropped away. I stood there alone and silent until its afterglow was completely gone. A few months later I was in Grauman's Chinese theater watching a movie with two friends when again there came that forceful leap. I told my friends, "I gotta go!" and ran out of the theater to catch a glimpse of God's passing. Though the magnificent sighting of God in the woods was never repeated, for the next four or five years I periodically experienced what I called its traces, tail-end or afterglow. Sometimes I saw more, sometimes less, but the effect was always the same: a profound love and longing for God, a quiet happiness, an uplifting, a momentary disinterest in the whole world. Equally amazing was the interior "leap" that could detect God's passing. The interior Power now seemed to act as a kind of alert system, and as long as that was all it did, its presence was fine with me. These experiences of God's passing were never predictable, they could occur any time, any place, regardless of what I was doing or where I was.

Initially I made a conscious effort not to look within, but in the long run it didn't work. I soon realized that the mere recognition of this Power was harmless; as long as we each kept to our own space there might be peace between us. With its sudden leap of joy, however, all other interests fell by the wayside, my cares dispersed in a knowledge above all concerns. Always this joy projected itself outward and upward in search of God, ever accompanied by an intense longing to see Him again. Far more impersonal than in my childhood, where it had taught me many things, this Power was now quite impersonal, left me to struggle alone with my problems. Obviously it had changed its behavior toward me. Apart from its sudden awakenings, it remained for the most part a quiet space within, akin perhaps, to the notion of a sleeping giant, an aloof Power unto itself. I say 'for the most part' because there was one other way it could affect me, which was when it acted like a powerful magnet drawing my mind inward and downward into an unknowable silence and stillness within. Needless to say, I dearly wanted to know the true identity of this Power. In time I was convinced it had some connection to God, but what this was I had no idea.

Shortly before the school year ended, an incident occurred that re-
sulted in some hard thinking about the man Jesus. My Christian faith was
called into question when I posed a particular question to Christ and got
a mysterious, terrible answer, one that would leave an indelible imprint on
my mind. My question was sparked by a playground incident when two
girls (sisters) became angry with me because every day in a game of dodge-
ball, I was able to hit them out of the circle. After one of these games they
came to me and said, "You think you're hot stuff because your father is
rich, but we've got news for you, Christ said it would be harder for a rich
man to get into heaven than for a camel to get through the eye of a needle!
He also said the beggar Lazarus went to heaven and the rich man went to
hell." "Yeah", her sister chimed in, "Christ loved the poor more than the
rich. You read the Gospels and you'll see this is true ... he was poor himself ... and said it was the poor who would inherit the kingdom of heaven."
"He also said you can't serve two masters at once", added the first sister,
"you can't be rich and love God too; ... he came for the poor, not the
rich ."

I don't remember what else they said, but I tried to assure them my
father was not rich, that he owed money to Barker Brothers Furniture
store–all the apartments came furnished. I also tried to tell them Christ
came for everybody not just the poor, but the bell rang and we had to line
up. Determined to have the last word, I said, "Well, I know one thing, I'd
rather be rich and humble about it, than poor and proud of it like you
guys, because the proud aren't getting to heaven either!"

In class that afternoon I put my mind to thinking up the perfect
rebuttal, some words of Christ with which to slay my friends after school.
The more I thought about it, however, the more I realized everything they
had said was true. Christ had, in fact, come to save the poor, the op-
pressed, the sick and the sinner, but since I was none of these things, how
had he come for me? Did he have less love for those who had not sinned,
were not poor, were not sick, were not a sinner? In my view, God loved
everyone equally regardless of their economic status, after all, God reads
man's heart, not their bank accounts. Thus God loves us equally in health
as in sickness, in joy as in sorrow, in good times and in bad. While man's
love could be fickle–loving God more at one time, less at another–God's

love was above such fluctuations; His was a steady and equal love. Although I believed this, it was still dissatisfying because it did not explain why Christ came and died to save those who had never sinned. If he truly died for all, then he had to have died even for those who had not sinned.

Now I had always thought the notion of Christ suffering and dying for my sins totally outrageous. To blame me (or anyone else) for his death made no sense, this was just someone's preposterous idea. What is more, as far as I knew, everyone strove to avoid sin (offending God). I knew my parents did, the saints and religious people did—all good people in fact. For myself, I was not conscious of having offended God, and did not regard myself a sinner, so how, then, is a non-sinner to look upon Christ's death? What would Christ's message be to us—more especially, what did it mean to me? No, there had to be another reason for his death, but what? The more I thought about these questions, the more imperative it became to find the answers. I knew that if I asked my superiors I'd get the same old answers, so I decided as soon as school was out, to go next door to the Church and ask Christ directly.

Blessed Sacrament Church was the largest in Los Angeles. To the right of the altar, was a life size crucifix from which Christ looked down with sorrowful glass eyes on anyone kneeling beneath. Since I was on crutches and not allowed to kneel, I stood under this gaze and began to ask my questions. No sooner had I started, however, than a wave come over me, a sense of some terrible tragedy that whisked away my questions as if they didn't count, were meaningless, childish, totally irrelevant. Before me there was only some terrible dark mystery. It was like a gray cloud, a mystery so deep my mind could not follow, couldn't even think. Though I had no idea what this meant, I took it for an answer of sorts, that left no doubt there was, indeed, more to Christ's death than I had ever known or been taught, more perhaps, than anyone had ever suspected. Though I did not know what more this could be, it occurred to me that the real tragedy of his death was that nobody really understood it! Though I wanted badly to know, yet nothing followed this experience but complete silence, seemingly a stubborn silence on the part of Christ.

While the effect of this experience left me with a subtle assurance I'd someday be privy to this knowledge—a true understanding of Christ's death–I took for granted it would only be in heaven. From that day, however, I never lost the certitude that the true mystery of his death was beyond any redeeming purpose, a mystery, however, not open to my understanding. Also, from then on, whenever I looked at a crucifix–which was always close by–it was ever shrouded in the same unknowable mystery I encountered on this day. Always it made me aware of my unknowing, a mystery, however, I was certain to know in heaven.

Realizing this impenetrable mystery had wiped out my questions, I thought that to get the questions out, I'd best move out of range of those glass eyes. So I backed up to the row of pews behind me. But as soon as I began my questions, I noticed the eyes were still looking at me, intently watching as if through their eyelids. I had never noticed this phenomenon before and decided I needed more distance. So I moved to the other side of the Church–the alcove of St. Ignatius of Loyola (it was a Jesuit parish)– but when I turned around to begin, the eyes were still looking. This gave me the goose bumps. For a moment I felt weak in the knees and almost bolted from Church. At the same time, however, I had a sense Christ wanted or expected something from me, yet nothing came to mind. Thinking I might somehow be imagining his gazing at me, I decided to move to the back of the Church. In such a large edifice I knew that even if the eyes were still watching me, I could not see them from such a distance, which proved to be true. Finally, from the rear of the Church I felt free to ask my questions: why had he died for those who had not sinned or never offended God? What was his special message to them–to me?

Though I had no idea how he would answer, I was sure I'd get one, so I sat down and went blank–to be sure the answers would be His and not mine. For some reason, however, I could not affect a blank mind for very long. Instead, I was aware of what a noisy chatter box my mind was, so I got up and paced back and forth across the back of the Church.

A long time went by, well over an hour. I grew increasingly impatient and decreasingly hopeful of getting an answer. It was as if Christ deliberately maintained a stubborn silence, yet He knew I was waiting and I knew that He knew, but how long could I hold out? I couldn't just let the matter go when everything in me cried out for an answer. Finally a thought came into mind: the reason Christ didn't answer was because there was no answer. He couldn't say how or why he died for me because he hadn't died for me at all! Then I remembered the words, "Many are called, but few are chosen," which meant that despite being called to be a Christian, I had not been chosen. Suddenly this explained everything. While my parents had chosen for me, God had not, which is why I could not understand Christ and why he did not answer. But if I was not a Christian, then what was I? Since my whole life had been inextricable bound up in a Christian life, it seemed to me that if I was not a Christian then I was absolutely nothing. Once again I experienced that same dark unknowable tragedy I had experienced up front. He had in fact answered me from the beginning, only I had not understood. This dark tragedy was not His, but mine, all mine–I had not been chosen, I was not privy to the true knowledge of Christ because I was not really a Christian. In short, I was nothing!

For a moment I felt poised on the brink of anathema, about to be cast into oblivion. I froze on the spot. The saving grace that broke through this horror was a powerful surge of anger and outrage, the likes of which I'd never experienced before. It was so powerful I didn't know what to do with it. Immediately I left Church, slamming its huge door so hard the whole edifice shook and trembled. I hurried away fast lest the Church collapse and I be found in its rubble.

I determined never to go back to Church again. I didn't belong, it would be hypocritical to pretend I did. After four blocks or so I stopped and looked up through the trees to catch sight of clouds drifting overhead. Nature, always so impervious to our fluctuating emotions and thoughts, always uplifting us beyond the mundane cares of life, its transcendent mystery ever there for us. I stood awhile just looking up to allow its mysterious detachment to dissolve my problems and restore a lost peace. I remembered God in the woods and thought to myself: since I've already seen God, who needs Christ? I can love God without him, despite him, I don't need Christ at all! After this there arose in me a great determination to love God, a resolution that brought me great joy, and with this, I continued home.

That night I told dad what the girls had said and what I learned in Church. I told him that although he had chosen the faith for me, somehow my baptism "didn't take," God hadn't given me the faith—"man proposes but God disposes." To his credit, my father was neither surprised nor disappointed, but dove into the issues. First he went over the various meanings of what it meant to be "chosen"; then, on the issue of original sin he challenged me to come up with a better explanation of the origin of evil, sin, and man's ultimate salvation. We also went over the whole issue of poverty, its different levels and various interpretations in the Gospels. In the end, he told me that people who didn't question their faith weren't worth their salt. As a supernatural gift, Faith was not dependent upon reasoning or understanding, and thus the mind would always be subject to doubt and questioning, a fact that neither negated Faith, nor was contrary to it. He reminded me that the revealed truths of our faith were profound mysteries ultimately beyond the human mind, which is precisely why they had to be revealed, and why we needed the gift of Faith. So dad encouraged me to question and not be afraid of doubts when they arose because our gift of Faith was sufficient unto itself. He ended by giving me Pascal's Wager to ponder, which goes something like this: If you live your life as a believer and it turns out to be true, then you have gained everything; if you live your life as a believer and it turns out not to be true, then you have lost nothing; but if you live your life as an unbeliever and it (the Faith) turns out to be true, then you have lost everything. Now I didn't quite get this. It seemed to me that if you lived your life believing something to be true when it was not true, then you've lived a lie, you've been cheated, and you may have missed out on a lot of fun. The idea of living according to something that was not true horrified me. No, I didn't think much of Pascal's wager.

That night before I went to bed I got out a piece of lined school paper, on one side I wrote down all the things I believed, and on the other side, all the things I did not believe. Thus I believed in God, the soul, grace, heaven, purgatory, the Sacraments, Mary, and so on. On the other side I wrote what I did not believe in—angels, devils, original sin, Limbo, Christ dying for my sins, and as for hell, well, I wasn't sure if I believed it existed or not. So I went downstairs and asked dad if we had to believe in hell in order to be a Christian. He said, "Well, the Church says you have to believe in hell, but it doesn't say you have to believe anyone is there." I was satisfied with this answer and put it on the side of things I believed in. When I finished my list and added everything up, I was happy to discover I believed more than I disbelieved, and wondered if this was sufficient to make me a Christian.

The over-riding issue, of course, was whether or not I honestly believed Christ was God. After all, God was not a human being–I had learned the hard way "God is a pure spirit that cannot be seen with bodily eyes"–so obviously, the physical, visible man Jesus could not be God. Earlier in life I had resolved this Jesus problem when I remembered that the human Jesus was dead and gone. He had returned to heaven whence he came, thus in heaven he was of the same divine status as before he came. I had no problem with this, yet the realization now hit me that, by definition, a Christian is someone who believes the purely human Jesus is God, and that even in heaven he remains forever as a human being. I didn't see how this could work, or how I could ever honestly believe this. Here I was confronted with the question of whether or not I was a Christian–did I believe the human Jesus was God or not?

After giving this question my best thought I decided that while I could not say "Yes," on the other hand, I also could not give a definite, absolute "No"–lest it be true and I be wrong. I felt there was something pompous and presumptive about closing the door forever on such a possibility. After all, God was the ultimate mystery with whom nothing was impossible, and who was I to say what He could or could not do? Then too, if I was not a Christian, then what was I?

I thought of all the Jewish people who had not believed in Christ, yet they knew God, loved God, led good lives, went to Church, prayed–did everything we did, only without Christ. It seemed to me that in the deepest sense I was really Jewish, I had to be. Jesus, after all, was a Jew, so if someone really wanted to be like Jesus, he too would have to be a Jew. This made sense to me, I liked the idea. If I'd been older I would have gone to the Synagogue and never gone back to Church. From this time on, I always thought of myself as a "secret Jew."

While I honestly wanted to get dad's help in this matter, I didn't know how to put the question to him. I already knew dad's view of Christ was that of a fighting Irishman chasing down the Pharisees of this world. To listen to him, the temperamental similarity between Christ and himself was strangely coincidental. For sure, however, dad was never hooked on any sentimentalism. Christ meant business, meant what he said, meant hard work, and those who didn't agree with him could just get out. Knowing his views, I had to put my question so as not to appear either wholly unbelieving or believing, which meant giving my question a lot of thought before putting it to him the following night, which I did. "Let's say," I began, "someone believes most of what the Church teaches, but not everything, does this mean he is not a Christian?" Instantly dad replied, "We don't understand in order to believe, rather we believe in order to understand. If you wait until all the understanding is in, you will never believe; if you are ever to understand there is only one way"–pounding his fist on the table–"Practice! Practice! Practice!" The emphatic way he said this cut out any further discussion. His answer was powerful. I understood it completely. While he had not directly answered my less than honest question, he wisely cut to the chase, got to the bottom of things.

Saying my prayers that night, I laid the whole issue before God: "If Christ is truly God, then you will have to let me know it. I trust you to let me know the truth and never let me believe anything that is not true. If Christ is to have any place or meaning in my life, you will have to give me this knowledge so I can believe; if you do not, then I will know Christ is not God and that I have no need of Him in my life." I totally trusted God to let me know the truth. It was inconceivable He would let me go through life believing something to be true when it was not. I could not base my life on somebody else's belief, never. I had to know for myself, and only God could give me this knowledge. This didn't mean I had to understand the truth, indeed, who could understand almighty God–Truth Itself? No, I simply needed to know the truth regardless of whether I understood it or not. I wanted to know the Truth of God, the whole Truth. There was no reason for God to keep it from me. As things stood, since God had not informed me Christ was the Truth, then there was no need to give Christ another thought. So trusting God to let me know, I went to bed with the issue resolved. I felt completely relieved of the whole matter and had no further problem with Christ. For years I neither believed nor disbelieved, but left the whole issue in God's hands and went on my way.

I might add, that while I certainly knew of the Trinity—Three Persons in One God—on several occasions, however, dad dismissed Its mystery as forever beyond the human mind. In his view, as the very essence of God, the Trinity was intellectually incomprehensible, unknowable. He might as well have said: "Don't bother to think about the Trinity, because you can't." Since he was up on every other theological doctrine, I'll never know why he was not up on the very one that had priority over all others, for without the Trinity, Christianity makes no sense at all. His rather easy dismissal of the Trinity was regrettable because I too, dismissed it as unthinkable and never gave it a thought. This omission, I'm convinced, left a big gap in my ability to come to terms with Christ and my Christian faith.

That Sunday—after the above incident—going to Church with my family was one of the hardest things I ever had to do. I felt it was totally hypocritical of me, even a sacrilege; getting through Mass was torture. I decided that during Mass I would mentally distract myself, pay no attention, keep other things or events in mind, which is how I got a terrible headache. I really wanted to tell Dad I couldn't go anymore, but I knew he'd either laugh or blow up, in either case, I'd end up going anyway.

Back at school, the dodge ball games went on as usual, and I continued to hit my friends out of the circle. Little did they realize what a can of worms they had opened; there is no underestimating the profound repercussions this whole incident had for my life. While prior to this I had never given much thought to my Faith, now I questioned if I even had it.

One evening at the dinner table—I don't recall what my parents were discussing—suddenly I heard mom say, "Why Mark Roberts, I do believe you love Our Lady more than you do Christ!" I thought, "Uh-oh, now he's on the spot! What's he going to say to that one?" Unless someone knew dad's enormous love for Our Lady, they would not understand the challenge mom presented him. I stared at him with baited breath. For a minute he paused as if thinking. Then, without a word, he deliberately resumed eating. I couldn't believe he wouldn't say at least something, so I continued to watch him expectantly. After another minute or so, he looked at me and winked, then went on eating. He never answered, never said a word. He wasn't about to defend his love of Mary, and indeed, he may well have felt more love for her than for Christ. To me his silence was golden, I thought to myself, "Good for him! I don't love Christ either."

Age 10

Age 11

AGES 11 & 12

The day before my 11th birthday dad asked, "How would you like a dog for your birthday?" I couldn't believe my ears! For years I had begged and argued for a dog, even when I thought it would never happen, I asked. After moving to the apartments there was even less hope of getting a dog. Still, if anyone asked what I wanted, I'd tell them the truth. The reason mom was always against it was based on her earlier experience with a dog when the older kids were young. She said that after a few weeks nobody paid any attention to it. She was the only one who cared for it, and the only one who grieved when it eventually died. No more dogs for her. I don't know what changed her mind, it may have been the Drudis' beautiful Springer Spaniel, the delight of us all. Mom and dad had decided on a smaller version, a Cocker Spaniel, and found a kennel in the valley that had several litters for sale. The next morning dad and I drove to the kennel and were ushered into a large room with about 15 puppies milling around. After playing with them, I picked out a two-and-a-half month black male, the terror of the group, and named him "Bruce", after one of Terhune's black collies. I had collected all of Albert Payson Terhune's books, and would have preferred a collie, but beggars can't be choosers. It turns out Bruce was a joy to the whole family, he added a lot of life to our house. Hands down, this was the happiest birthday I ever had, and Bruce, the best present ever received.

I loved that little dog so much, I felt guilty about it, genuinely concerned. One day, waiting at the bottom of the stairs for Bruce to make it down behind me, dad stopped to watch Bruce clumsily managing the stairs. I said to him, "You know, I think I love my dog more than I do

God." He laughed and said casually, "What you feel is puppy-love, whereas love of God is a strong will not to offend Him." Though I felt relieved, his remark turned out to be the most important piece of knowledge he ever gave me. I would even say it was the most important piece of knowledge I ever came upon in my entire life. It was pivotal, absolutely central, to my entire spiritual life. And not just then, but forever.

Thinking over what he said, raised a number of questions. While I never wanted to offend God, I couldn't see how merely the desire not to offend God could be regarded as love of God. It seemed to me one could abstain from sin yet never have a true love of God. On the other hand, why abstain from sin if you didn't love God? No, there had to be more to love of God than just not offending Him. Dad's remark, on the other hand, indicated that love of God was not a feeling or an emotion, but was a strong will to love God–this was important. His remark also brought up the issue of the different kinds of love we can have. Thus I knew I had an enormous love of nature, yet what I felt for nature was very different than what I felt for my dog, and different still, from what I felt for my family, and all of these were different than my love of God, which was not a feeling at all. No sentiment ever flowed between myself and God, rather, it was more of an innate attraction, a pull, a longing, something beyond mere feeling–in a way it was something beyond me, I really didn't know. At any rate, what dad had said so casually became an issue of great significance to me.

Either that night or the next, I brought up the subject of love after dinner. By this time I had already learned the traditional divisions of the soul's faculties into intellect and will (according to St. Thomas), or intellect, will and memory (according to St. Augustine), but what dad focused on this evening was the will as the faculty of love. In so many words, he told me: the will is the power-house of the soul that could move toward good or evil–do good or do evil. Love was the will's power to move toward the good, the highest Good being God, whereas its movement toward evil was a movement away from God. Love, then, was not an emotion or a feeling, nor anything produced in our minds or intellect; rather, it was the soul's power, its will, its determination, even its desire, for the highest Good, namely, God. So love of God was our determined will to seek the Good, move toward it and do it, do God's will that is, because God's will was always for our own highest Good, namely, for God Himself.

After this, dad launched into the age old dispute between the Dominicans and Franciscans. It seems the Dominicans thought the intellect was the soul's highest faculty because it was with that faculty we would see God in heaven–the Beatific Vision, that is. The Franciscans, on the other hand, thought the will was the highest faculty because it was the faculty of love, a love that would unite us forever with God's will–God's own love. From this it would seem that in heaven, where the intellect would be passive ("seeing" or knowing), the will would be eternally active, doing and loving whatever God does and loves. So which is higher, love of God or seeing God? While at the time this seemed like a frivolous dispute–because to see God is to love God–still, I got hold of something that became the mainstay of my life, namely: true love of God is a "will-to-God"–simple as that. Love of God is not in our heads, not a matter of emotions or feelings, rather, it is the will, that power house of the soul, our life's very energy, focused on God. That alone was true love of God. Nothing else.

It was from this discussion with dad, I picked up the one piece of knowledge that would become the back-bone of my life with God. I had long been aware of my own will-power. It was my experiential reality, virtually my life's energy that I knew to be somewhere in the center of myself. Over a period of time this identification of the will would have more meaning in my life than any other piece of information, data or concept, to come my way. Not for a moment did I think my will was in my head or thinking brain, on the contrary, it was a silent, unthinking power-house in the center of my being, and when its power was directed first and foremost to God, this was true love of God. From then on, for me, at least, love of God was a will-to-God.

I practiced becoming ever more aware of this, aware of my own will, its presence in me. I even set out to see if it was possible to focus this inner power on God at all times. Indeed, finding out if this was possible, was the most profound goal I ever set for myself. Intuitively I knew that my will-to-God was the door to a profound mystery, a profound truth regarding God and myself. It was as if I'd suddenly learned the secret code to everything important in life and how to live it. I no longer worried about loving God, because now I knew how. Now I knew what it meant, and I meant to do it.

I went on to discover that in its deepest sense, the will is not primarily the faculty of desire for anything known, but rather, the desire for something unknown, an innate longing for something that lies beyond ourselves, a longing for something we know is missing to us. This longing is always uplifting, never focused on anything in the world that we know of, and no matter how intense this longing, it is never a downer or saddening. It's a need to have something, know something, possess something, in order to fulfill ourselves, to be complete, whole, or totally satisfied. We may think at times it is a longing for beauty, truth, goodness and much more, but nothing short of God will ever satisfy. I particularly experienced this mysterious longing when out of doors, alone in nature, or listening to great music. For me, this longing expressed the true nature of the will, its deepest nature, which I knew as a longing for God and what I would always refer to as my "will-to-God."

* * * * *

Shortly after school was out for summer it was time for my next hip x-ray. After examining the results the doctor said the bone had completely rebuilt itself and I could discard the crutches. This news was not unexpected, for some months I had walked around the house and climbed stairs without feeling a thing. When mom asked the doctor if I should start out gradually, or if there were any restrictions, he answered with a resounding "No." I could do anything, take up any sport, the bone was as good as new, there would be no need for any further check-ups.

We took the crutches downstairs to the hospital supply store and left them with the man in charge–a donation of sorts–and so ended a two and a half year ordeal. Though I never heard from the bone again, certain leg movements had been restricted for life, thus I could never sit on the floor with my legs crossed, get into ballet and gym positions–all kinds of movements, in fact. Apart from sitting on the sidelines and watching my friends' ballet classes and tap lessons, I didn't miss much. One of the first things mom did, however, was sign me up for ballroom dancing–classical ballroom lessons. Sally and I went together dressed in our Sunday best, the boys in suits and ties, we learned to tango, waltz, foxtrot–all the classical steps. It was conducted with strict formality, virtually a class in manners and grace. Though probably not in my element, I enjoyed it thoroughly, we took several sessions of this class.

Because Sally's mom signed her up for sewing lessons–how to use a sewing machine and follow dress patterns–my mom did too. Sally did great, but for me it was total frustration. Mom also kept after me to sign up for a session at Camp Teresita Pines, where Marge had a summer job as a senior counselor. Marge had been to this camp a number of summers, more than any place in the world she was in her element there. This year, besides being in charge of a tent full of girls, she would also be in charge of horseback riding. For myself, I was not keen on the idea, I had been there once before when I was eight, didn't like it, and only lasted one day. Still, it meant getting out of the city, going to the mountains, being surrounded by nature, this much appealed to me, so I signed up and went off.

The only thing I liked about camp was its beautiful setting in the pines. I also enjoyed Mass in the outdoor amphitheater amid the pines. Lifting one's soul to God comes naturally in such a setting–so unlike city Churches where one has to make a concerted effort. Although we had little free time, I found myself a spot by a stream where I could go alone and become part of the scenery. (Actually, this spot was out of the camp's boundaries, which is probably why they could never find me.) The fact my sister was a counselor, however, proved a setback. She was extremely popular with all the girls, which meant everyone was disappointed when they found out I was nothing like her. I was constantly challenged by others to see how good I was at this or that, and, of course, I was no good at all. I did, however, enjoy learning the traditional camp-fire songs. With gusto, Marge and I would sing them together the rest of our lives.

An unsettling incidence took place after Marge got home from camp that summer. She must have had a bad case of nostalgia because she stuffed her side of our vanity mirror with camp pictures. And not little

2 by 2's, but more like 5 by 6's. I didn't say anything, but got out some of my dog pictures and filled up my side of the mirror. This left about a six inch square in the middle of the mirror–if you wanted to see yourself. When Marge saw this, she didn't say a word, so I took for granted she didn't care. A few days later, however, I walked into the room and noticed my pictures gone. Marge was lounging on the bed reading; I asked indignantly, "Where are my pictures?" She casually pointed to the waste basket. There they were, all waded up! Right in the middle of my chest I felt a burn. It wasn't painful, but given time, it was likely to burst into flame. Immediately I left the room, got out my Imitation of Christ, sat on the stairs, and cracked the book open to read the first words I saw.

The words said, "When thy neighbor smites thee on the right cheek, turn the left." Now this was anything but comforting. What I needed was something to douse the flame, merely ignoring the incidence wouldn't do it. Besides, if I let her get away with this, what might she do next? After being smitten on both checks, where would she hit me next? No, turning the other cheek was as good as asking for more, and I couldn't take what I already had. Then I pondered if anybody could really do that–turn the other cheek. Why should they?

Letting people get away with murder might not be good in the long run. No, this really wasn't good advice. And what about some of the other advice in the book? I flipped through the pages reading here and there and decided the whole thing was impossible. Nobody could live this way, the advice was impractical and unrealistic. Instead of dealing with the issues at hand, it would have us look the other way–look to God maybe, who didn't give a fig about Marge's tearing up my pictures–or possibly, my tearing up hers! No, this book was impossible, it couldn't help me anymore. Then and there I put it away forever.

For at least a half hour I sat there trying to figure a way to get rid of my anger. The only solution that seemed workable was to go into the room and do unto her what she had done unto me–wad up her pictures. But what if after doing that I still felt angry? Well, I wouldn't know until I'd done it, in which case, I'd have to deal with that later. So I got up, went into the room and grabbed her pictures, squished them up and threw them in the waste basket. Then I walked out, slammed the door, and sat on the stairs to wait for all the screaming. Well, I waited and waited, but nary a sound, not even a word from her, not then, not eve–evidently she had realized the justice of my actions. The reason for telling this story, however, is to say how it happened that I gave up on the Imitation of Christ. For a whole year it had been my mainstay, I knew it by heart, yet from this point on I would look back and wonder what, in heaven's name I ever saw in that little book. Whatever space I had been in–between the ages of 10 and 11–I would never be in it again. I only knew that the book could never speak to me again, and it never did.

* * * * *

The beginning of September Marge packed up and went off to board at Marymount College. Though she often came home on week-ends, I pretty much had the room to myself, which meant Sally could now occupy her bed. One morning the two of us were jumping on the beds, using them. like trampolines. We not only wanted to see how high we could jump, but see if we could do a flip of sorts and land on our backs. On my second or third flip there was the sound of splitting wood and the bed collapsed, in that same split second dad walked in–it seems he had been on his way in, anyway. I sat there stunned, both because of the bed and dad's timing, suddenly I burst into tears. "What are you crying for?" he asked. "Because I'm afraid you'll be mad at me." "Well", he said, "your fear is your own. I'm just wondering how the hell we're going to get the bed fixed!" Then he walked out and shut the door. Whether from relief or the ridiculous sight of the bed, Sally and I burst into laughter.

What I noticed was how abruptly I went from a feeling of fear to a feeling of laughter, which struck me as a bit miraculous. With his words, "Your fear is your own", my feeling or emotion instantly changed–but why? How did this work? I decided to ask dad about it. So that same night I asked him, "What did you mean when you said, "Your fear is your own?"" He replied, "Just that! You are responsible for your fear, not me. You were afraid because you thought I would be angry, but I wasn't angry, so you thought wrong. But even if I had been angry, your fear would have been your own, we are the cause of our own emotions, nobody else." "But," I countered, "other people can make us angry and afraid." "No-body," he replied, "can make you angry or afraid unless you let them. They can't even make you happy or sad unless you let them." He went on to explain, "Our thoughts and expectations govern our feelings, we think this or that is going to happen and we are happy or sad when it does or doesn't. How we feel is all up to what we anticipated, thought or expected to happen.

This was news to me. Big news! I'd never given a thought to my feelings or emotions, nor suspected there was anything I could really do about them. Yet he was saying that we alone are the cause of our feelings, nothing and no one outside ourselves were the cause. I said to him, "It sounds like we set ourselves up for our feelings, and the only way not to have them, is not to have any thoughts or expectations at all." He said, "Exactly! But who can live without thoughts and expectations? What matters is not that we have them, but knowing we are the cause of them, and not someone or something else."

I determined to test this out, find out if this was true or not. I wanted to see if it worked the way he said it did. I decided that for a whole week I'd watch every feeling I had to see if someone or something outside myself had caused it, or if it really was a product of my own thinking or expectation. What I learned was invaluable. He was absolutely right! I was amazed how it worked. In every case, I had set myself up for my own feelings and reactions. Thus I thought I could do this or that and felt disappointed when I couldn't. I thought my friends should do this or that and felt upset when they didn't. 1thought others would enjoy this or that and was hurt when they didn't. Always it was my thoughts and expectations that caused my feelings. But this is only half of what I learned. I learned that by not having these thoughts and expectations for myself and others I could be free of my feeling reactions. Though this was something I'd have to work on, the knack, I thought, was not caring about outcomes or other peoples' reactions, after all, they were as responsible for their feelings and reactions as I was for mine. If I didn't like something, that was my problem; if they didn't like something, that was their problem.

Although dad and I talked more about this, and mom chimed in with her dissenting views, the fact is: I had come upon one of the most psychologically significant and meaningful pieces of knowledge I ever acquired in life. Whatever my emotional life would have been without this knowledge I'll never know. I only know that the day I saw this truth I was forever spared half the emotional responses I might otherwise have had in life. In one fell swoop, I had been spared the experience of any deep or prolonged feelings regardless of reason or circumstance. From here on, I had a handle on my feelings and emotional experiences. What I learned turned out to be a grace in itself.

Not long after this discovery, I was in my bedroom when I heard dad on the phone downstairs shouting angrily, cursing, threatening to sue someone–take him for everything he had. Brother, was he mad! I sat and waited on the stairs for him to finish (he was hollering at some workman who evidently hadn't done a good job). When he hung up, I said to him, "I thought you said nobody could make you angry?" He grinned and answered casually, "He didn't make me angry." "Well," I said, "you sure sounded like it." "If I sounded angry, that was my choice." "But why would you choose that?" I asked. He replied, "Because sometimes it's the only way to get the job done!"

I went off and thought about this–thought about anger being his choice. Later I asked him about it. He said all his life his rule of thumb was to count to ten before responding to anything. This gave him time to choose his response, make it a deliberate choice. Naturally, I didn't believe he actually did this, but he said, "Try it!" Well, I tried it, and it worked, yes indeed, we can choose our responses or reactions. In dad's view, people who reacted instantly were at the mercy of their feelings and did not respond rationally. Whether we wanted our life to be governed by reason and rational choice, or by irrational emotions and feelings, it was up to us. Now this was another piece of knowledge that stood me well through life. Though sometimes it may not be possible to choose our feelings or emotions, yet we can always choose what to do with them–a choice always subject to reason. Despite dad's conviction that the ideal life was governed by reason and not emotions, he, nevertheless, could cry at the drop of a hat, and did so frequently. Mother, on the other hand, who believed in heart over mind, or feelings over reason, never cried a day in her life. Strange how this works.

* * * * *

With the onset of the war in the Pacific, yachts were not permitted outside the harbor. Initially we were permitted to sail inside the harbor and sometimes spent a day on the boat just sight-seeing. Since Los Angeles has one of the largest harbors in the country, there was a lot to see–ships from all over the world, battle ships, even the old galleons used in movies like "Mutiny on the Bounty." There were fish canneries, yacht clubs and, of course, the harbor seals and birds of the sea. Altogether we had some enjoyable trips.

When dad learned that boat owners could give use of their boats to the Coast Guard Auxiliary to patrol the coastal waters, he not only gave them use of our boat, but joined the Auxiliary himself. To pilot a boat, however, he had to get a special navigation license, which entailed taking a number of different classes. While these classes were held at different times and places around the city, one was a series of lectures at the Griffith Park Observatory a few miles from home. I think it was after his first class at the Planetarium dad asked if I'd like to go with him. So off we went.

The class was given in the circular domed room with a professor at a large console projecting his illustrations onto the ceiling. When the talk was over he said he was going to take us through the whole night sky. With that, the lights dimmed and stars began to appear. When the room was completely dark, the ceiling was packed with stars. Though the stationary stars moved with the ceiling; the planets took their own course, sometimes going retrograde through the sky. Along with this magnificent spectacle, they always played some appropriate music–that first time it was Elgar's "Pomp and Circumstance"–and afterwards, when the sun came up, the professor would wish us all a "Good morning."

I couldn't imagine anyone coming away from such a spectacle without being deeply impressed and uplifted. Afterwards, dad bought an astronomy book for himself, and bought me a board called a "Skyorama" (or something close), a movable map of the sky where you move the constellations and stars according to the time of year. To use it–holding it overhead–you only had to know where the North Star was. It didn't take long to find my way around the sky, for years I took this board with me wherever I went. My love of the stars, just gazing at them, was a big part of my life. I could never, however, look at nature with a purely scientific mind. The beauty and marvel of it always made me aware of its hidden mystery which I knew was God. In fact, I figured the reason nature always uplifted me was because of this hidden mystery. I was sure my love of nature was equally my love of God.

I accompanied dad to all his lectures. Our interest in Astronomy was probably the only academic subject we shared in common. I had a lot of questions to ask and sometimes he'd illustrate his answers with make-shift demonstrations, like using a light bulb (sun), orange (earth) and apple (moon) to show why we never see the back of the moon. He also got a long pole to point at some star and measure the angle between it and the earth. Although his pole was so long it bent over at the top, he swore his angles came out the same as the book. He also brought home a sextant he couldn't use because there are no horizons in Hollywood. Anyway, from then on, wherever we went, especially away from city lights, dad and I would always go for a walk to look over the night sky.

For a long time I had heard about the giant telescope atop Mt. Wilson, located in the Sierra Madre mountains above Pasadena. In his youth dad had hiked up the mountain to get a view of Haley's Comet in 19?? Dad asked mom to look into the possibility of a week-end trip to the Mt. Wilson Observatory. She found out there was a lodge with a few cabins, and once she was assured the cabins had indoor plumbing and a heater, she booked us for a week-end. On a Friday afternoon the three of us headed for the mountain–elevation 5,000 feet. On arrival we went immediately to see the giant telescope. I could only imagine what it would be like to sit alone in the silence of the night, perched on the telescope's high observation seat, the dome opened to the elements, just gazing at the stars. I compared this to an over-night vigil in Church, or the life of one of those early Christian ascetics I read about in the lives of the Desert Fathers. Such a life appealed to me so much, I determined then and there I wanted to be an Astronomer.

We also visited smaller observatories on the mountain and inspected the sun tower, which took constant pictures of the sun. Below the observatories were cottages where the astronomers lived, as well as a small community who lived and worked on the mountain. After dinner, a little group of us stayed for the lecture that followed. It was dark when we finally went outside to take in the mountain's unobstructed 180 degree view of the sky. The sight I beheld was the most spectacular phenomena I had ever seen, the sky so crowded with stars that I could not find the tiniest space between them. I had never suspected the heavens were like this, or that the earth was so hemmed in by stars. Even the simulated sky at the planetarium had not prepared me for this reality. When I came to the mountain I thought I knew my way around the sky, but here I was totally lost, didn't recognize a one. The thickness and density of the stars made them seem like a low ceiling overhead and that up a few thousand feet, one could all but touch the stars. There was every degree of brightness and size, even color. I couldn't get my fill of taking it all in. Merely focusing on a single star with the telescope, was not very interesting, rather, it was the whole panorama that was so uplifting. I wished I had brought a sleeping bag so I could lie on the ground and gaze at the stars all night.

Though later in life I had many opportunities to view the night sky from higher altitudes–also from sea and dessert far from cities–I never again saw anything to compare to this particular, spectacular night sky. The only way to account for this is that the atmospheric conditions must have been ideal–a rarity any place you go. After a while the little group dispersed, mom went to the cabin, and dad went back into the lodge to examine the latest scientific gadget called a "Television." This was my first view of that contraption–a lot of black and white fuzz with people talking in the background. I couldn't understand dad's fascination with it, so I went back outside and stayed up as late as I could, gazing at the stars. My dearest wish was to live on that mountain forever.

Coming home after our week-end on the mountain was a shock to my system, a literal come-down into ugliness, noise, routine and petty concerns. It took me days to re-adjust, yet even then, I felt my soul was still on the mountain waiting for my return. It would be another year, however, before this happened.

No longer restricted by crutches, Sally and I began making week-end excursions into the Hollywood hills where there was still a lot of open space. Sometimes we took pencils and tablets, find a shady secluded spot and sitting a distance apart–affected us. For my part, I found it impossible to write a thing. Becoming part of the scenery out of sight of one another– we'd try our hand at writing some poetry to express how our natural surroundings left me with a completely blank mind.

From earliest years I had pondered the experience of what I called my "blank mind." Initially, it only seemed to be the end of thinking, a point beyond which I could not go. All I had to do was try to think something through or try hard to understand something, and I would come up against a definite barrier, virtually, a blank wall. Because I had always been told "you're too little" or "you're not old enough" (to do this or that) I took for granted my blank mind was a matter of age and that one day I would outgrow it. But this never happened; instead, it grew with me. Though I kept waiting for some breakthrough in this matter, by the age of six or seven I gave up, and accepted it as the way things were. At times I was convinced it kept me from developing a profound thinking mind. Certainly it was no good in the academic arena.

There was something more to this experience, however, than simply a blank mind. I discovered that when I come to this end-point, it was not just the inability to go any further, it was also a point at which my mind stopped thinking altogether. I would even forget what I'd been thinking about. It was as if all I had to do was touch this point and everything in mind was instantly vacated, forgotten. The wall, then, was not just a barrier to thinking, it was the end of it, period. Although the nature of this wall mystified me, I had a suspicion that beyond it lay great knowledge, not ordinary knowledge, but one that could penetrate the mystery of the universe, God, myself; I often wondered what my life would be like on the other side. I also noticed that if I stayed at this point of no-thinking, I came upon a curious state of silence, which I came to think of as my "second mind" or "secret mind"–later, "silent mind." Though I sometimes wondered if everyone experienced this, for me it was simply a fact of life, one I had never been without, there had never been a choice.

When forced to listen to something boring, sometimes I'd deliberately go blank. On one occasion, being in a boring classroom, I put my head down on the desk and went blank. Almost immediately I knew I'd sunk lower or gone deeper than ever before. I didn't meet up with a blank wall, but kept going down into a deep well of silence that I found somewhat thick and heavy. To test the extent of the silence I first tried to remember getting up in the morning, but couldn't do it. Then I tried to remember the dress I had on, and couldn't do that either. Then I tried to remember the faces of my parents, and when I couldn't do it, I tried to remember my own face. And when I couldn't do this, I put my hand on top of my head to be sure it was still there. When I tried to pull out of this silence it felt as if some powerful force was holding me to it, wouldn't let me move out of it. I was grabbed by a fear I might be stuck in this silence forever–never be able to return to myself, never remember myself. In a moment of sheer panic, mustering all my physical energy, I leaped out of the seat and began taking deep breaths to get back a sense of myself I was so relieved, the fact I'd just made a big scene in the classroom was of no consequence. After giving me a look of total disgust, sister went back to her boring monologue.

After this I vowed never to go blank again. Yet despite my caution and vigilance, I sometimes felt a forceful pull into this silent state, the more I tried to resist the pull, the stronger the force became. Since I couldn't fight it, I had to go with it. Far from engendering fear, however, I found it a state permeated by the mystery of God. Since I would have this experience a number of times in the years to come, I might try to say something more about it.

First of all, I noticed there were two steps or factors involved in this experience. First there was the blank mind, then, a magnetic pull downward to the center of my being. My awareness was pulled downward, away from worldly awareness, even self-awareness. With my mind or awareness held to the depths–there seemed to be no further to go–what I encountered was not some "thing", nor no "thing", but just the opposite. At this mysterious depth was a pervasive sense of fullness, completion, an unemotional quiet joy, an other-worldly state I sometimes thought of as a gateway to heaven. I never doubted God had a hand in this experience, this was not merely the silence of a blank mind, but a foretaste of eternal life with God. This state could last 15–30 minutes before the force gradually subsided and I was able to pull out of it–get back to my usual self, that is. Afterwards, however, there was always a lingering aura or subtle trace of the experience that hung on for hours before it finally disappeared.

Several years later there was another change in this matter of a blank mind. Instead of a forceful pull into a silent mind, it was as if a gentle fog descended and shrouded my mind, overshadowing my thoughts and remembrances. No amount of effort could affect any recall until the cloud lifted or faded away. This was always accompanied by a quiet joy wherein I recognized God's unbidden presence. Though I did not appreciate the interruption, it was always gratifying to know God had not given up on me.

If there was any problem with these experiences it was their unpredictability and inconvenience—I could be playing ball, talking with a group of friends, or on a street car. If I was with others, I left, because the nature of this experience is loss of any interest in this world, the mind is not going to stay with it. It was as if a cloud had shrouded my mind with the message "None of this matters!" Once I was at the dinner table and had to push the food away and go up to my room. Lying in bed that night I thought about these experiences, wondered about their purpose and meaning in my life and posed the question to myself: "though these experiences come unbidden, yet given a choice, would I opt to have them?" Because they uplifted me to God, I valued them, but because they interfered with my life—never knowing when or where, always interrupting my thoughts, studies and occupations—no, I could never choose to live this way. These experiences, however, reinforced my early belief I was destined to die young. I thought it was God's way of getting me ready, and that someday one of these experiences would carry me right out of this world.

* * * * *

Either in the 6th or 7th grade, the last period of the day was PE. After some lazy half-hearted calisthenics we'd put our energies into a baseball game. Across the street from our yard was the Selma Elementary Public School. It got out a half hour before we did, and every day on their way home, a group of boys would stop and shout at us kids through the wire fence, calling us names like "Pope-dopes", "Cat-lickers"–all kinds of nasty things. This was their daily routine. For our part, however, we kids had learned to just ignore them. One day, however, I was standing in the outfield fairly close to the fence and decided to go over and challenge them: "If any of you would like to discuss or debate our religion, instead of calling us stupid names, meet me after school at the gate." Although about a dozen kids heard me, I never expected any of them to wait until our school was out. I was thus surprised after school to find 5 boys waiting at the gate. The first thing I asked was what religion they belonged to. No one answered. Then I asked what Church they went to. Again no answer. Then I asked, "Do any of you go to any Church at all?" One boy said he had been to one Church a couple of times, but didn't know its name. I asked them where they got their information about Catholics–from their parents, their teacher in school, where? It turns out they heard it from other kids. I told them that if they wanted to know what Catholics believed, it only made sense to get it from a Catholic who knew and practiced his religion, not from somebody who had not studied or practiced it. Since I, however, both knew and practiced my religion, I'd be happy to answer any questions they had.

Immediately one boy said accusingly, "You Catholics worship statues!" Looking around at all of them I asked, "Do any of you have pictures of your family or friends around the house–maybe hanging on a wall or on a mantle? Those pictures are not the actual people are they? No! So why do your parents keep these pictures around? To remind them of the people they care for–right? Well that's why we Catholics have statues and pictures of Christ, his mother and saints around our Church. They remind us of them, we care for them, but we certainly don't think the pictures and statues are the real people themselves!" Then I asked, "Have any of you ever been inside our Church?" A couple of them shook their heads, so I gestured toward the gate, "Come on, I'll take you in and show you around." But they said they had to be going home. I told them I was going in the direction of Highland Ave. and we could talk on the way, so we did.

As we passed a Protestant Church on the corner, I said, "They have a picture of Christ in there (The Agony in the Garden, I believe), but they don't worship that picture either. What all Christians, Catholics and

Protestants have in common is belief in Christ, they all worship the heavenly Christ, not some artist's picture of him. But you guys must know this, you're all Christians aren't you?" I looked around and saw only blank faces, so I went on, "At home have your parents ever talked to you about Christ?" No response. "Do they ever talk about God?" No response. "You believe in God don't you?" One boy said, "I don't know, my parents never talk about God. We're nothing, we don't go to any Church." My guess was that he was speaking for all of them.

It was obvious these kids knew nothing about religion or Christianity, and with one exception, had never been to Church. Based on this hunch I tried to give them a sense of the great Architect who made the world and whose mysterious presence was everywhere, even in ourselves. Whether they were just being polite or really listening, they offered few comments or responses. Three of them walked me almost to my doorstep before they turned up the street to go their own way. When we said goodbye, I told them if they ever had any questions about Catholics or what they believed, to wait for me after school at the gate. I never saw them again, nor were there any more kids shouting insults at us on the playground.

I stood there watching them as they walked up the street thinking, that if they looked back, I'd wave goodbye. As I watched them disappear I was overwhelmed with gratitude for my religion, my faith, my education, my parents, for I suddenly realized the difference between those raised in a religion and those who were not. While these boys may have been smarter than I in school work, their thinking evinced no depth, no insight, it was as if a whole dimension of their minds were missing. They couldn't seem to break through sensory data or get beyond what merely appeared. It was as if their minds were flat, one dimensional, capable of dealing only with the obvious. I was convinced that some part of their minds had failed to develop. It was my religion, however, its content and challenge, that had opened to me and everyone so raised, a profound dimension of mind and soul that could never be attained any other way or by any other means. Quite apart from its spiritual benefits and the variety of experiences it provided, my religion made me think and ponder, made me question and seek, it presented me with a whole different dimension of life, a way of seeing and thinking not otherwise available. Standing there, watching the boys disappear up the street, I was overwhelmed with love and gratitude for my Faith. At the same time, however, it was tinged with a genuine sadness for these boys who never had this advantage and would never know the joy of it.

Following this realization—the profound benefits of my religion—I came upon another, somewhat similar realization. After school one day I went across the street to an apartment building to visit my friend Nan. Her mother worked during the day and Nan was forbidden to leave the flat after school until her mother got home. Waiting for her mom, Nan and I chatted. We didn't go to the same school or have the same friends, but when Sally had to work—Sally was an extra at the studios—Nan and I were often together. I do not recall what set her mother off, but as soon as she walked in the door she lit into Nan with such verbal abuse I could not believe my ears. It was frightening; I felt terrible for Nan. Quietly I slipped out the door. Walking home I thought about all the parents I knew, most of them very nice, yet, by comparison, none could hold a candle to the caliber of my parents. Their intelligence and learning, their profound faith and generosity, their hospitality and good humor, their obvious love for one another, and the freedom they gave me—my list went on and on. Hands down, they were just two great people. Each in their own right, they were truly great. Nobody in this world could have better or greater parents than I. For some moments I was overwhelmed with gratitude and admiration. I had never realized this before or seen them in this light, but once I saw them for the great persons they were, my high regard for them never changed, if anything, it only grew with time. Whenever I thought back on all the graces God had given me, first on my list were my parents. Yes indeed, between my Faith and my parents, I had it all!

* * * * *

Though I was familiar with the children's version of the Old Testament stories and heard excerpts read at Mass, I had never read the Old Testament for myself. Since it was a book everyone else seemed to have read, I decided to read it front to back, if for no other reason than be able to say, "I've read it." I knew it would take some time to get through it, but using my free time, I calculated it would probably take a month at the most.

The reason this project took a full year is because I found the Old Testament so shocking in places it made me sick to my stomach and I had to stop reading. Sometimes it took weeks or a month before I could force myself to pick it up again. In places I thought it so filthy I felt guilty reading it, and hid the book so mom wouldn't find it in my bedroom–if these parts had any deeper meaning I missed it completely. That it was a "holy" book, well, I couldn't see that at all. I liked Joseph, but nobody else. I was impressed, however, with the scene of God's appearance on Sinai, but other than that, people's behaviors repulsed me. The shock and distaste was so great, that for the rest of my life I avoided it, couldn't stand listening to it, nor understand what anyone found in it. When it was read in Church or elsewhere, I went into my blank-mind mode because I couldn't listen. As for God's part in it, of one thing I w absolutely certain: "This God I have never known!"

God depicted in the Book was too awful to think about–angry, jealous, vengeful, killing masses of people by fire or water, this God was violent, terrible, frightening. To avoid this monstrous image I thought of the God I knew–brilliant, magnificent, above the fray, yet obviously caring and understanding. It seemed the God I knew and the One depicted in the Book were total opposites; certainly they couldn't both be true? Pondering how this could be, I thought of all the evils in the world–animal killing animal, man killing man, all the disgusting, indecent behaviors I'd heard about. How could God stand such a thing, why does he permit it? Then there is the hell He created for man, how could God enjoy heaven knowing all this misery was going on down there?

Thinking this over, a question popped into mind: "What if there are two sides to God, one glorious and magnificent, the other, terrifying and frightening, would you only want to know one side of God, or would you want to know both sides–know the whole truth of God?" With this question I suddenly felt cornered. If I only wanted to know the good and wonderful side of God and not the other, then I would spend my life knowingly living a lie, a lie because I had deliberately refused to know the whole truth of God. On the other hand, if I wanted to know the whole Truth, I would have to face the other side of God, which could be so terrible and frightening it might kill me. Now I understood the saying "See God and die,"–it literally meant die of fright! But immediately another question arose: "Well, would you be willing to die to know God–know the whole Truth and nothing but the Truth–or would you rather live a happy life and not know the whole truth of God?" Once again I felt trapped: if I said "no", then I deliberately chose not to know the Truth, but if I said "yes", this knowledge might kill me. But there was really no choice in the matter. When push comes to shove, I would rather know the whole truth of God and die of it, than to deliberately live without knowing the truth. No, there was no choice, I had to know the whole truth of God.

Getting on my knees beside my bed I said to God, "Yes, I would rather know and see You as you really are, no matter how terrible, even though it kills me, than to only know and see You in part." After that I braced myself for the killing Vision. I was ready, poised to die at that mo- ment–and fully expected to. Everything else in my life faded away, I felt no fear, only the tremendous strength and determination of the decision itself. I remained in that expectant stance maybe a half hour and couldn't understand why nothing happened; after a bit I decided it might happen later, perhaps tomorrow. So I cautiously got up and went about my busi- ness, expecting any minute, however, I might be confronted with the ter- rible Vision. After a few days of this, there came that subtle Laughter I'd heard before–indeed, heard many times in my life (though never with my ears)–and instantly I knew: there is no "other side" of God, no horrible, frightening aspect of God to see or know. There was simply no truth to such a notion. God had only wanted to know if I'd be willing to die to see Him, that's all the dilemma had been about. I also knew that although I would, in fact, die when I saw God, it would not be out of terror and fear, but from His overwhelming glory. I was even convinced the sole cause of death, everyone's death, was the vision of God. Thus I got the notion "see God and live", which meant to me, the ability to sustain the vision without dying. I wanted my whole life to be a preparation for that great day–to "bear the vision" and not die. Be carried into God's glory without missing a beat.

I would never again read the Old Testament. I never doubted Moses did, in fact, see the One True God on Sinai, and would ever regard the scene of Moses going up the mountain–and coming down–as the most dramatic and powerful piece of literature ever written. Some years later I also came upon a few Psalms that expressed what I was going through at the time. And then there was the day I remembered God's communicating to Elias in a "breeze"–an experience with which I could identify. But as for the rest of the Old Testament, literally if not viscerally, I had no stomach for it. I would always regard it as the history of a people, their experiences and perspective on events. In much the same way, I regarded the Gospels as a biography of the man Jesus and his biographers' understanding of him. In neither case, however, did I ever get a sense of anything holy or sacred about these stories. Certainly I knew they were not written by God–who doesn't talk or write. No, I would never be a Bible or scripture person. These books played no part in my spiritual life, nor would I have any understanding of those for whom it did.

One evening, listening to my parents talk about their personal rapport with God, it became obvious they were each talking about a different God. Each had different experiences, different views, a different rapport with God. I don't know how the discussion got started, but my ears picked up when mom said, "When I look deep into myself, I see God," and dad said, "When I look deep into myself, I see a potential devil!" Mom laughed, but I was shocked by the two of them. Did mom really see God all the time? What was that like? And as for dad, I never thought things were that bad with him. Yet I understood his predicament better than mom's vision. Dad was pretty keen on fighting the forces of evil both in himself and in the world; I was convinced his belief in original sin stemmed from his own personal struggles in this matter. Mom, on the other hand, never knew this struggle in herself, which is why she never believed in original sin–though she would never openly contradict any formal tenet of belief in this matter.

For mom, God was totally immanent or within herself, utterly close, personal, ever informing her of everything she needed to know to lead a good life, to guide her children, make right decisions and so on. For dad, on the other hand, God was utterly transcendent and ineffable, His unknown essence, the unfathomable mystery of the Trinity. Dad's guiding light was God's revealed truth via the Church. Listening to them go back and forth it was obvious that while there is only one God, everyone seems to know and experience Him differently. Though I could not relate or identify with either of their perspectives and experiences, yet, as a third party or middle term between the two, I had a peculiar sense of a responsibility being laid on me. Somehow I had to reconcile and integrate these two views and rapports with God—that is, to reconcile and integrate them within myself. How I could do this I had no idea, so I never gave it another thought.

With all this in mind, however, next Sunday in a packed Church, I marveled that despite a common belief in one God, no two people in that Church were thinking, knowing, praying, or experiencing God the same way. It was as if there were as many gods as there were people. When I first heard about the belief called "Polytheism" I was reminded of this phenomena. While people agree God exists, nobody agrees with the "who, what, or where" of God, thus for the sake of peace, the recognition of Polytheism was understandable—to each his own God. I would always think of polytheism as nothing more than everyone's individual view of One God, a reality as alive today as ever—only nobody wants to admit it.

After listening to my parents talk, I took stock of my own experiences and perspective of God. For me, although God was transcendent, He was also personal. As transcendent, I had seen God in the woods and glimpsed His passing. My life was focused on this transcendent, personal God. On the other hand, God immanent—that is, God in nature and all creation—was more impersonal, because this was God "Everywhere", a mysterious presence you could know and contemplate, but never localize as anywhere in particular. As for the inner "leap of recognition" I experienced with God's passing, I concluded this must be some aspect of God's immanent presence in creation (hence in myself). Gleaned from my own experiences at least, this was my understanding of the difference between God transcendent and God immanent—God without and within, that is.

Sometime after I turned 12, I made my Confirmation. Preparation for it consisted of all day Saturday classes given by a Jesuit priest. He passed out thick adult catechisms and said we'd be tested on its contents. His talks were actually very good. I studied hard for the test, which turned out to be so simple I could have passed it had I never opened the book. I'll never know why I took the name "Paula" as my confirmation name. I knew of no one who had this name. For sure it had nothing to do with St. Paul, whose Epistles I had never read for myself. The first time I heard the word "chauvinist", mom had used it to refer to St. Paul. To get a rise out of mom, all dad had to do was quote one of Paul's dictums about a woman's place in society. Mom didn't want to hear anything Paul had to say. In her books, his chauvinism was not Christ-like.

Dad, however, quoted Paul more than he did the Gospels. On one occasion he said, "My favorite saying of Paul's is, 'I have run the course, I have finished the race, I've fought a good fight, I have kept the faith!'" For dad, this was a cry of triumph, the greatest affirmation anyone could make at the end of his life. I thought to myself: "Good heavens, there's got to be more to life than just keeping the faith!" Keeping the faith is something I took for granted, there was nothing hard about it, certainly nothing to trumpet about. The idea that life's goal was to avoid sin and keep the faith struck me as simplistic, narrow and insufficient, surely we were created for more than that! Then I thought, "Well, if there has to be more to life than keeping the faith, what more could that be?" I went to my room to think about this and came up with what I thought was the perfect answer.

I imagined the scenario of facing God in heaven and His asking me: "Well, what have you done with your life?"–to merit heaven, that is. I would look him straight in the eye and, say: "I did it all! You made me human, so I lived it fully, didn't miss a thing!" This would certainly stump God. If he accused me of sin I'd say, "Well, that's all part of being human!" What could God possibly say to that? I waited for an answer. Without a word, however, God reached down and picked up a scroll, unfurled it with a snap, and held it in my face, "See, you say you lived fully, but look at all you didn't do, all you could have done, you missed this and that... "–the list on the scroll went on and on. I felt as deflated as a popped balloon, devastated in fact. But then there arose in me a great determination not to miss out on a thing, a determination to live fully and completely. To be exactly what God created me to be, no more, no less. If for Paul and dad, keeping the faith was their triumphant goal, to be fully human, live fully, that would be my goal. This determined conviction would never leave me. It was a goal that imbued all my actions and choices in life. In some respects, it made me fearless lest 1miss something or fail to experience everything possible–or at least make the effort.

I figured that to be fully human meant developing my brain to its fullest extent, testing possible talents I might develop, risking failures, never bogging down or repeating anything. If one door closed in my face, there were other aspects of life to be explored. As for keeping the faith, it would have been impossible not to, I had absolute faith in God. As for being a true Christian, well, only God could make this possible.

Sometime during this year I had a memorable "Church experience." It happened at the close of our Parish's "Thirty Hours Devotion," which entailed an unusually magnificent procession. Starting in the first grade, all Catholic school children took part in church processions–for Holy Week, Forty Hours, May Day, First Communion and other events. As a little one, I strewed flowers before the Blessed Sacrament; later, when I was older I either carried flowers or a candle; but after the fifth grade, being in the choir, I carried a hymnal from which we sang the traditional Latin hymns. On this occasion, processing up the middle isle and singing the Pange Lingua, I turned my head a bit to see the Blessed Sacrament coming down the side isle. Under the baldachin carried by the Knights of Columbus, wrapped in his elegant stole, the priest's face was hidden behind the large monstrance. On seeing the Blessed Sacrament I was caught up in such an onrush of exaltation and joy it was a touch of heaven. God's presence so palpable It filled the Church. I looked upward and saw what looked like a gray cloud of incense hovering overhead and, for a moment, forgot where I was. I wished I could have died then, it was a taste of glory. Having to stay on earth struck me as terrible. In a lifetime of experiences, this was unique because it did not involve me at all. I was caught up in the immense oneness of everyone and everything in God, caught up in the glorious end that awaits us all. The experience was also unique because it was the only one that ever produced tears–caught by surprise, overwhelmed by glory–I lost my voice as well.

For the rest of the day I just wanted to close my eyes and drop out of the world. Afterwards, though it was tempting to think I'd only been caught up in the beautiful pageantry, yet I had been a part of this same pageantry dozens of times before, and would be part of it for many years to come, but this particular experience never occurred again. While I never had the slightest fear of death, from here on, I looked forward to it because now I knew what it would be like. Of this, I never had a doubt.

Age 14

AGES 13 & 14

Shortly after our birthdays in May, Marge graduated from Mary-mount College. As valedictorian, she had been trained by the Sisters to imitate their same peculiar accent—part British, New Yorker, I don't know what—which amazed us; we were all very proud of her. Dad had planned a wonderful trip for the summer. Though he said the reason for the trip was to participate in a three day Triduum (short Novena) at the shrine of St. Anne de Beaupre in Quebec, I suspected his real reason was to have Marge visit the Mother House of the Maryknoll Sisters on the Hudson. Some years before, Marge thought she might like to join the Order, so perhaps dad thought a visit might renew her interest. Dad's reasons for traveling, however, were always a cover up, he simply loved to travel, no other excuse was necessary.

Unknown to me at the time, Marge had applied to enter Nursing School. My parents, however, objected, they wanted her to go to secretarial school instead—which never appealed to her. When I found out about this, I thought their refusal odd because mom told me that as a young girl she had begged her father to become a nurse. He refused, saying it was servile labor and no work for a lady, so he sent her to secretarial school instead. But that was 30 years ago, the nursing profession had come a long way, it was a profession of status, so why did mom object?

At bottom, mom's refusal was based on her philosophy of life: that only what was "natural" was truly Godly. Thus she said, "In every woman there is a God-given instinct to marry and have children, that's the way God made women, that's His will for them." To her, the pursuit of a profession or higher college degree was a waste of time, eventually a woman married and raised a family—a profession that required no degree and for which no college degree would be helpful. So in her view, because a higher education would only come to naught, it was a waste of time and money. This was what mom truly, honestly, believed.

Although dad evidently went along with her, he often commented with delight on the increasing number of women entering the professions—doctors, professors, attorneys—he had nothing but admiration for this new wave; and as the father of three girls, I know he was ready to go with it. We all had to live through the fuss he made when Gert left UCLA to get married. Mom, on the other hand, would stand her ground to the death—"It's not natural, I say!" The day would come, however, when both would regret their refusal to let Marge go into nursing. Unlike the rest of us, Marge would never go to battle for what she wanted, she never argued, demanded, or make a fuss about anything, yet within herself she harbored a deep resentment and we all know what happens then. Not long afterwards she literally broke their hearts. For right now, however, we were getting ready to embark on a grand trip which would take us most the summer.

From West to East we traveled by train through National Parks, stopped at major cities and, of course, visited all the Churches and Shrines along the way. It was a kind of circle tour: going up the West coast to Seattle (with a stopover in Portland to visit Our Lady's shrine), we took the ferry to Victoria, B.C.; after a few days we went to Vancouver where we took the train across Canada with stopovers at Lake Louise and Banff, then on to Toronto where we boarded a boat for a four day trip around the Great Lakes—with a stopover at Sue Ste. Marie to visit the graves of the Jesuit martyrs—and then up the St. Lawrence to Montreal, Quebec and the Shrine of St. Anne de Beaupre; after that, it was on to Niagara Falls, New York City, Boston, Chicago, Cleveland and home.

The most beautiful place we stayed was Lake Louise nestled in the peaks of the Rocky Mountains. Because the war was still on, the Chateau on the Lake was closed, so we stayed at a lodge down the road. There was still snow on the ground, the place was deserted, but the path around the Lake was open and on our first morning, we walked this path behind a fat waddling porcupine—with quills extended. In the afternoon we went back to see if the teahouse was open, it wasn't, so I spent the rest of the day walking in the woods and sitting alone by the Lake. If I could have lived anywhere in the world, it would have been here.

By far the worst experience of the trip was the five or six days spent in New York City, the heat and humidity were oppressive, and the Hotel's air conditioning was on the blink. Mom said it was the only mistake dad made booking the trip, all the other Hotels had been tops. Mom's philosophy of travel was: if accommodations were not as good or better than home, it made no sense to leave home at all. It was only by assuring her of the best accommodations dad was able to lure her into taking any trips. For dad, on the other hand, if seeing the world meant camping out every night, he would not have hesitated.

All in all, it was a wonderful trip, and because mom was an American history buff, I learned a great deal as well. On the way home she alerted us when the train was about to pass over the Mississippi river, so meaningful in American history and the country's terrain, yet its passing was a laugh. The train must have passed over at one of the river's narrowest points, and at a speed that, if you didn't look quick, you'd miss it. Apart from its muddy color, it looked no different than other rivers we crossed.

For me, the most outstanding experience was at St. Anne de Beaupre, though not at the Shrine itself. By the third or final day of the Triduum I could not sit through another long afternoon of sermons and devotions, so after lunch I told my parents I was going to hike up the hill beside the Church and would be back in time for Benediction. If I could not find them in the Church, I would meet then on the doorsteps when they came out. Since this was fine with them, I set out.

To the left of the Church, Stations of the Cross wound up a wooded path. The day before, I had noticed that after the last Station the path kept going upwards, I wondered where it went and decided that even if it went nowhere, I'd just keep hiking through the woods. It turns out the path ended at a gate in a low wall that surrounded what looked like a small Chapel in the pines. The gate was open so I went in, before trying the Chapel door to see if it was unlocked, I deliberately looked around for a name–to see if it was a Catholic chapel or not. Finding no sign, I thought

I'd have a peek anyway. Timidly I pushed the door open and was greeted with surprise and delight. Behind the altar were black grates with drawn back curtains, instantly I knew it was a Monastery of cloistered Nuns. Although I felt sure this was a Carmelite Monastery, with no sign, I had no way of knowing.

There was no one there, apart from some birds and the occasional sound of the breeze in the pines, there was not another sound. I knelt down and looked at the tabernacle to focus on the subtle Presence it ever seemed to radiate. I had few opportunities for unlimited time and quiet to focus on the Blessed Sacrament, the only other occasion was when I accompanied dad to the Plaza each month in the middle of the night for an hour of adoration. Other than this, Church was a busy place and rarely quiet, even with our frequent visits and thanksgivings after communion, time was always a factor, you'd just get into prayer and it was time to go.

I gave up the idea of hiking and decided to stay in the Chapel, to just sit and listen to the silence, enjoy the sense of being totally at home, utterly content and happy. I made no conscious decision to let my mind go blank, in such a quiet solitary setting, a silent mind is an automatic given, it just comes naturally. As I sat there, I never realized how deep and pervasive my initial sense of contentment and happiness had become, what I experienced came about so imperceptibly it might be compared to going outside at the crack of dawn, sitting there you do not actually see things getting lighter and lighter until of a sudden you realize the sun is in your face! The moment I became aware of this Sun–which seemed to have replaced the tabernacle–there was a shower of love and joy that filled the whole chapel. I was sure if anyone else had been there, they would have experienced it too. This radiant love was obviously not mine, it was God's–indeed, it was God. I knew then, the love with which I loved Him was His own love, the same love wherein He loved me. Because of this gift, I was now certain I could be a Carmelite, dedicate my whole life to loving God with the same love with which He loved me!

Sitting there basking in the joy of this love, I did not realize what had subtly taken place until the image of my parents drifted into mind. I had completely forgotten them, forgotten to keep track of the time. Instantly I thrust my body forward to get up, but could not move. It felt as if I was being held down by a powerful gravitational force. This was a surprise, because sitting there I had not noticed anything at all. I tried once more to get up, but couldn't. There was no choice but to stay there until I could move again, and so I did. It wasn't long, however, before I felt what could only be compared to a mild electric shock, after which I could move again. I compare this latter experience to an electric shock because the year before, fooling around with my old radio, I got a shock that went through my whole body and almost knocked me over—it even made a buzzing sound. Needless to say, I learned fast never to fool with electrical stuff. Though what I felt in the chapel was nothing like that, yet it bore a mild comparison. At any rate, whatever force had held me down, it was gone, I was free to leave.

When I blessed myself at the door I had the impression of a weight being laid on me, the thought of rejoining the world was so utterly repugnant I could only regard this weight as a cross. When I opened the door to leave, I noticed a low sign on the wall to the left of the door that read "Monastery of Discalced Carmelites." I just knew it!

Absolutely, this is where I belonged! From that day forward this knowledge—of becoming a Carmelite—was no longer in the back of my mind as something reserved for the future, rather, it was a sure knowledge in front of me at all times, a knowledge that affected everything I did and thought from then on. I knew that in that Chapel I had received a powerful grace, and unlike so many other experiences that came and went, this grace never totally disappeared; instead, it seemed to grow with time.

As I ran down the hill, I thought it ironic to be passing the stations backwards, for sure; true joy and happiness lie at the end of the Via Dolorosa, and none at the beginning. I looked at my watch, it was late, Benediction had long been over, my parents must be fuming. I could hardly believe I'd been in the chapel over three hours, it seemed no more than an hour. When I got down the hill and could see the front of the Church, I saw two solitary figures standing to the side of the front door, no one else was in sight. To dispel a scolding, I breathlessly told them: "There's a Carmelite monastery up the hill, I've been there the whole time." For a moment they were silent, then dad said, "We've already missed our train, but there should be another along any minute", so we took off for the train and returned to the Chateau Frontenac, our hotel in the City.

Not long after we returned home, it was time to get ready for school–the eighth grade this year. Three or four times a year mom took me on shopping trips to the big department stores, always before Easter and Christmas, usually at the beginning of summer, and again at the start of school. When we lived at the beach, it had been mom's custom to let me pick out a new book in the store so I'd have something to read on the streetcar going home, a custom she didn't change even after moving to Hollywood where we could walk to a department store. Since school was about to start, she took me on the usual trip and bought me a book. On the way home we walked the first block in silence, then she asked, "A penny for your thoughts?" Mom often asked me this, and I never hesitated to tell her, so I replied, "I was thinking about Mt. Wilson and wondering if dad would take us back sometime." Her response: "I just don't understand you!" Now I was pretty sick and tired of hearing her say this–for as long as I could remember, in fact–so this time I decided I wasn't going to let her get away with it, I asked,

Me: What is it you don't understand?"

Mom: If I knew, then I'd understand.

Me: Well something made you say that just now, what was it?

Mom: If I knew, I'd tell you.

Me: I think you just have a habit of saying you don't understand me when you don't know what else to say.

Mom: That's probably true, I don't know what else to say–because I don't understand you.

Me: Well, think about it. After you asked my thoughts and I told you I was thinking of Mt. Wilson, what didn't you understand about that?

Mom: (After a silence) I'm thinking.

Me: Do you think I'm a day dreamer or something?

Mom: Oh, no, that's Marge.

Me: What makes you think so? Give me one example.

Mom: Well, just the other day I asked her to go upstairs and get me something, a half hour later she calls down, "Mom, what was it you wanted?"

(Marge really wasn't a day dreamer, she wasn't one to fantasize. For whatever reason, Marge was impervious and disinterested in anything going on in the family, she was only in her element with her friends and never stuck around home if she could help it).

Me: So if I'm not a day dreamer, then what don't you understand about my thinking it would be nice to make another trip to Mt. Wilson?

Mom: (She thought a moment) I can't put my finger it, I don't know how to express it.

Me: Well something prompted you to say that.

Mom: If I had to put it into words, the best I could say is that 'you are never where you are'.

Me: In other words, my mind is never involved with what I'm doing at any given moment?

Mom: Not exactly, but I don't know how else to put it.

Me: Maybe you mean my heart and soul is not in anything I'm doing at the moment.

Mom: Yes, I think that's closer to what I mean.

Me: Well, it's true, but what's so hard to understand about that? We do lots of things we don't put our heart and soul into—like homework, eating, cleaning, in fact, most of the things I can think of

Mom: That's just it, one cannot find happiness when their heart and soul is not in what they are doing.

Right here I think mom put her finger on a profound difference between us. Mom obviously put her heart and soul into everything she did, cooking, shopping, praying, you name it. To be the best wife, mother, housekeeper, bookkeeper, friend, virtually everything she did, she threw her whole self into it, involved her whole being. In this she found a deep happiness, a spiritual happiness, of this I was sure. But I was a very different person, and that's what she couldn't understand. It would have hurt her, however, if I told her that the last thing I wanted to do with my life was live the life she did. I regarded her routine as boring and uninteresting, her life restricted to home, husband and kids, not really free. Most of her time was taken up with repetitive chores, useless chit chat, social niceties, nothing really elevating or inspiring. Dear God, there was nothing in her life that had the slightest appeal to me, the very thought of getting stuck in that rut gave me the shudders. But of course I'd never tell her this.

Me: You're right, that's just why I asked to go to Mt. Wilson, because that's where my heart and soul is. It's certainly not here–on Hollywood Blvd! I don't find anything around here that inspires or uplifts my heart and soul. While I'm not unhappy, neither am I really happy. You can only be really happy when you feel you are where you belong, where you are at home with yourself and your surroundings, which is not here in Hollywood.

Mom: Well, you can't always live in those kinds of places; you have to find happiness in yourself no matter where you are.

Me: Right, but if you have a choice in the matter, why not go there?

I don't know what else we talked about, but to the last, mom kept right on with her "I don't understand you." At least her admitting this was better than those times she thought she understood me, but didn't. Those times always turned out disastrous, really divisive. Mother meant well, she just tried too hard.

A few days after this conversation, out of the blue dad asked if I'd like to spend a weekend at Mt. Wilson. I was delighted, of course I knew I had mom to thank for this surprise. I think this was the trip we made shortly after a fire had devastated the area. As we drove up the mountain there were bins of food along the road for the hundreds of deer left without food. Sometimes we had to stop to let them pass, they were literally everywhere. The man at the desk told us that under the stairs of our cabin a doe had given birth to twins and that we could expect to see them around.

We had unknowingly arrived just in time to see a meteor shower that night, thousands of stars shooting in every direction. When one seemed to break loose and stream towards earth, there were spontaneous "Oh's" and "Ah's" from the little group gathered to watch the spectacular show–even mom was impressed. The only way I could account for my enormous love of the stars was my conviction that I loved them with God's same love, loved them no less than He did. This was the only possible explanation of why I had always loved not only the stars, but the sea so much–and the mountains, the woods, the clouds, the animals–it wasn't my love at all, but God's own love and His great gift to me. My goal on the mountain was to so strengthen my love of God that it would fortify me against the onslaught of trivialities that made up my life down the mountain. I wanted this love and God's Presence to always be as strong as it was on the mountain, because I knew from past experience how quickly this could ebb away when I got caught up in life's petty affairs. Though I had great determination in this matter, I begged God to help me so I might always have His strong love and Presence ever before me.

Sometime after school began, the subject came up of where I would attend high school the following year. At that time, our school (Blessed Sacrament) went through the 9th grade in order to accommodate those who would go on to the public high school, which started with the tenth grade. Unknown to any of us at the time, after our class finished 8th grade, the school eliminated its 9th grade altogether. I always thought the reason was due to our class's unruliness–the faculty had finally had enough.

To give some idea of a typical day in our class, here is mom's experience of it: "Something came up, dad and I had to leave in the afternoon and would not be back until after dinner. Before I left, I stopped by the school to give Bernadette the door key and some money to buy her dinner at the drive-in (two blocks from our house). I went to the Principal's office and asked to talk to her. I was told to go upstairs, turn right, and go down to the last room on the hall, #7. As I was walking down the hall, I noticed kids running in and out the doors, chatting and laughing–it was room #7. I took for granted Sister must have stepped out, but when one of the boys opened the door, I saw her sitting at her desk and kids milling around, it was bedlam. I asked the boy who came out if he would tell Sister that Bernadette's mother would like to speak to her for a minute. He flung open the door and shouted, "Hey Roberts, your mom's here!"

I don't know why mom chuckled every time she told this story, or why she didn't make a fuss about this terrible situation. Probably she knew I was just one of that unruly bunch–which was true–and she didn't want to make waves. I never got above a "C" in conduct–and got a "D" at least once. Although the Sisters labeled me "the instigator", this really wasn't true. I was very careful never to start anything, and never to finish it, but in between, of course, I certainly played my role in the fracas. In the four years at this school, the only class in which we didn't act up was Sr. Giovani's history class. She had a sharp tongue and knew just how to make a fool out of you in front of the whole class. Other than this class, however, we got away with murder. Sometimes we'd sit around and imitate the sisters and their attempts to control us, like old Sr. Gertrude, whose sole attempt at order was to make a fist, point her little finger at us and say, "Eh, lips quiet please!" it just cracked us up. Oh the stories I could tell! But enough of that school. Taking stock of my schooling, the truth is, I had learned nothing after the third grade, and I didn't look forward to spending another year in this school merely to have a good time. I honestly wanted to study, to take my education seriously, learn something.

Once dad said he wished he could have attended Catholic University in Washington D.C. For one thing, he thought they had the best motto or goal of any school–namely, that the primary goal of education was to instill in the students a love of learning. Since nobody could possibly remember all they had learned in their classes, they could and should, however, go on learning the rest of their lives. This was a love of learning for its own sake, not just to pass an exam, get a good grade, or even a job. Dad also said real learning didn't take place in the classroom by mere listening, but rather, in our own study and inquiry. Learning was totally up to us, not the teacher or the school, which is why the best thing any teacher or school could do was instill in its students a lifelong love of learning for its own sake.

Dad not only believe this, he lived it. He spent his whole life studying on his own. If there was ever a lull at the dinner table he'd challenge us kids: "If there is anything you want to know, just ask me, ask me anything and I'll give you the answer!" Usually that was enough to get the conversation going, but one day I decided to try and stump him, I looked through the encyclopedia for some data I was sure he'd never heard of. When I put it to him, however, instead of answering, "I don't know", he said, "I'll look it up and tell you." "But", I protested, "I thought you knew everything." He said, "I do! I know where I can find everything!" To him, knowing where to find the answer was as good as knowing it—the time between the two was irrelevant. One way or the other, dad would never admit there was anything he didn't know. But I took to heart what he said about learning, it struck a chord in me. As it turned out, there were few times in life I was not pursuing some subject or other, always out of personal interest and never connected to any school subject.

As to where I would go for the 9th grade, my parents gave me the option of either staying at my present school and entering Immaculate Heart High in my Sophomore year, or starting right out at Immaculate Heart as a Freshman. A possible third option that came up was attending Flintridge Sacred Heart Academy, a boarding school in the hills above Pasadena. This latter option was due to Marge's input, she had dearly wanted to go to Flintridge for her high school years, but at the time it seems it was not financially feasible. Without hesitation, going to Flintridge was my first choice.

While I would miss my class friends, another year of learning nothing wasn't going to do me any good. What's more, the same Immaculate Heart sisters who taught at Blessed Sacrament ran Immaculate Heart High School, and I didn't want to spend another year with them. Flintridge was run by Dominican sisters noted both for being highly educated and top educators; based on this alone, it behooved me to make the move. The idea of boarding, of course, conjured up all kinds of happy images, taken partly from Marge's experience, from books I'd read, and simply the sense of freedom and independence it would give. So while academic consideration came first, I also envisioned boarding as a fun experience. School would be an introduction to a new way of life, and above all, a life out of the city, close to the mountains. Yes indeed, I was ready!

After the first of the year, mom made an appointment to meet with the Principal of Flintridge–be interviewed, that is–look over the school, find out the requirements and, if everything went well, fill out an application. When we drove up the hill the first thing I noticed was the spectacular view of the Sierra Madre Mountains across from the school. I could see the sun tower atop Mt. Wilson and look down range to Mt. Baldy and beyond; the expansive vista was uplifting. Away from the bustling city and the world at large, this setting alone would have cinched the school for me.

As for the facility itself, this too was a bit spectacular. Originally built as the exclusive Flintridge Biltmore Hotel, it had gone under during the depression, which is when the Dominicans Sisters bought it at a low price, furnishing and all. Built on the side of a hill, it was a sprawling, spacious facility of Spanish architecture set off with patios and gardens, an Olympic size pool, tennis courts, stables, cottages, and a charming octagonal glassed-in dance pavilion which the school converted into a music conservatory with practice rooms. A bridge over the main road led to guest bungalows nestled in the hills, which housed all but the senior students. (Seniors slept in the main building so they would not have to go outside or walk the distance to the classrooms located at the lower end of the main building). Inside, it looked like a hotel, the tall lobby windows looked out on the mountains, to the right of the lobby was a huge vaulted lounge or ballroom. The wood paneled dining room had a high vaulted ceiling and an inner balcony from which an orchestra could play, but which the sisters converted into their private dining room. The bedrooms were unusually spacious, each with their own bathroom and balcony. From just about every room in the place, however, there was a view; obviously the Hotel had been built to take advantage of this view.

On that first visit I was both surprised and worried to learn there was no immediate or easy acceptance into the school. They needed a lot of data on me and my parents before I could be considered. I was worried because when they got my school transcripts with its D+ average, two red E's and a C or D in conduct, they had good reason not to take me–no use ruining their good academic reputation on someone like me. My only re-deeming grade was in Religion, which for my 12 years in school, were straight A's. This didn't mean I actually studied or even liked these clas-ses–which were the most boring–it simply meant I already knew my reli-gion and didn't have to study it. What I learned at home from dad, my own reading, and above all from practice, was beyond any "religion" I could have learned in school. For me, school religion was just so much watered down repetition. Sometimes, however, when I was actually listen-ing, sister would say things I knew were not true, which got up my dander. On such occasions I always clarified things with dad who merely shrugged his shoulders at sister's ignorance. "But the kids?" I said, "They'll think she was right." "Well", he said, "it goes to show, you've got to question what you hear, ask around, inquire, find out for yourself."

Where my A's in religion always came in handy, however, was when dad, after looking over my terrible report card would hand it back saying, "Well, as long as you know your religion that's all that really matters." Once after witnessing this, mom said to me, "You've sure had it a lot easier than the others!"–my brother and sisters, that is. "If they had brought home a report card like that, your dad would have exploded. He was hard on the others, but it seems by the time you came along, he just gave up."

Despite my bad academic history, mom took home the Flintridge application. We were told that once they had made their decision we would be notified by mail, either with a rejection slip or a formal invita-tion, that's the way it went. Months went by without a word, I pestered mom to call the school, but when she did, she was only told we would be notified in due time. Finally, sometime in May came a beautifully printed formal invitation to join their student body. It was a happy day, I was wonderfully relieved and could hardly wait till school began.

Toward the end of the eighth grade some of us in class were invited to a party at Billy Westland's home. We had often been to his home for afternoons of ping pong, other games, or just a get-together, but this time it was to be an evening party with dancing and eats. Billy's father had recently died, so along with his mom, his Jesuit uncle was there to chap-eron. I was not near as interested in dancing as I was talking to Billy's uncle in the kitchen, so after a few dances I had a chat with his uncle and later rejoined the kids in the living room. I don't know what had happened between times, but things had gotten a bit rowdy. As far as I could tell, some of the boys were out to kiss the girls, if not all of them, at least some of them. When I reentered the room it seems the boys instantly challenged one another to see who could kiss me. This situation had happened once before in my own home. Three of the boys—who I knew well—had followed Sally and I home after school. When they started getting silly, we beat them off and kicked them out. The present situation, however, was different. For one thing, there were about five boys in on this challenge, and for another; I didn't want to cause a big scene and ruin Billy's party. I decided the best thing was to go home. I was afraid, however, that if the boys saw me leave by the front door, they would come after me, and since it was several miles to home and already after ten, I didn't think this a good idea. So I got my coat from the bedroom and climbed out its one-story window, but no sooner was I out, when the boys spotted me and started shouting, "Get her!" "Run her down!"

I was not a sprinter, but I gave it everything I had, all the time asking God to help me. After a block or more the boys gave up, but I kept running, changing directions at each corner to be sure I couldn't be found. A block or so after I stopped running, I experienced not just the familiar leap, but an explosion that knocked me off balance and left me sprawled on someone's front lawn. I may never know how it actually worked or what exactly happened, I only know this much: the Power within seemed to burst out of me and stand before me as a blinding light, the wordless knowledge it conveyed went something like this—using my own words: "I am your true life, you belong only to me, I will have you." This was no loving encounter, on the contrary, this Power meant business; it was definitive, almost scolding. As the brilliant light before me, the inner Power had clearly identified itself as God, and for a moment at least, my brain was too stunned to doubt It. The experience was both spectacular and sobering. I lay on the grass a while before getting up and starting home. By the time I reached home, however, I had already begun to question if "what" I had experienced—seen—was really God or not.

I had good reason to doubt. After seeing God in the woods–which is when the interior Power reappeared–I took for granted the interior Power was not God, thus I determined to ignore it completely. God in the woods was utterly transcendent to me, not in me, as was the interior Power. Also, God in the woods had identified Itself as God whereas the inner Power had never done so. For another thing, I knew from past experience this inner Power could disappear on me, and as the worst experience of my entire life, I wasn't going to put myself in any position where this could happen again. But here now, for the first time, the Power had momentarily identified Itself as God (the Light). Its message had been for me to stop ignoring It and to focus on It as the true love of my life. But I could not do this, it was impossible.

While I knew God was both Everywhere and In all things–and in the Eucharist as well–having seen God in the woods so brilliant and transcendent, I took for granted I had "openly" seen God Who-is-Everywhere and In all things–that is, "openly" seen God without the medium of nature or myself standing in the way. In other words, though we can see God in and through creation, yet this is not seeing God "openly" or without a medium. So while God was the uplifting mystery in nature and in myself, still, God was only mediated and not as He truly existed beyond creation. Such, as least, was my view and understanding of my different experiences of God.

There was no question the Power within had some special connection to God, I regarded it as a kind of grace or some part of me specially created by and for God, but as for the Power itself being God, I couldn't accept that. Once before I had turned my eyes away from God transcendent and focused, instead, on the interior Power, and–poof!–it vanished on me. No, I'd never make that mistake again.

Following this experience, uppermost in my mind was the need to find out the true nature of the interior Power. It had been a mystery from age five, and since it obviously played some part in my experiences of God, I couldn't see spending my whole life not knowing or not understanding its true nature, its true place in my life. But how could I obtain this knowledge? I decided only God could resolve this dilemma, only He could inform me of the Power's true identity. The only problem, my glimpses of God were so fleeting, quick and unexpected. He never stopped for me, didn't even notice me. So I decided to pray God to stop long enough to answer my question, let me know the true nature of this mysterious Power that obvious knew Him better than I did–after all, if it were not for Its leap, I wouldn't know God was even passing. So from this time on, my quest for the true identity of this Power was my top priority. I constantly prayed God to let me know and was ever on the lookout for any opportunity to ask Him. Sooner or later I was sure God would give me the answer; I felt this unknowing was an impasse that in some way kept me from growing, from moving on.

Some time that summer Mom received a list from Flintridge of things I would need to bring with me, several of which we had to shop for. One item was a long formal gown for attending concerts, the theater, or special school functions; another was an   English riding habit–if I wanted to take riding lessons, which I did. Fortunately, Marge already had boots and jacket, so mom only had to buy me a pair of jodhpurs. This expenditure, however, turned out to be a waste of money, after one semester of harrowing experiences I quit riding–once I clung to the mane of a saddleless, run-away horse that galloped for miles at full speed. No, I much preferred tennis; on weekends I was able to take lessons at the courts up the street from our house.

The only sad remembrance about the day I left for school was waving good-by to Sally. My heart fell as I watched her disappear from sight. I was waving good-by to an irreplaceable childhood friend which no future friendship could duplicate. In the next years I rarely saw Sally, from that point on our lives diverged in very different directions. One thing that always remained, however, was my genuine love for her; I would never think of her without the warm experience of a loving heart.

There were no day students at Flintridge, everyone boarded. The girls came from all over the state and out of state, from Mexico and Central America. One of the girls in my class made the trip to the States on a Banana boat from Costa Rica, where her father had a banana plantation. While some of us lived close enough to go home on weekends–I was about 20 miles away–the majority only went home for Easter and Christmas vacations. We were about 25 girls in the freshman class, and while we would all make special friends, the policy of changing rooms and room-mates every semester made us a rather homogeneous group. Although our days had a schedule, there was no regimentation, lining up, no one following us around, checking up on us, there was a lot of free time and choices of activities. Although from my first to last days at Flintridge I attended Mass every morning, the student body was only required to attend on Fridays. At gym we chose our own activities—swim, play tennis, organize a ball game—there was no lining up for calisthenics, in fact, some seniors students were often in charge of our gym period. We were also on our own for breakfast, we could come and go in the dining room as it suited us—or not come at all. For the other two meals, however, we were seated together at tables of eight, began and ended our meals saying grace, and always had to dress for dinner—no uniforms.

The school rooms took up only a small space of the whole facility and were located at the lowest end of the main building—about 9 rooms and a library is all there was to it. During school hours, a visitor could look around the whole place and miss the school entirely; they might not even see a girl or hear a sound. Nevertheless, we were down there about five hours every day, plus a study period every evening from 7 to 8. During school hours there was one free period where some of us went to practice music or drama, while others went to the library or sat on the lawn to study. Every day I hiked up to the music conservatory above the pool to practice. Though all the rooms had a view, I would choose a room where the piano faced the mountains so I could play and look at them at the same time. Playing what I liked, composing and singing, this was one of the most enjoyable hours of my day.

A highlight of my years at Flintridge was the student body's weekly instruction in choral singing conducted by Roger Wagner. At that time he was still starting out and not too well known, but even had he never become famous, what he was able to do with our motley group was short of miraculous, we surprised ourselves at what we could do. Every year he brought his initial choral group up the hill for an evening concert, and one our girls eventually joined his Master Chorale. The sisters frequently brought in vocal or musical artists for an evening's concert, but what was purely optional was taking in an opera or concert down the hill in Pasadena, for which our parents paid a special fee. Mom was only too happy for my exposure to great music, renown artists and good stage productions. Apart from this, however, we students sometimes put on our own evening recitals and drama productions. For a small school, it was rather outstanding for what it offered in the area of music and drama.

Altogether I cannot think of a single negative thing to say about Flintridge or the years I spent there. With the exception a little glitch during the last months–a later story–I was always grateful for the experience, the happy memories, and those who made it possible. For me, at least, it was the perfect place to be during my adolescence years. Though structured from behind the scenes, the atmosphere was free flowing and engendered a sense of being on your own with free choices regarding your time, friends and activities. There was nothing rigid or restrictive, no talk of discipline or threat of what would happen if we didn't do such and such. No one spelled out the rules, and I never heard of anyone even being scolded. The girls seemed naturally well behaved but then, they had all been hand-picked, and not only for their first year, but for all their years at the school. Every year we had to wait for a formal notice to arrive in the mail that spelled out our status–be invited back, or not.

Flintridge, however, would not have been the school it was without its also being home to a community of sisters–by my count, at least 20 or more. Because of this, the facility supported two separate and distinct ways of life. No more than eight sisters were involved in full time teaching, both the principal and librarian taught part time. Besides this, there were 4 or 5 retired sisters, one of whom was superior of their community, along with 4 or 5 German sisters who had immigrated during the war and were responsible for all the dirty work, so to speak. Of these, two or three worked full time in the kitchen, one was in charge of the gardens, another in charge of cleaning the facility.

Apart from the Principle, whose room was in the senior's hall, and the three sisters with us in the cottages, the rest of the community lived in a strictly cloistered portion of the main building–the entire east side that slopped downhill. None of us ever saw past the door marked "Clois-

ter." Although I do not know the Dominican Rule, I know they daily recited the Divine Office, a portion being said before Mass in the morning,
Vespers sometime before diner, and Compline I believe, said either before
or after the evening rosary–which some of us girls attended. What I found
most impressive, however, was their chanting the Salve Regina at the end
of Vespers. Over their white habits they donned a black cape, and lining
up on either side of the isle with candles; they chanted this ancient hymn
to Our Lady. Half of the year the chapel was dark except for their candles.
The first time I saw this, I was deeply touched by its beauty and–solem-
nity. Altogether, the community gave me some insight into the more
prayerful life of the Dominican Order.

In the sisters' refectory or dining room, they ate in silence while
someone read to them. After their meals, the sisters silently processed two
by two through the halls to the Chapel where they said some prayers.
Seeing them coming down the hall, we girls quietly stepped aside and
waited for them to pass–we called them "penguins" because of their while
habits and black mantles. When those who taught were not actually in the
classroom, they were expected to live the community life, which meant
they never mingled with the students and were rarely seen. The only one
available at all times was the Principle. Even the sisters who slept in the
cottages with us only arrived before lights out and departed before any of
us were up. There's no underestimating this community's impact on the
life and atmosphere of the school, though we didn't see a lot of the sisters,
we were aware that they lived a spiritual life, kept a Rule, and were dedicated to their community life. Under a single roof then, there were two
different life style's going on at Flintridge, and while this could not be
ignored, most students never gave it a thought or paid any attention to
the sisters' community life.

Without this background of the sisters' community life, Flintridge
probably would not have been the right place for me. Their prayerful life
was far more meaningful to me than learning math and history. I came
away with a great respect for the Dominican Order and never forgot the
motto on their coat of arms, which the sisters translated: "Share What
You Contemplate." But if I could understand their contemplative side, I
could never grasp their teaching side, or how sharing the contemplation

of God had any connection with sharing a knowledge of math and history. The fact these sisters saw a connection, must have been part of their vocation which, obviously, I never had. My gratitude would not be for their classroom lessons, but the spiritual atmosphere and example they lent to the school.

While I enjoyed kneeling or sitting alone in the Chapel, which was off the inner courtyard opposite the girls' recreation room, I also felt close to God sitting on the hillside just looking at the mountains. I found several hidden places on the side of the hill where I could either sit or lie down without being seen. There's no telling the many hours I spent there just looking. The mountains drew me like a magnet, drew forth in me a mysterious longing, a love and uplifting I could only feel, but not understand. I recognized this mysterious attraction from my years by the sea, it was the same, only now I felt it imperative to know what there was about nature that caused this, and what was it in me that had this affinity or connection to it? I was sure this phenomena—my experiences in nature—had a meaning or purpose in my life, but what? Compared to my experiences of God, the experiences on the hillside were of a totally different nature, and though I intuited a connection, I did not know the nature of this connection any more than I knew the true nature of the Power within.

Something else I enjoyed on the hill top was the night sky. Above the city lights and smog, the stars were brilliant—though not as thick and spectacular as on Mt. Wilson. During my second semester, on weekends when Mom had nothing special planned, I often took a bus to the Planetarium for the afternoon lecture and show. I also brought my "Skyorama" and flashlight back to school to identify all the constellations and their major stars. In winter it was already dark when we finished dinner, so I'd spend the time before study-hall at this task—also after our 8:30 dismissal and before lights-out. Before long I had so mastered the sky map, the night sky became as familiar to me as the key-board on my typewriter.

Sometimes after dinner I was joined outside by Sr. Antoinette, who taught Latin and English and was one of the study hall supervisors. She had taken Astronomy courses, was familiar with the night sky, and could fill in a lot of history and statistics. Above all, perhaps, she gave me the correct pronunciation of the names I had only learned by reading. Usually a group of girls would gather around to listen. I was convinced the school should have offered a course in Astronomy it would not have been beyond any of us and of interest to many.

My first retreat experience came sometime during Lent. For a whole week, school and all activities were suspended; we ate in silence while someone read over the dining room speaker. That first year the Superior's Jesuit brother gave us several talks each day, but apart from Mass and evening Rosary, we were basically on our own with a lot of free time. While we were not asked to keep silence in our rooms, we did it anyway. The previous week we had been asked to pick out some spiritual reading for the retreat, but going through the library both at school and at home, nothing appealed to me, so I decided to take along a couple of dad's astronomy books. When he saw my pile he got out another book he'd found at the Planetarium and handed it to me, "I thought it was a good book, see what you think of it," so I put it on my pile. Its title, I believe, was Man Does Not Stand Alone.

As it turned out I read this book several times, it was not only factually interesting, but spoke to my own perspective on the universe. Although the book's agenda was to convey to the ordinary lay person all the information and technology man would need to go to the moon, the last chapter revealed his personal perspective on the universe as the creation of a marvelous designer, an unfathomable intelligence that could only be "God." This view permeated the book, it was a perspective much like my own; I felt certain the author would not only understand my own particular love and–experiences in nature, but may well have had them himself. During the Jesuit's talks, I sat with this book open on my lap and read.

I spent all my free time out of doors, usually on the hillside reading or just looking. The universe not only spoke of God, elevated and drew man to God, but I was convinced it had an immediate, almost concrete connection to Him. God was more than just nature's backdrop, its creator and sustainer, God was also a kind of sensory, material veil though which the eyes of the soul could see him. Thus I was convinced something in or about me was physically, not just spiritually, looking at God. How all this worked of course, I hadn't the slightest idea. I was sorry when the retreat was over; ending on a Friday it was an abrupt transition from its silence back to City life. One good thing, at home I could talk about the book with dad. He was delighted I enjoyed it; the two of us made a trip to the book store to see if we could find more books like it.

Something odd happened one day in Sr. Bernadette's math class. She had given us class time to work on our homework assignment, the room was silent. I was sitting alone in the back row under one of the windows. In order to listen to the silence I let my mind go blank, but as soon as I did this I experienced a forceful pull inward and downward to behold a blaze of light. On seeing this, it felt as if a dazzling meteor had struck the center of my being, and in that same instant, the window pane behind my head blew out, shattered into a million pieces. Everyone was startled, especially myself. The glass sprayed all over me, it was in my hair, on my arms, books, lap, the floor. Immediately I jumped up to shake it off and turn around to look at the window. Sister also jumped up, came down the aisle and said rather angrily,

Sr.: I hope you know you'll have to pay to have the glass replaced!

Me: But I didn't do it!

Sr.: Well you're the only one in that seat that could have done it.

Me: But how?

Sr.: I don't know, maybe you hit the window with the back of your head.

Me: But my head couldn't reach! (My head could only have hit the jutting window sill).

Sr.: Then how could it have happened?

Me: I don't know.

Sr.: Well you must have done it because nobody else is back here or near the window. The school will be sending your parents a repair bill.

After that she sent someone to get the janitor–I never knew if my parents were billed or not. While I had no physical explanation for the window, my impression of the experience was that God Passing By had descended (maybe even come through the window) and united with the Power within which caused a kind of explosion. That's all I could think of. I was certain this experience was the two together, the Transcendent and Immanent and not simply one or the other.

I might add, located down the hill in Pasadena was the Cal Tech Jet Propulsion Laboratory which was constantly letting out sonic booms that shook the whole school. Nobody would have been surprised if this shattered a window now and then, which was probably the first cause we thought of when the glass shattered. Yet there had been no sonic boom, no earthquake, the window had shattered amidst stillness and silence. What I couldn't get over, however, was how irrational Sr. Bernadette had been about the whole incident, she never even asked if I'd been cut or hurt. By and large however, Sr. Bernadette was okay, though she didn't know her math. She was the school librarian and was good at recommending books to me. She kept me updated on the newer books the Sisters were reading in their refectory. About this time she told me they were reading Walsh's biography of St. Teresa of Avila, but since it was a big fat book, it would be months before it ever reached the school library. That weekend I asked dad if we could go to the Catholic store downtown and look for the book. Always happy to have an excuse to browse around the book store, we went that weekend and, as usual, came home with a load of new books. Though I enjoyed reading the biography, I could never relate to her experiences or particular spirituality. I picked up on the titles of her own books, however, and made a stab at reading her Way of Perfection which I found too dry and uninteresting to pursue.

About two months into my first semester, I unexpectedly received the second best present in my life. For Religion class we were given the assignment of outlining the four Gospels—due by the end of the semester. Since I was taking a typing class, I spent my free time in the typing room working on my outline. That weekend at dinner, I told my parents what I was working on at school; immediately dad asked, "How would you like to go down to Sears and pick out a portable typewriter?" I didn't have to answer, only to ask "When?" He said, "Right now, after dessert." So leaving mom to cleanup, we drove down to Sears and picked out the best, most recent style portable typewriter and brought it home. I would always count this as one of the most important gifts of my life. After that, having to write anything by hand became anathema, my hand could never keep up with my mind, thus the typewriter opened up a freedom of mind and expression I could never have had otherwise. When typing my mind functioned differently, whereas writing by hand so stifled my brain I avoided it whenever possible. Apart from this, my typewriter spared me from having to sit in the typing room at school and dad's office at home, instead, I could find myself a corner anywhere, even outside, and go to town. Needless to say, my religion assignment turned out beautifully with Christ's words written in red; I received a big red "A" at the end of the semester.

But if this gift was the best thing that happened in my freshman year, it was unfortunately offset by two rather bad events at home. First, I lost my dog Spot—so named because she was part Dalmatian. Three years earlier we had opened the door one morning to find her, still a puppy, on our doorstep. At first we tried to ignore and shoo her away so she'd go back home, but she never left. We inquired up and down the block and at the pet store, but no one recognized her, and so she became part of the family. Mom and I just loved her, but dad had reservations because she didn't like the postman—or any delivery man—and sometimes chased people on bikes. One day she bit a biker in the butt and tore his pants, the man threatened to sue us. As long as I was at home I could keep an eye on Spot, but mom and dad were not so vigilant, and after her next offense, dad gave her to one of the workmen on the premises. When I learned of this I got the man's address, took a taxi to his home—clear across LA.—and brought her back. But Spot kept running and jumping at passing bikers, so the next time it happened dad took her away for good, but refused to say where. All he assured me is that he never took her to the pound—which was true, because I visited all the pounds in the L.A. area. If he told me he had given her to somebody, he probably thought I'd find out who, and go after her again. I never understood his secretiveness, it would have been easier to know she had been put to sleep than constantly imagining her lost someplace, unhappy, or possibly mistreated. The whole thing was heart breaking; I gave dad a black mark for it.

The second upset is when I came home one weekend and found Marge gone. When I asked where she was, I was told to read the telegram on the living room coffee table. In about ten words it said she had just been married and would not be coming home. To say it was a shock would be putting it mildly, it was a tragic, heart-breaking blow, less for me, of course, than for my parents. They sat there while I read the telegram without offering a word or comment, not then, not ever, the deed was done and that was that. We had only met her husband several times when he came to pick her up for a date, there was never a hint she was even thinking of getting engaged, much less married, not a word from her at all. I don't know how I landed in such a secretive family; it was always the cause of frustration and heart-break.

When I went to our room and saw all her things around–she took nothing with her knowing she'd never be back, it was as bad as if she had died. With Marge gone, I realized my family life was over, merely living with mom and dad was not family life, not at least as I had known it. My strongest links to the past were gone, now I was the only one left to leave. Lying in bed I tried to think of something positive about it all, but not even the fact I now had the room to myself was consoling. Suddenly I remembered the Monk! I got out of bed, took him out of the drawer and set him up where I could see him, tomorrow I'd give him his permanent place on the wall. The next day, however, mom told me to wait until she had packed up Marge's things; it was just too soon to spread my own stuff around. When I came home the next weekend not only were Marge's things gone, but the bedrooms had been switched. I was now in the front bedroom where the windows faced the street. Although the room was larger and looked beautiful, I was now without my view of the Deodar trees, the sole uplifting view in all of Hollywood. Well, the Monk would just have to be my substitute for something uplifting to look at. So dad and I installed him on the wall where I could see him from my bed, and there he stayed for years to come before I moved him elsewhere.

With a room of my own I could bring a girlfriend home from school for a weekend. My first choice was Maria Lopez, my first room-mate. No one ever had a worse case of home sickness than Maria, who was from Mexico City. When she wasn't hanging out with her older sister–a junior at school–she was in our room moping and crying. Any time she'd try to tell me about her home or background she'd break into tears, and every night–for weeks–she cried herself to sleep. At first I tried to be sympathetic, but since it didn't do any good, I spent my time in the next room where the whole cottage seemed to congregate because there was always something crazy going on there. It was several months before there was any breakthrough with Maria, which happened at gym when I asked her if she wanted to swat some tennis balls. With a racket in hand, Maria suddenly came alive with an energy and aggressiveness hard, if not impossible, to match. After that she joined our jump rope gang–between classes, six or seven of us would rush outside to the patio for a quick game–which Maria thoroughly enjoyed. As it turned out, I would rate Maria as one of the most spirited, fun loving, happy girls in the school, she was gung-ho and game for anything. The first time I asked her to come home with me I thought she'd want to ask her sister or perhaps call her parents, but instead, she responded with an immediate, enthusiastic, "Yes!" So home we went, and not just that weekend, but for as long as I was at school she came home almost every weekend. From the first it was obvious Maria was not a guest, she was family, she belonged, she was the sister I had lost with Sally. During the week we never hung out together or ever again shared a room at school, but between Maria and I there would always be an unspoken, enduring sisterly bond.

Catalina Island: Age 15

AGE 15

Because the war was over we could take out the boat again. This year I spent almost half the summer at Catalina. The first trip over dad was too busy to stay with us, so he left us moored in Avalon bay for two weeks while he returned home. When he came back we sailed to the Isthmus (a harbor near the northern tip of the island) where we met other members of the family—now married with children—who booked rooms on shore. At the Isthmus we could swim from shore to boat, altogether this reunion of the whole family made for a happy time. After this trip I returned for several more weeks with Aunt Mabel and Uncle Joe on board. On one outing that summer we had some tense moments when Lee, taking a bunch of us for a ride around the harbor, ventured outside into dangerous waters. As we left the harbor the fishermen on the rocks waved us back, gestured frantically for us to turn around, but Lee kept going. It was a stormy sea with high winds and giant swells, no place for our small boat. Once outside we hit the waves with such a resounding bang we had to hang on for dear life, yet I didn't see how Lee could turn the boat around without its being swamped. Uncle Joe kept shouting at Lee, "Remember your baby, we can't hold on to him anymore!" I don't know if Uncle Joe was actually scared, or just using the baby as an excuse, yet it struck us funny and relieved the tension. That Lee was able to turn the boat around, told me all I ever needed to know about his expert seamanship.

The end of August school began with a happy reunion of schoolmates. My roommate this semester was Pat Travis who, next to Maria, became my most endearing friend. Although Pat was the brightest and perhaps the most sociable in the class, her most outstanding feature was her keen and subtle sense of humor, her perspective on the world seemed to verge on the humorous. Pat was highly verbal and the fact she loved to argue and debate–about anything–is what made us a match. We would sit on our beds facing each other and deliberately choose a topic to discuss–politics, psychology, religion, whatever–and if we had to quit for gym we'd resume as soon as we got back, then go right on after study hall that night, and end up after lights–out in our walk-in closet where we'd sit on the floor, snack, argue and laugh till the wee hours. Although pretty serious about our topics, sooner or later we'd break into such belly laughs it brought us to tears. After lights-out it was all we could do to muffle our laughter and not get caught–as Pat would say, "We must be careful to laugh at the right time!" Often the night watchman banged on our wall to warn us we could be heard. I never had so much fun with a roommate, there we were, the academically brightest and dumbest thoroughly enjoying each other's company.

The night watchman, Mr. Barth, was part of the Flintridge scene. With his flashlight and gun he was up all night making the rounds of the entire facility. Though we never saw his gun, we often heard him shooting into the air when the coyotes got howling too long or too close. Every night he monitored the girls' walk between the main building and the cottages across the road and was responsible for locking the main door after we left. Once I was late and found the main door already locked. After I ran to get the principle who unlocked the door, I had to wait until Mr. Barth got there to escort me over the bridge to the cottages. Besides a walkie-talkie he had set times for being at set places during the night so the sisters would know approximately where he was–if needed. He was also the one who checked up on "lights out" since none of the sisters left their rooms to check on us, in some of the cottages there were no sisters at all. So Pat and I figured out Mr. Barth's time schedule for passing our cottage and would be quiet until he passed. Mr. Barth, however, must have caught on, because he would sometimes return unexpectedly and bang on our wall, which always cracked us up, yet he never ratted on us or issued a complaint.

Pat lived with her grandmother who owned and operated an exclusive Sanatorium down the hill, thus she lay claim to psychological expertise, liked to play psychiatrist, and took a particular interest in analyzing me. She was the only person with whom I ever talked about myself, more especially, my divided self—the one on the outside that everybody saw and knew, and one on the inside, my real self, that nobody ever knew and was even a mystery to me. Right off she said I had a dual personality disorder, but I told her this was impossible because the inside person had no personality at all, it had no such outward expression and that was the problem—the outer did not express the inner. I illustrated this with a couple of experiences, like when the outer was totally silent, only the inner remained, and when the outer got going again it did not express the inner; nor was the inner ever really interested in the outer, seemingly had little to do with it. I felt the two should be in harmony so that the outer expressed the inner, but I didn't see how this could be done, if ever. Furthermore, it seemed to me I had three possible types of unity:

1. Being one with nature—which I experienced by letting its marvel and mystery sink into me, impress itself on my spirit to become a part of it, no different than it.

2. Being one with myself—a kind of interior absorption or awareness where externals were forgotten in an experience of fullness, completion, a centralized coming together of mind and will, a whole person for whom nothing was impossible,

3. A oneness of both of the above, which was greater than either. In this experience a mysterious power could bring everything together in an uplifting greatness and overflowing joy that surpassed myself. I was sure God was the source of this oneness because only His Power could gather everything into a Oneness beyond mere personal unity.

One thing I had noticed the year before was that beginning each day with Mass was a source of unity and personal integrity, but a unity that seemed to dissipate as the day wore on and once again I was rushing here and there, chit-chatting about nothing and throwing myself into numerous activities with wild abandon. By the end of the day I felt myself scattered, goal-less, without accomplishment, utterly dissatisfied. I desperately wanted a life wherein I felt I could be true to myself every moment of every day. To help myself in this matter, I spent more time out of doors where I could read and study alone or chart the stars at night. Initially I found this helpful toward maintaining the unity I so desired.

Because the mornings started out so well, I decided that instead of going to recreation after dinner, I'd join the sisters each evening for rosary in the chapel. I found this a quieting effect; in the red glow of the sanctuary lamp, not only my outer but inner vision was focused on the tabernacle, and from this solitary gaze came a sense of unity, a concentrated wholeness which, alas, I could not hold for very long. Sometimes, however, this silent gaze lasted and I would stay in the chapel after everyone left. I often experienced real joy being alone with God in the silence of the dark chapel. During the study hour that followed, I tried to maintain this inner sense of unity by avoiding influences that might distract me; still, by the time of lights-out, I was my old scattered self again.

Pat took a lively interest in my search for personal unity. From what she said, however, it was obvious she never experienced any such division within herself, thus I didn't see how she could grasp my real dilemma. At any rate her theory of how to get it together was the altruistic approach. She said concentration on self was a dead end, a circular affair that would never let us out of ourselves, it was only concern for others that would eventually lead us out, and in so doing, heal all divisions, thus her advice was "forget your self and be concerned for others." "But", I responded, "If I could really forget my deeper self it would also mean forgetting God." This surprised her–did I think my deeper self was God? No, I didn't, but it was only the deeper self that wanted to know, love and serve God, whereas by contrast, the outer self was concerned primarily with itself, its external image and desires. As for altruism, even an atheist could be altruistic, God wasn't needed for that kind of life; in fact, such a life might he an escape from having to deal with the inner self

I told her that it was going out to others that mainly created the division in the first place. Being at the service of everyone else, giving them my time and attention and trying to make their interests my own, only scatter my forces, pulled me in different directions, sapped my strength and mentality, in short, it was no good for creating in me any sense of personal unity. Pat responded by saying that the other option–staying alone and aloof–was merely a failure to come to terms with one's self and others. It would lead, she said, to introversion and ego-centricity and only create larger problems than the one I was attempting to resolve. But how could I help others when I had first to help myself, or help others get it together if I didn't have it together? According to Pat, however, the way to get it together, to realize unity in ourselves, was by going out to our neighbor, and there, between us, lay the impasse. It seemed as if Pat had been born an integrated person and, indeed, she came across as far older than her years–she was fifteen at the time. Even later in life Pat was the same integrated individual, in this matter she was ageless.

Coming back to her altruistic argument, she used charity as the unifying force, which was difficult to refute. Once she said, "The only one who can help you is God. He is the only reality we have, and when we know Him we can see His reality in ourselves and in other people, and did you ever think that the 'deeper person' you feel in yourself could be God?"

Her question took me by surprise, while I knew my deepest self was not God, I was reminded of what mom said to me years before–"You'll never find your true self until you find God." The God I experienced, however, was certainly not my self or any part of myself, but that my deepest self was "that" unknown aspect in myself that experienced God, well, this was probably true; I took for granted, however, it was some aspect of my soul, but not an aspect of my psyche. Her question, however, put me on the spot because now I had to verbalize the difference between God and my deeper self, both of them a mystery to me.

For the months we roomed together the subject of my divided self was not only a frequent topic, but a standing joke–she referred to me as a "psychiatrist's dream." While nothing she said was actually helpful, she enabled me to express my problem, hash it out, which of itself was rather enlightening. Putting my experiences on an intellectual level, having to articulate them, get them across, even defend them, made them much clearer to me, in this respect Pat was very helpful. Although my problem was not the only subject we discussed, yet things always had a way of getting back to my "case history" as she called it. Once we were arguing about the policies of two opposing politicians, and when things got heated I suddenly said, "You want to know what I really think? My deeper self doesn't honestly give a damn about either politician or their policies. It doesn't matter who wins because it's not going to affect me one way or the other." This ruined her train of thought, but only for a second, then she shot back, "You know what I think? I think your deeper self is just a cop-out for not being able to deal with the real issues of life." So there we were again, back to that inner self business.

Without question Pat was one of the most brilliant, well-rounded, self-possessed persons I ever met. She did indeed have it "all together" with no hint of duality in her being. What was most noteworthy, however, was her exceptionally strong Faith which I thought might be why she never experienced any dichotomy in herself. For her to live and act was all an expression of her singular Faith, for her, there was no inner and outer. Seeing this made me question my own Faith, and by faith I do not mean belief, which in my view belongs to the outer person, whereas Faith was somehow the very life of the inner self. At any rate, I felt my Faith was not as strong as hers, so perhaps Faith was her secret and my problem. Once, when I suggested she watch out lest the mental illness of the Sanatorium's patients rub off on her, she said, "Perhaps that's the supreme sacrifice of this vocation: to know others think you are odd, but let them do it anyway." I found this remarkable.

Although the next semester I only moved across the hall from Pat, we never again enjoyed our discussions together. Though ever good friends we basically went our own way. I might add, her older sister, then a senior and the school's student body president, joined the Dominican Order after graduation. This sent her grandmother through a loop because the oldest had been groomed to take over the Sanatorium when she retired, and now this plan was shot to pieces. As it turned out, the responsibility fell on Pat and though she was perfect for the job, I always felt it terribly restricted her life. She not only took over the Sanatorium at a young age, but took care of her aging grandmother and saw to all the family affairs. Since her younger sister also joined the Dominicans, and her brother lived in New Zealand, the whole burden fell on Pat alone. She was never really free, not at least, in the outer sense of the term.

Some months into the school year we were assigned oral reports for our American history class. I don't remember my topic, but I remember wanting to make a good impression on the teacher and get a good grade. When my turn came I couldn't have been better prepared or more sure of myself. Everything went well until I made the mistake of glancing out the window. Although the windows overlooked the mountains, this day I merely noticed that the window was open. I thought I either saw or felt a breeze come in when suddenly my mind shut down completely. It was as if a mysterious waft of fog had beclouded my mind and pervaded my whole person. I looked down at my notes but couldn't read them, they were a jumble of letters. What also surprised me was that I didn't care, instead of trying to get back on track or at least offer a quick conclusion–I could not have remember the topic anyway–I just smiled at the teacher, shrugged my shoulders and abruptly sat down. I felt I had been ushered into a dimension compared to which nothing else had any meaning whatsoever, an ethereal dimension free of mind, desires, emotions, everything.

As soon as class was over I went to a solitary spot on the hillside to be alone with this unique experience. I knew myself to be in some mysterious state, a buoyant, joyful, uncaring freedom where no worldly concern could touch or involve me. My whole being was pervaded by something unknowable, something I could only compare to a breeze because it was lightsome, gentle, exhilarating and refreshing. Above all, it engendered an overwhelming love of God, so much so, this breeze seemed to be love itself, a love not engendered by myself, but by God. Though I didn't know why I had this experience or what its purpose, no reason would have had any meaning anyway, because the experience was IT–an end in itself. It took about a week before this experience completely wore off, slowly it ebbed away until one day it was completely gone.

The after effect of this experience–indeed all my experiences–was the sense that some abiding change had been effected. I was never able, however, to pin point "what" had changed or how I was different. Since there had been no physical, intellectual or emotional change, I knew it to be much deeper, a change in some unknown depths of my being. What I carried away from such experiences, however, was an abiding knowledge. For one thing, I knew God to be the sole cause of the experience, and as such, I marveled God cared enough to cause it on my behalf. At the same time, however, this knowledge laid a certain responsibility on me to never let God down. Though I never thought I could be worthy of such a touch from God, I determine to live so as not to be wholly unworthy. In this way, at least, I could show–or better, live–my gratitude.

Another piece of knowledge was the existence of some hidden purpose down the road. God didn't reveal himself for nothing or merely for my enjoyment, no, this meant serious business, it had a purpose. Because the experience was a piece of heaven I firmly believed I was destined to die young and God was just getting me ready–warning me in a .way. Because I believed this, I wanted to live in constant readiness–as dad often told us kids: "Live each day as if it were your last." Now I understood why.

Needless to say, every experience informed me that a different dimension of life existed, a dimension of human possibility not only for life in heaven, but life on earth as well. Although this dimension (or state) has no concern or connection with earthly events, at least it could be known or experienced while still in this world. Knowing I could not cause this state or enter into this dimension of my own accord, I nevertheless wondered how I might prepare for it. I simply could not go on my way as if the experience had been a mere blip in my life's history, on the contrary, every experience engendered a tremendous energy and desire to pursue God, to know and love Him with my whole heart, mind and soul. The nature of gratitude seems to be: give as you have received.

It was over Christmas vacation that God affected a major breakthrough in my life, it occurred at the Planetarium one Saturday afternoon. The importance of this breakthrough cannot be appreciated, however, without understanding my particular and immediate dilemma, because what I saw and learned was the resolution of this dilemma.

The Dilemma

For years I had pondered the true connection between "God Passing By" and the Power within. They were two different experiences, seemingly from two different sources, each playing a different part in my life. The Power within was abiding, close and personal, while God Transcendent or Without, was only known in Its Passing, glorious but aloof, and relatively impersonal. Though there were times when the interior Power seemed to impress on me that it was God, the impression did not last, there were a number of reasons for this.

4. 1. As a child I had learned to keep a certain distance from this interior Power (or Friend) because I knew it could overpower me, take me over, thus there was a certain fear of it. It was important the Power keep its own space so I could have mine.

5. 2. Later, in the greatest crisis of my life, when the Power suddenly disappeared and left a black hole in its wake, I knew it could never have been God because God would never do such a cruel thing. I wanted nothing to do with any God that would come and go, for this reason I kept my eyes on the God who had always been there for me–God in nature.

6. 3. I knew God was "Everywhere" in creation or nature, indeed, I had seen this at an early age, God in the sea had even cured me. Though God in nature was a wondrous, mysterious presence, it was somewhat impersonal, aloof, and nothing like the personal Power within. So God's presence in nature was not the interior Power, of this I was certain.

7. 4. Following God's revealing identity in the woods (God Passing by), I was more certain than ever the Power within had not been God. How it happened that at the moment of this revelation (in the woods) the Power suddenly returned–after an 18 month's absence, I could not figure out, I simply determined to ignore it. Soon, however, it was obvious it had some connection to God. It was constantly interfering in my life, always popping up–"leaping"–importuning me, and at times had inundated me with a longing and love of God I could hardly contain. On three occasions it seemed to leap

out of myself and appear before me (a brilliant, blinding light) as if it were God itself–God in nature and God Passing rolled into one. For some moments I knew it was God, yet afterwards I reverted to my skeptical position. At one point I figured the Power was probably some grace or gift God had implanted in me and what I experienced was this grace responding to God. If only I knew its true identity, however, I could understand the part it was meant to play in my life. I was never sure what my rapport with it should be or what expectations I might have of it, in short, I needed to know its true place in my life with God. How to attain this knowledge, however, was my particular dilemma. For a least a year or more I prayed every night that God would enlighten me, let me know the truth in this matter once and for all.

* * * * *

As time went on, the need to know grew more imperative. One day I both knew and saw I had come to a point in my life where I was absolutely stuck, a point beyond which I could not go or make any further progress until this mystery of the Power had been resolved. I cannot describe how I knew this, but it was an unmistakable moment of truth as clear as the hand before my face. I determined that the next time God Passed By I would ask Him: "What is this in me that knows you? What is its connection to you?" Because God's passing was always so swift and unexpected I was afraid He'd be gone before I could get the questions out, still, I had to try. Thus I had my questions poised and ready months before the following event took place.

Saturday afternoons during Christmas vacation I would take the bus to the Griffith Park Observatory for the lectures. This particular Saturday there were many visitors, and though the lecture hall was almost full, I found a seat about the middle of the third row from the back. As usual Dr. Mueller was giving the lecture–a gracious man always available to answer my questions after the lecture. Halfway through his lecture, however, there came the familiar "leap", instantly my whole body was poised to run outside to catch a glimpse of God passing by. This time, however, I held to the arms of the seat undecided whether to go or stay, when I saw God's Passing anyway–as if through the room. Though I fully expected this

Passing to be as swift as a meteor, to my amazement It stood still as if deliberately hovering for a moment, so I shot out my questions "What is this in me that knows you? What is its connection to you?"

The answer I received was not conveyed by any word or intellectual means, instead it was conveyed by what I saw, a knowledge by seeing alone. What I saw was the enactment or movements of God that conveyed a knowledge of how God works or how He manifests Himself, virtually moves to manifest Himself. In this movement I saw that God Passing by was also the Power within (my Friend), One and the same God only two different Manifestations, hence, two different experiences. There was another part to this enactment that I failed to recognize or comprehend, possibly because I was so over-whelmed with the initial knowledge–namely, God on the inside (the Power) and God on the outside (Passing or Transcendent) were One and the same–I didn't expect anything more. So even though I saw something more and knew I'd seen it, it meant nothing to me at the time. My questions had been answered and I was so wild with joy I could not sit still another second.

I felt like shouting "hooray!" and must have said something aloud because the man next to me turned and gave me an impatient "Sh!" I had lost all interest in the lecture, I wanted to go outside, be alone in nature to relish this joy and new knowledge. I'm afraid I stepped on some toes making my way to the isle; with only the red exit sign in view, I made my way to the door and opened it just enough to squeeze through so the light would not disturb the darkened room. Then I ran across the rotunda and out the front door into the bright sunlight where instantly I was struck blind, the pain in my eyes was excruciating. To get out of people's way, I felt along the top step to one side where I sat down and put my face in my hands. People going by asked "Is there something wrong?" "Can I help you?" It was embarrassing, I couldn't even look up at them, only shake my head "no." At least five minutes went by before the pain decreased and I peeked between my fingers to find out if I was ever to see again. After that it took maybe 10 minutes or so before things returned to normal.

Despite the physical set-back, the spiritual joy was unabated. As soon as I could squintingly see, I looked out on the hillside. Though visually it was the same as ever, I was now seeing it with a new knowledge. That God's presence in nature was the same as in me not only accounted for the mysterious affinity I had experienced with nature all my life, this same Presence was the Leap within, the interior Power, my old Friend—and God in the woods! An analogy of this new knowledge might be that of a balloon where the (divine) air on the inside is the same as the (divine) air on the outside, yet the experience of this air is very different. The air on the inside seems to be circumscribed, intimate, personal, responsible for our life's movements and the object of our interior focus. The air on the outside, however, is everywhere, infinite and immense, relatively impersonal, and though we live and move in it, it is too vast to ever be the object of one's focus. These two different manifestations of God account for two very different experiences of God—inner and outer.

It was about five miles to home, but since I was in no hurry to get back, instead of taking the bus I decided to walk. I had a lot to think about and wanted time to relish this new knowledge alone and out-of-doors. That night, trying to recapture what I'd seen, I knew there was some aspect of it I had failed to grasp; I blamed myself for being hasty and running out too soon. Once I saw how God Within and Without were the same, I was so overcome with joy it didn't occur to me God might have something else for me to know. So while I knew some part of this knowledge was still in the clouds, I trusted if I really needed to know, God would give it to me.

With this new knowledge a central piece of my life's puzzle had fallen into place. Now I could see how years of experiences fit together, marveled at the different ways God had revealed Himself, starting as a little one. I saw a kind of developmental progression, how God had been teaching me, preparing me at each step, I had not gone from one isolated, disconnected experience to another, on the contrary, each experience had been a step on a specific path. First there had been God in nature (in the sea), then God Everywhere, then God in me (the Power), and finally, God beyond me and nature (God's Passing by), to finally see how these all fit together, all God's revelations, was like the revelation to end all mysteries.

But surely God didn't go to this trouble for nothing, it was all part of some great Plan, a particular work He was going to accomplish come hell or high water. Although I could never make out this purpose, somehow I felt we were getting close and that before long I would know the great Plan. Although a bit skeptical of what lay ahead, I felt game for anything.

Several days or a week later (I do not recall) it suddenly dawned on me: God Within and God Without, but what about me? What was my eternal connection to God? Because God is within doesn't make Him a part of me, or me, a part of Him. Like air in a balloon, the air is not the balloon; so too, between God and me there was no intrinsic or eternal connection at all. The very fact of God being within and without obviously left me out; if I died or disappeared, God would go right on as if I had never existed. In the end I would cease to exist and God would go on without me—without the whole of creation in fact. With no real or true connection to God, creation was just a temporary showcase, here today, gone tomorrow. This not only made creation expendable, but God as well—with no eternal connection why bother to know and love God at all? It made no sense!

The instant I realized this, it felt like my stomach had dropped out. I had no abiding existence. In truth, I was nothing, counted for nothing. Without God, or if there were no God, it would have made no difference because I would have missed nothing. But to know and love God and then cease to exist, would be to lose everything; better, I thought, not to have known God at all. For me, of course, it was too late, because I knew God, the lack of an eternal connection was not only terrible news for me, but for all creation as well—it didn't even speak well for God Himself. It seemed pointless and cruel for God to lure and lead us on, knowing all the while we were ultimately assigned to oblivion. If this were the case, God had no right, reason or purpose to reveal Himself to a single human being. I reasoned God would not have revealed Himself to me for nothing, or if I were only to come to naught. It simply flew in the face of common sense for God to waste time on someone bound for extinction. No, I did not believe God capable of such a cruel trick, nor could I accept my ultimate extinction. I was sure all creation had some eternal connection to God, but what was it? Prior to this I'd never given a thought to my connection to God, but if I had taken it for granted, I could no longer do so.

The knowledge I received at the Planetarium had obviously been insufficient, there had to be more to it. Though I tried repeatedly to re-capture the "enactment" I'd seen at the Planetarium–in hopes of seeing the part I missed or did not understand–this proved impossible because it left no imprint on my mind. Though trying to describe it to others I might use words like "light" and "cloud", this is not what I saw at all. The truth is: I saw God's own enactment, movement, manifestations, that was IT, no other words apply. While this new knowledge had been a profound revelation, the answer to a lifelong question, it had created a worse di-lemma than the one before, a dilemma that required I ask God yet another question, demand another answer. I determined to ask God, "What am I to you?" "What, if any, is the true connection between us?" I was sure He would give me the answer, after all, my life was at stake. Although I needed an immediate answer, because the family had plans for that day, I decided to stay up all night and pray God to give it to me. Right now, my life was on hold.

Every bedroom had a crucifix on the wall–about 18 inches or so–and sometimes I knelt there to say my rosary before bed. This night I knelt to pray God for an answer, and vowed not to get up until I received it. If I had to stay there the rest of my life, no matter, people would just have to come and physically remove me. I posed my question not to the crucifix, but to God transcendent ("God-Without", "God-of-the-woods", or "God-Passing by"), after that, I waited in silence. I did not have to wait long before high up behind the wall somewhere, came a swift, straight, brilliant beam of light that passed downward through the center of the crucifix and on into the center of myself. I was hit with such force I fell backward against the maple bed post; it was as if I'd been struck by lightning. Instantly I recognized the Trinity–God Transcendent, "God Passing by" (the Father); God Immanent, the Power within (the Holy Spirit); and between the two, Christ. Though I had blessed myself ("In the name of the Father, the Son, and the Holy Spirit") thousands of times and knew the Trinity to be the lofty mystery of God, I had never given it any real thought–indeed, dad often said the Trinity was "unthinkable."

Seeing the Trinity in this light, however, it not only took on meaning in my life, it became central to it. But as regards Christ's place in the Trinity and what he revealed of God's mystery, I was a complete blank. It bothered me that the Light had passed through Christ, after all, he had no place in my life or experiences, I never thought of Him, never felt any need for him. So what was he doing in the Trinity, what was his role? Above all, what did his place in the Trinity mean to me? I could not think of a thing.

Initially the revelation of the Trinity had not seemed to answer my question, instead, it posed another: "What was Christ's connection to God Immanent and Transcendent?" Instantly I set myself the task of trying to figure this out. I wracked my brain for at least two or three hours. Just having to think about Christ was tedious, his life had always been dry and uninteresting, yet I forced my brain to go over everything I knew about his life, his works and teachings, yet none of them spoke to me of his part and meaning in the Trinity. After several hours my brain was on fire from sheer strain. It reached a point where it could no longer move at all. There was no choice but to despair of the whole issue and crawl into bed, my brain just wanted to relax, sleep, forget about the whole thing. Once in bed, however, it took hours before my brain began to relax, and there set in that rather pleasant feeling of slowly drifting off to sleep. But no sooner had I reached this point, when something came into my mind from the outside—above my head on the pillow—which informed me:

Christ in the Trinity stands for you and all creation, He is your true and eternal connection to God, the link between God Within and Without. His humanity is the vessel, the meeting place where God within and without have fruition and become One so that everything created and uncreated is united and One. To know this same fruition as Christ knew it, the vessel must be perfect as he is perfect. Christ is the medium through which the vessel (me) could become one with its content (God). Transformed into Christ, His place in the Trinity is also your eternal place in the Trinity.

Words cannot say how this actually came to me, it was simply a clear knowledge given all at once and not in words. To me it was a com-

plete revelation, the whole plan of God in a nut shell, ingenious, magnificent and definitive. Christ was not merely a medium between God Within
and Without (Father and Spirit), rather, He represented all creations in-
clusiveness in God's Oneness. Thus for me, the way was to become as
Christ, one with Christ, because He was my true connection to God and
in the end, my eternal place in the Trinity. (I might add, while later I would
see and know Christ, it was never Christ alone, but solely in His oneness
with Father and Spirit).

I was now wide awake and knew exactly what to do next: I had to
make my peace with Christ, and then, I had to follow. My life was settled
once and for all, now I knew "the Way." Though it was almost four in the
morning I got up, dressed, and walked to Church to make my peace with
Christ. A dense fog hung in the air, despite the street lights I couldn't see
but a few feet in front of me; if there was anyone else out, I never saw
them. I knew the first Mass was at five, and that the sacristan often opened
the doors early. When I got to Church he was just opening it so I walked
into the beautiful, warm, empty Church and was inundated with joy. I
liked to think Christ was as happy to see me as I was to see Him.

It was almost noon before I left Church. On the way home, looking
up at the sky, I recalled the terrible incident years before when I realized
I had not been chosen, was not really a Christian. Here now, after years
of knowing I was not a Christian, there came the happy thought, "Now
I'm a Christian!" But no sooner had this thought entered my mind than it
was instantly blown out: "No, you are not a Christian yet, you are only
becoming one." Though a bit sobering, I understood perfectly. The term
"becoming" meant I was on "the way" and that being transformed into
Christ was a progressive journey, not a one-time event or grace. Until this
transformation was complete, until I had followed Christ to the very end,
only then could I honestly say I was a Christian. So despite my "conversion experience"–which is how I referred to my experience of the Trinity–
I was still just a neophyte, the merest beginner.

My understanding of following Christ meant to live as He had lived,
that is, live in oneness with the Father. I knew Christ never prayed to
Himself, worshipped Himself, did His own will or even pointed to Himself; always he directed himself to God His Father. To follow Christ I

would also focus my life on God the Father, not on Christ. Due to the nature of my conversion, however, my focus would always be on God as the whole Trinity, not singly on the Father, Holy Spirit, or Christ, rather, it was the glorious mystery of the Trinity that became central to my spiritual life. But if the Father and Holy Spirit were not a mystery to me–indeed, they had been part my life from the beginning–I would always be confronted with the mystery of Christ. I did not see Christ either within myself or without (transcendent), thus I could only think of Him as beside me–like a brother–he was "that" mystery of God into whom I must be transformed. While I had no idea what the end of this transformation would be like, I knew it would not be a transformation into Christ's humanity, but into his divinity. As I saw it, no one could fully know Christ until they had been fully transformed into Him, until then, everything known of Christ was incomplete. But if we do not know the fullness of Christ ahead of time, still we can do as He did–love God (his father) as he did.

I would always regard Christ's human personality as a passing earthly persona. When one is perfectly still–mind and body, silent and alone–there is no personality to speak of, thus personality is one's unique way of expression; it is what others see and know of us, nothing more or deeper than that. Besides, it would have made no sense to be transformed into the past physical and psychological personality of the human Jesus, after all, he had his human nature and I had mine. Knowing his humanity had been transformed (deified), I believed that as it went for him so it would go for me–though I had no idea how this worked.

Obviously, my love of Christ was never for the historical personality, but rather, for the divine Christ. What was important to me were not his words, but who he was, the mystery of his incarnation, death, resurrection, and certainly, His Eucharistic presence ever with us. Right off, I regarded the Eucharist to be my true link with Christ in the here and now; it was the way into His divine mystery. I was sure that in the Eucharist I would learn everything I ever needed to know about Christ and thus, for me, the Eucharist was "the Way."

My conversion, of course, cannot be understood in the usual sense of someone newly embracing a religion, a spiritual life, or a turning away from sin. Rather, when I saw how God worked, His plan for creation and Christ's place in it, I also found my place and set out to take it. Fortunately, prior to my conversion, the practice of my religion was well entrenched; for years I had gone to daily Mass, been involved in all the practices of the liturgical year, prayed daily and made visits to the Blessed Sacrament. I was also well educated in my Faith, familiar with the lives of the saints, in short, prior to my conversion everything was in place. Like a fledgling bird I had only needed a push to fly, and my conversion was that push. Once I took off I never looked back, never hesitated or harbored a doubt; I knew my direction, knew the way, and just as the bee flies, I headed straight for my eternal home in the Trinity.

The revelation of the Trinity literally changed my life overnight. Where some people might struggle to become detached or find it difficult to drop everything in order to follow, the nature of this experience was an automatic falling away of everything. Of its own accord, my burning desire to be transformed into Christ eliminated everything in life not conducive to this end. Nothing else held any interest for me and fell away as so much waste of time. To follow meant leaving everything behind, getting rid of everything, it meant material and spiritual poverty, and with this singular focus, my life was automatically simplified.

The first thing I did was empty my book case and make several trips to Pickwick's used book store where I sold my prized books and put the money in the Poor Box at Church. Then I gathered up the few pieces of jewelry I had and gave them to Gert for her little girls—she had four. The next day I met two girlfriends, told them I was getting rid of most my clothes and asked if they'd like to see if there was anything they could use. A day or so later when mom saw my empty closet, she was angry and told me in no uncertain terms, "Until you can pay for your own clothes don't be giving away the ones I buy." If mom never understood me before, from here on it would have been impossible anyway.

After I distributed my nick-knacks and keepsakes, the only thing left was my typewriter, as long as I had to do school papers, however, I'd keep it to the last. After that I racked my brains trying to think of something I owned or was attached to so I could get rid of it, but the only thing that came to mind was my picture of the monk—but who would want him?

Certainly I'd never throw him in the trash! I decided he'd just have to be buried with me, so he stayed on the wall. Once my room was cleared, while it didn't look like a cell–with its flowery drapes and bedspread–it did look like a guest room. I decided to sleep on the floor because it was uncomfortable and kept me awake so I could commune with God until the wee hours. When winter came, I deliberately slept next to an open window where I got a bad case of arthritis, but this too, served as a constant reminder of God.

If I had little to give up for God in the material sense, I could certainly forfeit some of my little pleasures, although here too, there wasn't much. I decided not to eat the things I liked and only eat the things I disliked, which meant eating just about everything since I never enjoyed food anyway. The most abhorrent thing I could think of eating was a raw egg, so I got one from the fridge, cracked and swallowed it whole. Because it came back up, I got out another egg and then another, yet I never succeeded in keeping an egg down. The main items left on my worst menu list were milk and meat; that eating this didn't make me sick was a grace in itself.

Since my foremost goal was to be aware of God every moment of the day, I spent all my free time in Church where it was silent and I could be undistracted and alone with God. Prayer and solitude were the most basic needs of my interior life. Following my conversion I was inundated by the Presence of God, especially in Church where I'd be flooded with love and joy radiating from the Blessed Sacrament. I had already learned that talking to God was not as satisfying as simply remaining in His Presence, thus our conversation was simply the flow of love between us. After four full months of this delightful prayer I had my first experience of God's seeming "absence"–which I later learned was called "aridity"–a story I leave for later. In turn, however, God's love generated in me a great desire to keep myself strictly disciplined in order to be faithful to His graces, and also to do what I could to return His favors. I took on a program of "penance"–another name for self-discipline–not because of any sins, but because I had a strong will to gain perfect control over myself and, above all, assure God by my actions of my determination to deny myself everything on His behalf.

My focus on the Eucharist, the glorified body of Christ, was not a focus on His past or the scriptural images people often have of him, rather, in the Eucharist my focus was on Christ as he is now (and ever) in the Trinity. Because his earthly body had been deified (made Godlike) I took for granted his transformed body was now part and parcel of His divinity. In short, I would never feel any need for the historical Christ, even though I realized that without His incarnation we would never have known the Trinity and God's plan for creation. It would be several years before I came across the term "Logos" used for the divine Christ; it would have been helpful if I had known this term earlier because I would have recognized it as the term for the divine Christ in the Trinity—as set apart from the purely human, historical man Jesus.

Back at school I mapped my day to spend as much time as possible in prayer either in the Chapel or on the hillside—and do the minimum of study of course. I was up with the sisters in the morning and the last one out the main door at night—Mr. Barth always knew he could lock the door after I left. While I didn't deem fasting necessary—because the food at school was so bad anyway—I did abstain from the more edible dishes and eat the smelly things nobody wanted. I avoided wasting time on social distractions which didn't interest me anyway, and took opportunities here and there to sacrifice my worldly comforts, likes and desires. I simply wanted the freedom to focus my whole being on God day and night. The immediate goal was to be constantly aware of God's presence which, at this stage, seemed to require my mind be free of all worldly distraction. In time, however, I learned how to focus my will on God at all times and not depend on my mind. Altogether I was learning a great deal in the months following my conversion, learning my limits and potentials, the obstacles to be overcome, learning about God and myself, indeed the essence of a life of prayer is a constant learning experience.

Though I always knew I had a cell waiting for me in Carmel, it was probably a month or so after my conversion before I decided the time had finally come for me to occupy it. Carmel was the only place I knew where I'd have the freedom to pursue my goals without distractions and interruptions. I didn't belong in school anymore, nor at home, the only milieu I knew I'd be at home in on this earth was Carmel. So I wrote to the Prioress (the Superior) and reminded her of her promise years before when she told me that whenever I was ready there would be a cell for me. I told her I was ready now and only wanted to know how soon I could come. Easter was about two months away, and I thought Easter Sunday would be a glorious day to enter, other than that, I could not see waiting longer than after school was out that year.

I thought it odd I had to wait almost a month before receiving a reply, and was disappointed at the two sentences it contained. It said that the Prioress who had promised me the cell was no longer Prioress (the sisters elect a new Prioress every four years), and that if I was interested in finding out more about their life and vocation, I should call and make an appointment to see her. Although this struck me as rather cold and abrupt, I called immediately and made an appointment for the following Saturday.

Instead of my usual Saturday trip to the Planetarium, I took the bus to Alhambra where the monastery was located. When I first saw the building from down the street I experienced a nostalgia, a longing to be living their life now, truly this is where I belonged. The extern Sisters–Ignatius and Aloysius–gave me the grand welcome, threw their arms around me as if I was a long lost relative, and scolded me for not having come to visit them sooner. They also told me the story of the first time dad brought me to visit them after I was born. As each child came in the door he pointed and said, "This one will be a Holy Name Sister, this one a Jesuit, this one a Maryknoller", and pointing to me in his arms, he said, "This one will be the Carmelite." They laughed and went on telling stories about dad's visits in the early days and how they first met mom–which was after their marriage when dad brought her to tour the new monastery before it was closed to the public. Finally a little bell rang at the turn and we were informed Reverend Mother (the Prioress) was waiting for me in the parlor. From behind the grate Reverend Mother greeted me cheerfully, asked about my parents, talked about praying for me during my illness, asked about school and so on. The first chance I got I asked

Me: Do you have a vacancy?

RM: Yes we do

Me: Please reserve it for me. I would like to come as soon as possible.

RM: Have you finished High School?

Me: No, but I'm not interested in it anyway.

RM: Oh, well, you have to finish High School.

Me: Why?

RM: We don't want dumb Carmelites in here.

Me: I don't think going to school will make me any smarter or any better prepared for this life.

RM: Well all the sisters here finished school, why should you be an exception?

Me: You really mean I can't come until I finish school?

RM: Yes.

(This was an uncalculated blow, it meant waiting more than two whole years! She might as well have told me to wait fifty.)

Me: What if I could finish school next year, would you take me then?

RM: As long as you have a diploma I see no problem. But tell me, what do your parents think?

Me: I haven't told them yet.

RM: (Shocked) They don't know you want to enter Carmel? Well you should tell them as soon as you go home.

Me: They won't care. I thought I'd wait until I talked to you to be sure you had a place and would take me. I also wanted to tell them when I'd be entering.

RM: You have to understand that your entering is not solely up to me. Before we can decide on your vocation you will have to meet with the sisters on our community counsel, and after that, meet with the whole community who will then vote on whether you come or not.

Me: When can I meet them?

RM: If they are not busy, maybe you can meet the counsel sisters next
          time you come.

Me: How soon can that be?

RM: How about a month from now?

Me: That's a long time.

RM: I think you have time ... but if you like, in two weeks we have a
          special Feast Day, another aspirant is coming to visit, so perhaps
          the two of you could meet one another. She's finishing high
          school this year and may enter this summer.

I assured her I'd be here. After this we probably spent an hour talking, during which she got around to the proverbial question, "Why do you
want to be a Carmelite?" In part of my reply I told her how difficult it was
to be a contemplative in the world–all the noise and distractions, scram-
bling for time to pray, no solitude, all the social obligations and interruptions at home and school, last but not least, it was difficult to keep my
mind on God when I had to read Shakespeare and do math problems! In
Carmel I'd be free of all that, free to be aware of God day and night without interruption.

Before I left she told me to remember that God's will for me right
now was to be in school, and by doing my very best I could be assured of
fulfilling God's will. I did not want to argue with her, but staying in school
was no longer God's will for me, clearly it was the will of others. If God
wanted me in Carmel–which I believed He did–then staying in school
wasn't doing His will at all, but of course I never told her this.

On the way out Sr. Ignatius looked at me eagerly, "Well, when are
you coming?" I told her if I had my way I'd be there at Easter–in a month
or so. "Wonderful!" she said, clapping her hands. "But", I added, "Rev.
Mother wants me to wait until I finish high school–two more years!" Sister made a sour face but said nothing. Once again I was showered with
religious hand-outs–cards, leaflets, relics–then they hugged me and said
they'd pray I'd come back soon to stay forever. They were the only two
(of three) people in the world that ever encouraged my vocation, in the

ordeal ahead they were the only ones who sincerely shared my ups and downs.

That night at dinner I told my parents where I had been and what I intended to do with my life–be a Carmelite. They evinced no surprise, their facial expressions didn't even change. When it was obvious they weren't going to offer any comment I said, "Well, what do you think?" Dad raised his eyebrows and replied, "It's your life, if you need my consent you have it." Then I looked at mom, who was staring at her plate with pursed lips, "If you really want to know what I think", she said, "I think this idea will pass in a year or two, so I'll wait until then before I say any more about it." I pressed her, "Well what if next year I still want to be a Carmelite, what are you going to say then?"

She replied, "I don't think there's going to be a "then", so I can't tell you now what I'd say "then." And that was the end of talking over my vocation with my parents, and not just then, but forever. For them, the subject was strictly taboo, a no-no. Whenever I made some reference or comment about Carmel it was instantly followed by a deafening silence. The whole thing was downright strange, I knew there had to be some kind of conspiracy going on between them, and in this I was not mistaken.

When I first began spending long hours in prayer I thought it might be helpful to read how the saints and other religious people went about it. Looking over the books in dad's library I spotted St. Ignatius' Spiritual Exercises and began to read. I decided to try these exercises, follow the instructions step by step. I waited some weeks before starting because I needed a week of free time, so I set a particular date to begin, and in the meantime, fairly memorized the initial instructions.

By the time the day arrived to start the Exercises I had high expectations and never doubted it would be a good experience. What appealed to me was the possibility of sharing Christ's human experiences, not just his oneness with God and all its joys, but also his sufferings. Since the initial exercise suggested focusing on the scene of Christ's agony in the garden, I decided to do the same. The Church was all but empty when I arrived. I sat down in the second pew in front of the large crucifix beside the altar–the same crucifix mentioned early in my life. I had seen pictures of Christ in the garden, his eyes looking up to heaven, his hands resting on a large rock, so I closed my eyes and tried to bring this image into view. It never crossed my mind that this first step would be difficult, yet it was; I could hardly get the picture in my mind when it would be gone. Trying to hold on to it was a terrible struggle, a genuine mental strain. Even when I retained it for a few seconds it was neither clear nor up close. I kept fooling with my mind as if it were a camera trying to focus in on a distant picture in a museum. I had to start over and over just to get a picture, any kind of picture. I had no choice but to settle for a completely lifeless holy card picture I'd seen, and looking at it was like being forced to stare at a bad watercolor in an art gallery. I stared at this picture until it became a blur. I thought I could finally go on to the second step of pondering what Christ must have been experiencing at this time. But this is where I came up against a stone wall—my mind would not move, I could not think at all. When force didn't work, I tried just being quiet to see if anything in the picture might move, or move me. But nothing moved, not the image, not my mind, not my emotions, nothing.

After a bit I realized the picture was literally stuck in my mind, glued there, so I could neither get rid of it nor move my mind at all! Because of the exertion of getting a picture and then forcing my mind to think about it, my head felt like a ball of fire. Though I'd never had a headache in my life, I deemed this something worse. I was sure, however, that once I cleared my mind of the picture and went out into the fresh air, everything would return to normal; but it didn't happen. Though I went outside, the picture remained stuck in my brain, refused to budge or disappear, which left my brain in a terrible, painful condition.

By the time I got home there were sharp stabbing pains in my head, my brain could not relax a bit. Immediately I made an ice pack, lay down in my room and put it on my head. When mom asked what had happened, I told her, "I just tried to meditate." She responded, "If you'd asked me first, I could have told you it wouldn't work"—evidently mom had also tried and failed. Anyway, I lay in bed totally thoughtless for the next 24 hours, lay there mostly awake because sleep would not come. The next day, however, I was able to sleep most the day. It was three full days before my head—brain, mind—returned to normal.

This was not just an unforgettable experience, for the rest of my life whenever I so much as heard (or saw) the word "meditate" or "meditation" I had an unconscious visceral reaction, a knee-jerk reaction, a negative "conditioned response." The instant my brain encountered this bad word it spat it out, rejected it, and I would physically shudder. It was as if the word "mediation" hit a brick wall with a bang. On the other hand, I learned a great deal from this bad experience; for one, I would never, ever force my brain again, regardless of the subject matter. For another, it dawned on me that all my life I had never had the ability to form or retain mental images, never developed an imagination. I could not remember a single instance of imaging anything, always my mind depended on a physical or sensible prop. Even my memory was without images, what I recalled was always the event–what I'd heard and its effect on me–but not figures and never a single face. Evidently people have different brains, different minds. Something else I learned is that prayer is not something that can be taught or learned as a spontaneous expression of our rapport with God, prayer defies all methods and particular ways. I now realized that my prayer life depended on God's grace alone, and not on anything I did or tried to do. Thus to wait upon God and His good graces would be my sole approach to a life of prayer.

Since we lived in a Jesuit parish, the next time I went to confession I complained to the priest about the Exercises. To my surprise he responded:

Fr. Forget it, women don't have the kind of minds to meditate anyway; they shouldn't even try the Exercises.

Me: Then at the beginning of the book it should have said 'for men only' because I nearly lost my mind.

Fr: By all means avoid it like the plague! How old are you anyway?

Me: 15

Fr: For heaven's sake, forget all this prayer business, go out and have a good time!

Me: What for?

Fr: You've got plenty of time before you have to start thinking about your spiritual life.

Me: At what age should people start thinking about their spiritual life–18, 19, when?

Fr: Whenever God calls them.

Me: He never calls people at 15?

Fr: You think he's called you?

Me: Of course. I've already applied to become a Carmelite.

Fr: A Carmelite! What good can you do for the world locked in a monastery for the rest of your life?

(These were fighting words).

Me: I know one thing, the Carmelites have done more for me than you have. Apart from insulting my intelligence, what have you done for me? Nothing! I'm going to ask the Nuns to pray for you.

After that I walked out making a mental note never to bring up my contemplative vocation to a Jesuit again. The few times I thought a Jesuit friend might be understanding I was always met with the same old rejoinder, "Fine, so you are a contemplative, now tell me, what are you going to do for the world?"

I would liked to have found an understanding priest with whom I could talk about my vocation, ascetic practices and later, my prayer problems, and though I tried on a number of occasions, they all came to naught. Their whole attitude was "Come on down to earth and be like the rest us"–as one put it. Sometimes things would go well until they asked my age, when their attitude abruptly changed. One of them said to me, "Listen sis, I know your type, see? There's lot of kids like you with the same mistaken ideas, see? Now cut it out, see? If you've got any virtue at all you'll prove it by obeying me, see? Now are you going to do it?" I asked, "How can I obey you when, in conscience, I do not think you understand me." He snapped, "Ah, they all say that!" "Then", I said, "I owe you no obedience when you can't even believe what I tell you." Another one told me: "Just be like the other girls, never be singular, obey your superiors and be humble, that's all you can do for now." Still another said, "It will blow over, youth is unstable." Now if denying myself a candy bar upset these priests, what would they say if I told them I ate bugs? My attempts to find an understanding priest or confessor were fruitless, I gave up. Since I'd always gone it alone anyway, the failure to be understood, believed or helped was just par for the course. Besides, what difference would it make if they thought I had a vocation or not? Either way their opinion meant nothing to me, as long as I knew I had a vocation that's all that mattered.

From the beginning, my goal was to be aware of God's presence every minute of the day, thus my rule of thumb: eliminate every activity that did not promote this focus, and include only those that did. There was no way this goal could be accomplished as long as I maintained the status quo or went along with the usual routine at home and school, more often than not, my goal and the status quo were at odds. The old activities no longer interested me; my mind, will and heart were not in them, they were occupied elsewhere.

Love of God (or better put, my "will-to-God") created in me an enormous strength, an unbeatable drive and will. A way to both test and express this was by rigorous self-discipline. Like an athlete in training I began testing my strength of will, always in search of something I could give up for God by either denying or going contrary to myself. The athlete who does not continually challenge himself has no way of knowing his potential–or his limits–and thus he will never know how far he can go. Was there anything I could not do for God, or give up? The only way to find out was to test myself. There was no place in me for any compromising arm-chair spirituality, there was only rigorous testing, self-sacrifice, actual doing. Love is not a one way affair, it is not just taking from the other, but giving–giving to the loved One everything we have and are.

To this end I not only gave up the few foods I liked, but ate anything that repulsed me–bugs, dirt, a stray hair, raw eggs, a blind grab into the garbage pail. There were pebbles for under my knees when I prayed at home, thorns to hold in my hands, my dad's belt for a discipline, a few hours of sleep on the floor, and only cold showers. It goes without saying

I took every opportunity to practice virtue—patience being the most diffi-cult—by helping others when I could, and once, deliberately humiliated myself when I asked six girls chatting in a room at school if I could go around and kiss their feet, which I did. I greatly appreciated they're not snickering. In short, I took every chance to thwart my own will and de-sires, and when I noticed I was attached to giving up things, I would take them back (reverse myself) just to offer up my feelings of guilt about do-ing so.

What I wanted was to gain perfect control over myself, be master of the ship, because with this power in my hands God's wish was my command. I knew, of course, I would never have complete control be-cause my life did not belong to me alone, my power flowed from Him. My strength was not my own, it was only borrowed, given to me to use, not to possess.

More important than external mortification, however, was my con-cern with internal attachments. While I had no attachment to people or things, there were subtle attachments to my own self image—did I think I was somebody special in God's sight? Did I honestly think I was chosen above others? Did my practices make me feel good about myself or make me pleased with myself? Was I attached to my experiences of God? Was I sincerely seeking God for His own sake or solely for my own? I had a lot to discern within myself, and what I found is that in everything there was always some "me" in it. At one point I realized I actually liked doing penance and denying myself; where initially these practices had been new, challenging and difficult, now they were as easy and ordinary as the com-mon life they had replaced. This, however, only put me on the look-out for ever new and more difficult practices to add to my repertoire.

Earlier, when I was ten or so, I picked up one of dad's old books and read about the lives of the early Fathers of the Desert. I thought their penance and mortification so outlandish I took the book to the kitchen and read to mom while she cooked dinner. The two of us laughed heartily, what crazy guys they were! We couldn't figure out what any of it had to do with love of God or what they thought they were accomplishing for God, themselves, or the world. Now, however, remembering this earlier incident and thinking about these old men, I understood them perfectly, all that drive prompted by love of God had to be expressed somehow. Without a doubt I knew I had it in me to be an outstanding ascetic, given the chance there was nothing I could not have done. Right now, I dearly wished I lived in their days and in their neck of the woods, because in the age and place where I lived, I was clearly out of place.

Just before school was out for the summer I came down with a terrible case of scruples. For more than four months I had held to my daily schedule of prayer and practices with great fervor and determination. Initially, if due to some school event or no fault of my own I could not fit something in—say I missed the rosary that night—this omission only reinforced my resolve not let it happen again. After a while, however, any omission in the schedule and I became so cast down I could hardly pick myself up, it took all my verve and nerve to get back on track, start all over again. Sometimes I felt so terrible about missing some small practice, it was as if I'd let down Almighty God and the whole world. The only one I really let down, of course, was myself, and I knew it, but knowing this didn't help. While I would not go so far as to say I had a case of self-hatred, I could not have been more discouraged or disappointed in myself.

My situation might be compared to someone on a strict diet who, having eaten some forbidden food or taken a double portion, kicks himself around for the rest of the day and is ready to throw in the towel. Or again, my schedule was like a row of standing dominoes, if one went down, they all went down, the game was over. The discouragement and self-incrimination that followed the smallest omission made it difficult to pick myself up and go on. Things reached such a pitch that if I ate an extra serving of mashed potatoes it was as bad as a mortal sin. The whole thing was preposterous, a genuine torture. I knew my omissions never warranted such a reaction, yet my efforts to be flexible, to let it go, treat it nonchalantly, didn't work at all. At first I tried eliminating some of my practices; still, any omission in the remaining practices had the same effect. It became obvious that whether I had five or five-hundred practices, made no difference, a single omission and I'd be devastated. Obviously I had become attached to my own ascetic practices, attached to the point that if I so much as missed an opportunity I felt guilty and discouraged.

After giving the situation my best thought, I decided the fastest way out of this rut would be to abandon my schedule and practices in one fell swoop, this way, with no schedule or practices at all, there could be no omissions–and no scruples. This would be a drastic measure and I did not know how long it would take before I would be free again–free to carefully and cautiously adopt a more flexible regime. I was determined, however, that if it took a year, then so be it, because I couldn't go on living this way.

Ceasing all practices and disciplines may sound easy, yet it was the most difficult task I ever had to do. It meant not even going to Mass or trying to think about God, it meant taking on all the things I now disliked–because my tastes, interests and goals had changed–and putting off all the things I now liked. It was a complete reversal of my true life. Trying to adjust backward to my former life was a reverse process–literally penance in reverse. Trying to revert to a life in which I no longer had the slightest interest or enthusiasm required a discipline far greater than the one I had taken on for my spiritual advantage. In short, I had to forfeit what I enjoyed and take on what I no longer enjoyed.

The irony of this situation was not lost on me. Now I had to eat what I had formerly liked whether I wanted it or not–which made me sick. Having to listen to my classmates' awful music in the rec. room instead of being in the quiet chapel was torture. I searched the library for unholy books to read, and even sleeping in bed instead of on the floor was uncomfortable. Filling my free time was especially problematic because it went against the grain of what I would really have liked to do. Despite the difficulties, however, I never suffered a single scruple, and because of this, I knew I must be on the right track.

I know the exact moment I was freed from my miserable condition. I believe it was on the night of the third day (after the reversal). I experienced a sudden release comparable, perhaps, to having a load lifted from your soul accompanied by a surging sense of joyful freedom. I recognized the hand of God in this release because I had experienced it before–and would experience it a number of times again. It was as if God had said, "Enough of this!" and that was that. Though initially wary and cautious about resuming my practices, there was really no need, the whole problem had disappeared and never returned. I was gloriously free!

Having to go through this ordeal taught me a great deal about myself and how best to live my life, it also gave me insight into the lives of other spiritual people, especially the great ascetics and saints. I could always detect varying degrees of scrupulosity in what they said about themselves—moaning and groaning about what miserable creatures they were, beating their chest over nothings, constantly self-deprecating (a subtle form of self-absorption) and so on. Either they honestly didn't believe God had forgiven their sins, or else they had a bad case of scruples. As for the ascetics, I understood how they could become dominated by their own practices. The strong willed, tough minded types are the more likely to go to extremes, become compulsive and nearly die from their own determination. I know because I could have gone this same way. Over time, however, I carne to regard ascetic practices as belonging to a beginners' milieu, an important and necessary first stage of the spiritual journey. Without the self-discipline needed to unify my energies to focus my whole life solely on God, I would not have been ready to move into deeper waters. Finally, however, I reached a point where I could not discern what I really liked or disliked any more, and at this point my ascetic practices didn't do anything for me, they did not seem to bring about any progress or make any difference to my interior state. From here on, come what may, I could take it or leave it.

AGE 16

I was able to work out a way to finish high school in three years. A diploma from a public school required fewer credits than a Catholic school, so by adding up what I had, and what I needed, with two courses over the summer I could get a State diploma after my junior year. I made an appointment to talk with a counselor at the local high school–Hollywood High, a block from home–to inquire about getting a state diploma and enrolling in their summer school. The counselor was very helpful and assured me that with the addition of two required courses (possibly three, I don't remember) I could get my State diploma the end of my junior year. One of the courses I needed was Civics which Flintridge only offered during its senior year, and the other course, I believe, was English (American Literature, I think). At any rate, I signed up for all the courses I needed. Though spending my summer studying was not a happy prospect, the idea of waiting another year to enter Carmel was even worse.

As long as I was at school Mom paid little attention to my eccentricities and new life style, she was waiting patiently for it all to blow over. Once at home for summer, however, when she had to live with me, she became increasingly upset. I had no interest in company, friends, shopping, entertainment, going here and there, in short, I was not very companionable. Although she didn't know half what was going on, she evidently saw enough that disturbed her, obviously I had changed. Unknown to me at the time, she called Carmel and virtually accused Reverend Mother of putting me up to the whole thing. She asked Reverend Mother if she had suggested that I fast, do penance, or otherwise live like a nun at home. Rev. Mother was shocked; she knew nothing of my daily life and denied suggesting anything to me. Mom asked her, "Then where do you think she got all this from? Who put these ideas in her head?" It never occurred to mom that God might be behind it; given her view, my behavior was not in accord with anything God would want, require, promote or even approve of—not for herself, at least.

For her part, Reverend Mother thought I might be trying to copy the lives of the saints I had read about. She assured Mom, however, it was a capital offense to undertake any discipline without the consent of one's confessor—and who might mine be? Mom didn't know, so Rev. Mother said she would look into the matter, if I didn't have a confessor then she'd recommend one who "had his feet on the ground"—her exact words. In the end, the two agreed I should be sent to someone to "have her head straightened out"—also their exact words.

On my next visit to the monastery Rev. Mother started right out telling me that one of the requirements for entering was to have a recommendation from my confessor, someone who had known me for at least a year, was familiar with my interior life, and could discern if I had a true vocation to Carmel or not. She ended with the question: "Do you have such a Confessor or know someone like this?" No I didn't. She went on, "Well, I know someone you might like to meet, one of our Carmelite Fathers down the street." (The Discalced Carmelite Fathers ran St. Therese's parish, a few blocks from the monastery, they were also the nuns' confessors). "If you like, I can give him a call to see if he can stop by and meet you." I said, "Fine." She left the room, made the call and came back, "He'll be here shortly."

Father Columbanus must have been sitting by the phone, because in less than ten minutes he walked in. (Later he told me the meeting had been set-up ahead of time, and that Rev. Mother told him about my mother's call and her complaints.) At that time Father Columbanus was thirty-five, short, with dark hair, he had arrived from his home and Monastery in Ireland only a few years before. He walked in without a smile and spoke to Rev. Mother with an air of reverence—no familiarity. My first impression of him as a "serious person" endured for all the years I knew him. I would never know anyone who took his Carmelite contemplative vocation more seriously.

After being introduced, Rev. Mother told him I would like to come and see him, to talk over my vocation. He said, "Fine," told me to call for an appointment, then bid us goodbye. For Rev. Mother, everything was settled, if mom called again she could now refer her to Fr. Columbanus. This passing from mom to Rev. Mother to Father happened a number of times until, in the end, Fr. Columbanus got fed up and put his foot down—something I never thought him capable of doing. Because I noticed Rev. Mother and others referred to him as Father "Columban", whereas his real name was Columbanus, when I asked him about this, he said, "It doesn't matter what I'm called, the kids in the schoolyard call me Father Column-bum."

I almost dreaded my first visit with him. I was convinced he would only give me another version of the old line—just be one of the bunch, go along with the crowd at school, do whatever your parents and superiors say, just going to Mass and saying the rosary are quite enough—something like that. Since I could never buy this line and had no intention of following it, my main concern was how to respond. Should I tell him the truth or say nothing? If I told him I could not take his advice, he'd tell Rev. Mother and I'd never get in. On the other hand, if I let his advice go in one ear and out the other, it would be dishonest to let him think I was living a life I wasn't. Which should it be? Since what was at stake was my Carmelite vocation, I decided to say nothing, give him no back talk or cause for complaint. If things didn't work out, I'd just shop around for another priest.

It was a warm day, without a smile, but a friendly "Hello," Fr. opened the screen door of the rectory and led me to a side room with a long conference table. He sat at one end and I, in the middle. Without another word he simply said: "Tell me about your prayer, how do you pray or what do you do when you pray?" Nobody had ever asked me this before; I had never thought about it, much less expressed it. Still, it was not hard to answer. "When I pray in Church I focus on God's presence in the Blessed Sacrament, at home I focus on the presence of the Holy Spirit in myself, and when I'm out of doors I focus on God in nature (in my view, the pre-incarnate Logos). I almost always feel God's presence which is sometimes intense and sometimes not, and I often express my thanks and love. Once in a while I feel no special Presence at all, but express myself anyway, knowing He is present whether I feel it or not. In any case, since I figure God already knows how I feel or what I will say, I sometimes don't express anything at all, say nothing, but just remain silent in His presence. Pretty much that's how it goes."

After that he asked, "How much time do you figure you spend in prayer every day?" That answer took some calculating because it depended on whether I was at home or at school. I figured no less than 4 to 5 hours in Chapel or Church every day, also, several hours before going to sleep each night; and at school, at least an hour or two out-of-doors every day.

Next he asked, "How long (weeks, months, years) have you been spending this amount of time in prayer? Is there any particular experience you recall that got you started?" Briefly I went over my "conversion experience" which had been about five months before. I told him that because of this, my real focus in prayer was always on the Trinity, never on the separate Persons. Thus whether my focus was on God within or without, it was always on the oneness of the Trinity.

The rest of his questions were easy to answer, except one that he popped rather suspiciously: "Besides spending time in prayer do you practice any special disciplines or perform acts of mortification, like fasting and abstinence–or wearing a hair shirt?" (He smiled at this). I asked eagerly, "Do you know where I could get one?" "Yes I do", he replied, "but I wouldn't give it to you." He went on to tell me that Carmelites have never gone in for special ascetic practices, it's not their spirit and not in their Holy Rule. Since just keeping the Holy Rule had produced Saints, obviously this was all God required. I asked where I could get a copy of the Rule because I'd like to follow it right away and not wait. He said that at our next visit he would bring a copy and we would map out my daily schedule according to the Rule making whatever modifications necessary for my situation. This prospect delighted me, to live the Carmelite Rule now, right now, it was too good to be true, what a wonderful man he was!

We had already spent over two hours together, but before parting I had to ask him an important question: "Since I've answered your questions truthfully, now please answer mine truthfully: do you think I have a Carmelite vocation?" With emphasis he replied, "You definitely have a Carmelite vocation, a strong vocation." After a pause he added, "And the next time I see Reverend Mother I'm going to tell her so." I then asked how soon I could come back to see him, "In three weeks, same time, same place." From then on I went to see him every three weeks.

Meeting with Fr. was not just a joy and a relief, it was a grace for which I would ever be thankful. In him I had the sole, strongest ally I would ever have in my contemplative life. Also, I would never meet anyone who had more experiential insight and understanding of the path mapped out by St. John of the Cross, in every sense, Father was the Saint's true spiritual son. His knowledge of this particular path could only have come through his personal experience, from living it. This meeting, however, with the man who had his "feet on the ground" did not, I'm afraid, "straighten my head out" as mom had hoped. When I told her he was going to help me live the Rule at home, she threw up her hands in horror and walked away. After all the fuss she'd made, nothing really changed.

Earlier I mentioned my first bout of "aridity"—which at the time might better have been called an "anxiety attack." It occurred almost four months to the day after my conversion experience. There was nothing about it I would call arid or dry, rather it was a sudden complete disappearance of God. I had gone to Church to spend a few hours in prayer, kneeling down and looking at the tabernacle I projected my whole heart and soul toward God, but where I had always been met with His welcomed response, today there was no response; it was as if he was not present at all. Then again, it was like being in the presence of someone you love who deliberately ignores you, it was bewildering to say the least. My first thought was "What have I done? How have I displeased Him?" I thought back over my preceding days but couldn't find anything I'd done wrong, so what had happened?

I begged God to explain His coldness, give an account of why He did this—or else make it good again. For one hour (12 to 1 o'clock) I remained in this anxious state, demanding, bewildered, with no insight or understanding. I had never heard of such a predicament. Finally, God must have had enough, because abruptly He put in his appearance, which was more than a relief, it was the greeting of two lovers returned from a bad trip apart, a meeting so delightful it was almost worth the separation.

My first take on this experience was that God was only testing me, yet when I thought this over it didn't make sense. You only test someone you don't trust, someone whose infidelities don't warrant your trust. Since I had not been unfaithful, I put this reason aside. I had already learned that the purpose of my spiritual experiences had been to teach me something, give me some knowledge I needed to know, so this is how I judged the event. What I definitely learned was that my attraction to prayer, even my prayer itself, was solely a grace from God, for without it I couldn't pray and would not even have wanted to. Although I already knew this, yet experiencing just an hour without this grace brought it home like nothing else. I decided that if it ever happened again, I would know it was His doing, not become anxious, and take it like a soldier.

Three weeks later it happened again, only this time it lasted two whole hours. While I didn't take it like a soldier, my anxiety was at least replaced by impatience–waiting, waiting, trusting God to respond in some fashion. This was not so much an experiential absence of God as God's unresponsiveness. While tempted to mistake this for God's indifference, I eventually took it for God's own silence, the way God really is. Two weeks later this arid state lasted six hours, and while patiently waiting, it struck me God was saying "go deeper." He wasn't going to reciprocate my emotional outpourings because his real Presence was deeper than that, thus to encounter God I had to move to a deeper dimension of myself, which, for me, was a move to my unfeeling center or will-to- God. Gradually I learned to be with God on this deeper level, which was sometimes wonderful and sometimes just an arid silence.

At first these bouts of aridity would come and go, but gradually they were more come than go, and increasingly difficult to live with. This absence would last a full day, then two days and so it went until, finally, this became an abiding state in itself, a far deeper state, however, than the one I had begun with or had ever known before. At such times my prayer was a silent waiting, a prayer-of-the-will (a will to be with God, to love God) which was like a steady, but dry flame within.

Because of this aridity my prayer life was completely simplified, it opened a new and much deeper dimension of God and myself where I was learning to find Him without emotion or thought in simple silence and stillness within. At the same time, however, just as the aridity became increasing tedious, so too the intermittent consolations became increasing profound, sometimes even spectacular. It was as if there was a certain proportionality between the intensity of the aridity and the periodic encounters with God, thus the deeper more prolonged the aridity, the more glorious God's breaking in.

Because I felt the need for some insight into what was going on, I searched through numerous books on the spiritual life but found nothing helpful or explanatory. One day, however, after begging God to send help, and trusting Him to guide my choice, I decided to go to the school library, stand in the doorway, randomly focus my eyes on a book—any book—and take it down. The book I focused on was on a top shelf against one of the back walls. Keeping my eyes on the book so as not to lose sight of it, I groped my way around the book stacks to get to it. Seeing me feeling my way around, the librarian, Sr. Bernadette, broke the silence, "What are you up to now?" she demanded. Without taking my eyes off the book I told her I had to get down a certain book and needed a ladder, so she got up and brought me one. The book's title was Life of St. John of the Cross by Fr. Bruno O.D.C. I knew the name of the Saint because dad had three volumes of his works in his library, but all I knew about him was that he was a Discalced Carmelite—which I thought a nice coincidence. Though I would be delighted to read about his life, I was a bit disappointed, I wasn't looking for a biography, but for information about what was going on in my spiritual life.

It didn't take more than a day before I came to Bruno's short exposition of John's written works that included something about his "Nights." A few things he went over seemed to address my situation perfectly, and with this knowledge I was greatly encouraged. I decided when I got home to get down John's books. It was with hopeful expectation the following Saturday, I took out the first of Peer's three volumes, Ascent of

Mount Carmel. I not only found it dry reading, but was convinced he had written it for the criminal element in society, terrible sinners, the worst of the worst. Some of the sins he described I'd never heard before and had to look them up in the dictionary. He went on and on about people's sinful lives, what they owed God, and why they should reform their lives—if for no other reason than fear of going to hell! I kept thinking he would eventually get to the spiritual life, so I plowed through chapter after chapter and was increasing shocked that such sinful ingrates existed.

I made myself read at least half the Ascent before putting it back on the shelf. No, John of the Cross was not for me, he didn't address my spiritual life or give me any insight into God's way in my soul. Between this book and Bruno's Life, however, I picked up on the term "aridity" and though I never thought it an adequate or good description, I adopted it as a term for the periodic absences of God that I experienced. Since I knew God was not absent–couldn't be, in fact–the term "absence" was not true; on the other hand, to experience the absence of a loved Presence is a little more than "arid", dry, boring or dull, it can produce a nostalgia that sometimes made me sick to the stomach. At the same time, however, this seeming absence actually increased my desire, intensity, energy and toughness of soul. Anyway, I settled for the traditional term "aridity" and thereafter referred to my experiences as "bouts of aridity."

Before the onset of these bouts of aridity I had read St. Teresa's Way of Perfection and found that, according to her descriptions of the various levels of prayer, I was already enjoying "unitive prayer." My understanding was that this prayer belonged to the "Unitive State" which she seemed to regard as the highest possible–as far in the contemplative life of prayer as anyone could go. At first this did not seem right to me, but I thought, "What if she is right? What if I am already in the Unitive State?" My answer: "It doesn't make any difference; all I know is that there has got to be more to the spiritual life than the Unitive State!" (Further to go that is). Although down the road I realized I was not in the Unitive State, still, this mistake had consequences in that I never placed any value on the Unitive State or even getting there. It never struck me as remotely relevant or important. Apart from heaven–the only definitive end there is–my life was ever focused on the present moment with no concern for anything down the road. Besides, from the age of seven I was convinced I would die young, so there was no use even looking down the road.

It was not long after my initial bouts of aridity, in late June I believe, I made my first trip to see Fr. Columbanus—to get my "head straightened out." I have already spoken of our first meeting, so it must have been at our second meeting I told him about my occasional "bouts of aridity." He thought this was great, right on target, par for the course, and the worse, more prolonged these bouts, the greater his delight. Over the next year and a half the aridity grew worse, not because of any absence of God, but rather the absence of a peaceful interior silence I felt I needed to encounter God—it was always as if God was out of reach or I was never silent enough. Father not only listened carefully to my descriptions, but actually counted the days and weeks between these tough bouts. "Now let's see", he'd say, "it lasted 10 days this time, but only five days the last time you were here...I think we are making progress." When I told him "I can't stand this type of progress" he introduced me to what he called his "Get Tough Program", which I will speak of later.

Every time I went to see him he started out asking how my prayer was going: "How long did the aridity last this time and how did you handle it? How long did you spend outside this arid state and what was your prayer like then?" In time I noticed he had a kind of mental calculator for all this, so I asked him what all this calculating was about. He was surprised I had noticed, but explained it was to gauge where I was on the path—the path through John's Dark Nights that is. He said I was going along just fine, my experiences were all very typical, expected and ordinary, after all, I was treading a well-worn path. That all this could actually be calculated in days, weeks and months (maybe even years) greatly surprised me. I said, "Well, if you can calculate it, tell me what to expect next month and above all, how long will it take to get to the end?"

He replied that while the stages of the path could be calculated, its timing could not. Time largely depended on us, our cooperating with God, our fidelity to the practice of prayer; our fervor, determination and perseverance, all this was up to us. On one occasion he told me that in his own Novitiate in Ireland, "If a novice had not reached infused contemplation after two years, he was dismissed. He was told that while he likely had a vocation, it was not to our Discalced Carmelite Order." (Many years later when I quoted this to another Carmelite priest, he said, "How things have changed! Today, if after two years a novice is still with us and has all his buttons, we thank God for that!")

I had no idea what "infused contemplation" was, had never heard the term before. When I asked about it, Fr. gave me a formal definition I could only relate to the balloon experience I had when I was five–the infusion of that mysterious Power. I told him about this experience and asked, "Do you think this was infused contemplation?" He only said, "For sure,"–though I detected a suppressed smile on his face. "Well", I asked, "what happened to it, why did it disappear four years later?" All he said was, "God is never absent, He did not disappear, you just had to grow up." This answer was not satisfying, but I didn't press the issue. Later, of course, I learned the Passive Dark Nights are "infused contemplation", thus infused contemplation is not merely a passing experience. Over time I became familiar with contemplative language and terms, also the stages and paths elaborated by St. Teresa and St. John of the Cross, the two founders of the Order of Discalced Carmelites. Because of this, there developed between Father and I an almost non-verbal understanding, neither of us had to say very much to be understood and know we were understood. I might add that our rapport was never that of student-teacher or confessor-penitent, or even advisor-advisee, rather, it was two dedicated Carmelites talking together, the older more experienced graciously taking a keen interest in a younger, more inexperienced fledgling. Father never advised me to do this or that or told me to do anything, there was never any chit-chat or mere social exchange. Father was a good questioner, however, always he got right to the point. It goes without saying, he was a good listener.

I would always be intrigued by Father's calculating the progressive ascent of the Dark Nights, for him it was as predictable as a timed mechanism. As we went along his calculations went something like this: initial aridity, one day a week, then 2 days a week, then three, and so on. At the same time there was also the reverse occurring: some experience of consolation one day a week, then one day every two weeks, then every three weeks, and so on. While I could see we were headed for zero, at the time

I had no idea what this meant or where it would all end up. Due to these calculations, however, Father knew ahead of time what I had to report, a fact I found amazing and tremendously reassuring. He had absolute confidence in this whole business, and I had confidence in him. That it was possible to calculate the onset and progress of the various Nights was the most extraordinary piece of knowledge I ever encountered in the spiritual life. It poses the possibility of there being tighter guide lines than the path alone with no time factor. That our progress, be it slow or fast, is up to us, means everything depends on our response to God's grace, whether it is total, half-hearted (sporadic), or downright slow (endless excuses). The fact the path can be timed according to our response means the time it takes to get to the end is proportionate to our response. Thus our response is the time gauge for the whole journey, it sets the pace. This answers a lot of questions regarding one's progress, it also has implications as a practical tool for discernment, insight, advice, foresight and much more, its importance can never be overstressed. I marveled at this knowledge gleaned from Father, it is not common knowledge, nor can it be found anywhere in contemplative literature.

When I set out to lead a spiritual life I had no knowledge of any particular path or way, Christ said "I Am the Way", so He was It (for me, the Eucharist) and that was that. I took for granted that differences in spiritualties were due to people's individual temperament and response to God, it never occurred to me there were certain paths people shared in common, with stages, similar experiences and the same problems. To know other people are going or have gone the same way is helpful; that they didn't collapse or wimp out, that despite everything they endured to the end, what could be more encouraging and stabilizing than this? It gives one the hope "if they can do it, so can I!" In all my reading and searching, however, I never found any saint or books on the spiritual life I could relate to, no one going the way God seemed to be leading me, no one who shared my experiences.

The next time I went to see Fr. Columbanus I complained about this, "I've read all the Saints and their books, but there is no one in the Church for me." As soon as I said this Father replied, "I know someone! Wait here." He left the room and returned with a book, put it on the table in front of me and said, "She's for you, you'll understand her." The title was The Spiritual Doctrine of Elizabeth of the Trinity by Pere Philipon, 0. P. "Unfortunately", he said, "1 can't loan it to you because the Fathers will give me holy heck if they find it missing from the library. But you will probably be able to find a copy in a Catholic bookstore."

That night I told dad about the book, and the next day we made a trip to the Catholic bookstore downtown and found it. It would take many pages to say what this book meant to me; perhaps all I need repeat is Father's words: "She's for you, you will understand her." In the whole Church, I fit in more with Elizabeth's spirituality than anyone else, it seemed we had been given certain graces in common. In this young French, Discalced Carmelite nun, I finally found a kindred soul. Down the road I would be equally grateful to St. John of the Cross for his book, The Spiritual Canticle–I virtually lived the book. Together, these two books were my sole reading during the next ten years, in a way they pretty much summed up my journey. I should add, however, that while Elizabeth's retreat notes were beautiful–choice scriptural excerpts–what I found most insightful were Fr. Philopon's theological commentary. For the next year and a half this was the only book I read–over and over. There is no telling how much this insightful commentary meant to me. (Though written in 1937, its first English publication, I believe, was 1947. It has long been out of print).

Summer school was barely over when it was time to return to Flintridge, my last year there. I was glad to get back, it was easier to live the Rule there than at home where mom spent much of her time thinking of things for me to do. One of the first things I did was to go through my class schedule with the Principle, Br. Benigna, and double check my credits to be sure I had everything necessary for a State diploma the end of the year. I had no choice but to let her know my plans for entering Carmel.

I had never before had any dealings with the Principle. Apart from greeting her at the front desk on return to school every Sunday evening, we had no dealings with one another. As moderator for the senior class, there was no reason or need to talk with her, in short, she didn't know me at all. As the one in charge of the whole student body, however, her presence was all over the place, so I could not help but observe her and form my own impressions. While obviously highly competent and brilliant, there was something in her rapport or demeanor I found unattractive. In my view she had the veneer of those who never say what they are really thinking, people who have determined to make a good appearance despite their true thoughts and feelings. I never found her approachable and when she asked why I chose the Carmelites instead of her own Dominican Order, she obviously didn't care for my simple answer. Knowing that the Dominican motto was, "Share What You Contemplate" I said to her, "Teaching school would not be my way of sharing what I contemplate." If the sisters who taught math and English, for example, were sharing what they contemplated, it missed me completely. Their motto sounded good, but obviously it didn't work.

All she said was that she hoped I'd consider changing my mind. At the same time she assured me I could be given a State diploma after my junior year and promised to take care of the matter for me—do all the paperwork required. On at least three occasions she gave me her verbal promise to take care of this, she also personally promised my parents and sent a letter to the Monastery to assure them as well. As it turns out, however, she did absolutely nothing, never lifted a finger, totally ignored my parents' face to face request and later calls. As far as she was concerned, I was nothing but a high school dropout. My initial distrust of her had been totally verified.

Although the first semester was marked by several extraordinary graces during prayer, other than this, life seemed to go smoothly until after Christmas when everything erupted. Before giving an account of this eruption, however, this may be the only place to say something about the extraordinary experiences mentioned.

From the time of my conversion God had showered me with many graces—no two alike—the most important being some new knowledge of God and/or myself. There were also a few outstanding graces wherein their full relevance was not understood for many years. While in the years to come the following experience would become a kind of gauge of my interior progress, at the time it occurred, however, I did not know this—could not have known it.

Kneeling alone in the quiet school Chapel, a great force came down on top of my head that stopped my brain and all its functions. I could not move my mind, a superior force, strong as steel, but light as a cloud, had overpowered it. It felt as if giant hands were holding my mind in a vise. I looked upward a little over my head to see a shaft of light a few feet before me. It seems a wide ray of this light had come down and penetrated my mind with a force that held it immobile. This condition may have lasted no more than one or two minutes, after that, the force gradually lessened and things eventually returned to normal.

I had no understanding of this experience or what it was about, I only knew it was God's doing—a powerful doing. For my part, I had no response at all, no emotions or any movement within, it seems the force had immobilized my whole being, not just my mind. Afterwards, my mind remained stunned and did not get back to its usual form for a full day. When I could think about it, my first question concerned God Within, where had It been during those moments? I had not experienced its familiar Presence nor could find any connection with It and the brilliant Light. At the time, I had no answer for this. If there is any problem with such an experience, it's that: it ruins one's appetite for anything else or anything less. Compared to this, all experiences of God's Presence, love, joy—you name it—is sheer aridity; I took for granted I had experienced a foretaste of a state down the road, most probably reserved for heaven, since such a condition was obviously not compatible with continued life on earth.

The next time this occurred—six months to a year later—while my mind was immobilized, the force was not as heavy and only accompanied by a dust of light that permeated my mind—no external, brilliant Light. Over the years I periodically had this experience and noticed the ever lessening degree of force or power it took to immobilize my mind, Finally the day came when it hardly took any force at all. Once I realized the progressive nature of this experience, it became like a gauge of my journey. Thus what initially had been so spectacular and obviously supernatural, eventually became unspectacular and came about almost unnoticeably, easily. Still, this total cessation of mind was never a state I could have brought about by myself. If I learned anything from this experience, it was the difference between what I could do and what only God could do. No effort on my part could ever be a match for what God could do in a split second.

As to the benefit of this type of experience, apart from revealing the marvel of God's doing and the enormous love it engenders, in time its repetition would act as a kind of gauge. If we think of the spiritual life as a path between ourselves and our eternal life in God, no one knows at any given moment where they are on this path, they do not know how far they have come or how close they might be to the End. It is only when, God permitting, we come to the top of some hill (some high point) and can look back, that we get a glimpse of how far we have come. As for the path ahead, this cannot be known before it has been traversed–lived. So the only gauge possible is the difference between where we are now (at some given moment) and where we were back when. My initial experience in the Chapel was just such a gauge; I knew where I was at that moment and clearly knew the distance between it and where I had been before. So too, given this same experience years later, the difference between it and the earlier experiences were obvious. Having said this, however, a gauge serves no real purpose on the journey. Merely to realize one has come a ways is not really helpful, in truth, the journey would have been the same had there been no gauge at all.

Shortly before Christmas I was introduced to the entire voting community at Carmel. This was the first or second time I had met them as a community. Before the community could vote on my entrance, however, I would need a medical and dental report, as well as a recent hip x-ray because of my earlier bone disease. So in January I went around and had all the exams. The one nice surprise was an unexpected chat with Dr. Wilson, the bone specialist, who after seeing my hip x-ray said, "Only an experienced specialist looking at your x-ray would know you ever had a problem." After that, he sat me down and asked many questions about the monastic life and what had attracted me to it.

It was our regular family doctor who started all the trouble. It seems my blood test indicated I had a case of pernicious anemia. Immediately the Dr. called mom and literally gave her hell–"Peg, what kind of a mother are you? I'm shocked someone in your economic class would have a child with this problem. Why aren't you feeding your children healthy foods and monitoring what they eat? I thought you knew better"–he went on and on. Finally he prescribed one iron pill a day for a month, and another test after that. He ended saying, "If you can't feed her spinach every day, then have her drink a can of carrot juice instead."

Mother was shocked, embarrassed, and madder than a wet hen. Unknown to me, the first thing she did was call Rev. Mother and ask her what kind of priest she had found for me that would allow me to fast and become anemic? She was sure it was all his fault. Rev. Mother was also shocked–at my anemia, at mom's accusation, and above all, at that man down the street with "his feet on the ground," she was sure Father must have given me permission to fast or something. Mom told her I could never enter now, and that I might never be able to survive on the Nuns' diet. I don't know what else she said to Rev. Mother, but after hanging up, Rev. Mother immediately called Fr. Columbanus and told him my mother's accusations and asked if there was any truth to it. Father, in turn, was shocked, of course he had never given me any such permission. As soon as he hung up he called me, "Bernadette, I want to talk to you as soon as you can get over here," that's all he said. Although I knew this whole thing was much ado about nothing, still I was on the hot seat, the focus of everyone's suspicions. But if they were waiting for answers, so was I. I never had any symptoms of anemia–never felt tired, lacked energy, lost weight. I told mom the doctor had probably read the wrong chart, after all, he was an old man obviously overdue for retirement. In the meantime, however, I took my pill and drank my can of carrot juice.

The ride to see Father was one of gloom and doom. Although the whole thing was ridiculous, if it hadn't ruined my chances of entering Carmel, it at least put a stopper on the process. Rev. Mother already told me my entrance–tentatively set for two weeks after school was out–had been put on hold. Even if we didn't know what caused the anemia, I'd just have to eat humble pie anyway–eat a lot of everything in fact.

Father met me at the door, "Well, you blew it! I don't know when the sisters are going to take you now." After we sat down he said nothing, but seemed to be waiting for me to explain myself. So I started, "I'm sure the doctor was mistaken, I never felt sick … my mother just doesn't want me to enter ... Rev. Mother said they would have to put off my entrance…" I talked myself into a hopeless corner of despair, and with no place left to go, put my head in my arms on the table and burst into tears.

After a bit I realized I did not have a handkerchief, and there was no way I could look up at Father with a snotty nose; I thought of getting up and running out of the room. At that point, however, a handkerchief was thrust in my hand, which I pushed back across the table—what would he do afterwards with that filthy thing? But it was put back into my hand, "I want you to use it!" he said. Without lifting my head I used it, but afterwards I was too embarrassed to look at him, didn't know what to say, it was a moment of self-hatred. I focused on folding the handkerchief in my lap as small as possible so he'd forget it and I could take it home, wash and return it. The silence in the room was deafening. When I finally raised my head and gave him a quick look, his eyes were the essence of kindness and I detected a suppressed laugh. I defrosted and involuntarily sighed, glad the whole thing was over. He learned back in his chair, and with a loud sigh said, "Bernadette, Bernadette, what am I going to do with you?"

That was the question. What could he do—what could anybody do now? I was surprised that after his long pause, Fr. already had an idea in mind; he had prepared his case ahead of time. He began:

"You know, I think this whole thing may be my fault. Sometimes we directors think we're doing alright when, in fact, we need more help than we can give to others. We think we know the whole story and the ways of the Holy Spirit, and we do not. My position with you was not that of a superior giving you an obedience to do this or not to do that, the director's position is to watch and see how the spirit moves in order to help you go along with its interior movement. But I think now this is not enough. The last few days I have been thinking about this problem and about you. I knew ahead of time exactly how you would feel, none of this really surprised me, but I had to think not only of your direction, but of my own direction in your regard, think of the best way we can go on from here. In examining my possible failures in directing you, I came up with what I think is a perfect solution."

He got up and went to a small table in the room, took a small book from the drawer and laid it on the table before me. The title read, The Rule and Constitution of the Discalced Carmelite Order of Our Lady of Mount Carmel. "From now on", he said, "this will be our guideline, the Holy Spirit will have to fall in with it. For the entire Carmelite Order and its Saints, and now for you, this is the Great Way, a sure and proven path, we can't miss. We'll study it together and adapt it to your present life so you won't have to waste any time or energy deciding what to do or what not to do. The Rule has a grace of its own that will carry you along without your even knowing it–as we often say, "Keep the Rule and it will keep you." Believe me it works, I know, and I'm confident it will work for you."

I was delighted with this plan. We not only went over the monastic day as applied to my present life, more importantly, Fr. stressed its whys and wherefores–goals and spirit of the Order. He gave me the little book to take home and study saying we would discuss some section of it every time I came to see him. The Holy Rule had a profound meaning for Father, he loved it and never tired of going over its benefits. The Rule was like a divine guarantee, a path of holiness and sanctity that led us into the eternal depths of God. This is why, at our first meeting, he would have me keep the Rule as much as possible while still in the world, and why I lived it long before I entered.

After briefly going over the Rule, Father asked for my menu, especially the foods or meals I didn't eat or had "given up." I assured him I had never tried to fast, not at least in the Church's definition. Apart from one big meal a day, I didn't know how the Church's fast worked since I'd never had to observe it. But between being a picky eater, not eating between meals and passing up things I especially liked, this must have done the trick, either that or they made a mistake at the lab–my mistrust of doctors was not unfounded. I told him I made a point of eating the things I hated–meat, milk, eggs, cheese–and had gone so far as try swallowing raw eggs. All my life, food had been a problem, so most of it was a penance anyway. He asked what foods I had given up.

Me: Well, ice cream, for one.

Fr: From now on eat it! What else?

Me:	Hmm…chocolate pudding, it's one of the few edibles at school.
Fr.:	Eat that too.
Me:	Then there's pumpkin pie sometimes.
Fr.:	Never pass that up!
Me:	Oreo cookies
Fr.:	Eat those for penance

(The list went on until finally I said:)

Me:	If I eat all this stuff I'll bust.
Fr.:	If you do it will be your own fault, you should not have given up eating anything without asking me first.

We didn't talk about prayer that day, he gave me a talk on the meaning of true mortification which was not in external disciplines which were our own choosing, but rather in interior discipline, detachment and surrender to God which was God's choosing. I recognized what he was saying and promised I wouldn't do a single external thing without asking him. (I will admit, however, I was reluctant to ask his permission about petty things. Sometimes it's hard to draw a line in these matters, and I didn't want another case of scruples.)

It had been a difficult meeting, and when I knelt for his parting blessing–his "special Carmelite blessing" I called it–he blessed me with unusual fervor. Laying both hands on my head, which he had never done before, he said, "You belong on the Mountain!"(Carmel). I was very touched, interiorly I even felt his blessing. Once out the door, I ran down the steps and was half way across the parking lot when he called me back and held out his hand. Without a word, I put the handkerchief in it and took off again.

Since the iron pills had only been prescribed for a month, after the next medical test, the results came back perfect: no anemia. That it took such a short time for a cure made me suspicious, things could not have been as bad as the doctor made it sound. After telling me "no more pills" the doctor told me to be sure to eat my spinach and continue drinking a can of carrot juice everyday–"canned penance" I called it.

The doctor's report was sent to the sisters, and during my April visit, Rev. Mother told me the sisters had voted me in. I was overjoyed and utterly grateful. She set the entry date for June 15th, about two weeks after school was out, and suggested I bring mom to see a postulant's outfit so she could have one made for me.

When I left the monastery I walked down to see if Father was home so I could tell him the good news. Because he was busy, I sat on the front steps and waited. When I told him the news he was delighted and suggested we go into Church to thank Christ and our Lady. "Now", he said, "you will be under her mantle with the rest of us." (For Carmelites, Our Lady of Mount Carmel is like a mother hen who gathers her Carmelite chicks under her protective mantle–I once saw lovely picture depicting this). So kneeling at the altar with Father, who shared my joy, was like a grand finale, a glorious ending to a long saga–my worldly life.

When I told my parents the good news, dad lifted his eyebrows, suppressed a smile, but said nothing. Mom nodded her head in acknowledgment, but made no comment. When 1 told her about the need to have a postulant's outfit made, all she said was, "Alright"–so much for sharing the good news with my parents! Although they must have realized how obvious and ridiculous their conspiratorial silence appeared, it would have done no good to call them on it, indeed, it might only have set off an explosion. For my part, however, nothing could dampen my joy, Carmel at last! I knew the day I entered would be the happiest day of my life.

Age 17

AGE 17

Around the first of May, several weeks before my birthday, I reminded Mom of my postulant's outfit which still had to be made. We were at dinner when I asked: "When are we going to go to Carmel to see the postulant's outfit? We've only got about six weeks left, don't you think we should get started?" There was that deafening silence again, but I stared at her expectantly. In turn she stared at dad as if waiting for him to answer or say something. When I looked at him, however, he was stubbornly looking down at his plate. Finally mom put her hands in her lap and looked at me. "Your father and I have planned a wonderful birthday surprise for you, but we didn't want to tell you until we got closer to your birthday. We have planned to take you on a trip to Europe; we'll be visiting Lourdes, Lisieux, Fatima, Rome, and other places you will enjoy. It will be a kind of Pilgrimage and birthday present in one."

Me: It sounds like a wonderful trip, but no thanks, I'd rather be in Carmel.

Mom: You can always go to Carmel, but you wouldn't always be able to take a trip like this.

Me: I'd rather be in Carmel than take a trip anywhere in the world.

Mom: You've got a long life ahead, what's a couple of months? You would have wonderful memories for the rest of your life.

Me: No; I'm going to Carmel, besides, sometimes memories can be a distraction.

Mom: Oh for heaven sakes, you can be so stubborn! Why don't you ask Reverend Mother and see what she thinks? 1bet the sisters would like you to go, after all, it might be your last chance.

Me: I don't care what Rev. Mother and the sisters think; as long as they'll take me in June, I'm going.

Mom: Well, we're planning on leaving a couple of days after school is out, so if you enter on the 15th we won't be here.

Me: (I was shocked). Can't you wait and go after I enter?

Mom: No, it's all planned, the reservations have been made. If we don't leave by that date we can't go at all.

Me: Well, you don't have to be here when I enter, Lee can drive me to the Monastery.

Mom: Just think it .over; there's still time.

Me: I don't need any time; I don't want to go.

Mom: Let's see what Rev. Mother has to say.

I don t know where mom got the impression Rev. Mother had some influence on me, she didn't. My relationship with Rev. Mother was friendly but rather business like, we never discussed anything spiritual; she never inquired about my prayer life or daily schedule. On my monthly visits I rarely saw her anyway, she'd send the Novice Mistress or one of the Counsel sisters to talk to me–which I preferred. Mother Agnes and especially Sr. Regina spoke wonderfully of the spiritual life, they exuded the Carmelite spirit, and nobody knew John of the Cross and his path like Sr. Regina. I loved talking to her.

At any rate, Mom was off base thinking that by her becoming good friends with Rev. Mother I could somehow be influenced. It was the other way around; it was Rev. Mother who was influenced by my mother. On my next visit to Carmel I was told my entry date had been postponed. Rev. Mother said the sisters thought it best to wait until my parents returned from their trip so they could be present when I entered. She urged me to go with them and said I could enter when I got back. She then reset my entrance date for the first week in September.

I was crushed. I thought it weak of Rev. Mother to give in to mom; and as for mom, this bid for time was all part of her little scheme. She could not understand why going on a trip, even a pilgrimage, did not appeal to me. My days had long been geared to living the Rule and I wanted nothing more than to live it without the unending string of worldly distractions and interruptions. Besides, if I had wanted to go someplace I could have spent the summer with Maria at her family's summer home in Acapulco. For several years she had urged me to come, she even tried to entice me with pictures of her lovely home and gorgeous yacht. Maria's mom made a special trip to our home to importune me, but my heart was not in it, I knew where I belonged.

By this time it was pretty obvious mom was bitterly opposed to my entering Carmel, yet she would never admit it or discuss it. Later she told me her reason for never talking to me about it: "Because you were always so stubborn, I knew that the more objections I raised, the more stubborn you would become and the more determined to enter." This was the way she judged me all my life; she could never grasp her own faulty reasoning. I said to her, "If you really believed I was determined to enter Carmel because you objected to it, then it follows that if you had encouraged me, I would not have entered—does that make sense to you?" Since it didn't, she put it off with "There's no use arguing with you. I learned that long ago!

It seems anytime I didn't go along with her, mom labeled me "stubborn", a label she also gave dad and anyone she couldn't bring to her way of thinking. When I was little, she was convinced I would not eat my vegetables and meat solely because she wanted me to! It never occurred to her I didn't like the taste. To assume people only hold certain tastes, views, desires or whatever, for the sole reason of opposing someone else, is patently ridiculous. That some of mom's likes and dislikes never set well with me is a fact she either could not comprehend or stubbornly refused to believe.

I always thought if mom, instead of playing her silent game, had openly discussed things with me or asked questions, she might have gained some insight into my vocation. As it was, her silence closed the door on this possibility; in her mind, an honest discussion of differing views amounted to "arguing" and she couldn't stand that. So mom's complaint of never understanding me was her own fault, she never give herself a chance.

As things turned out, mom and dad went on their trip while I boarded at Immaculate Heart High School, about five miles away, where I lived in the novitiate, the only non-religious in a community of a hundred sisters or so. I do not recall how I pulled this off–getting to stay there–since the school did not take boarders. Perhaps the sisters thought I wanted to enter their Order, I don't know. I took another class in Latin–my fourth year–because as the language of the Divine Office I knew it would be helpful. (I already had three years of Spanish as well). I could have stayed at home, however, since Lee and his young family were staying there for the summer, but I figured living in the novitiate might be a little more like living in Carmel than staying home where there was a constant need for a baby sitter. As it was, several times that summer, Lee, Gert, their spouses and friends went off for dinner and a movie leaving me with five crying little kids under the age of five. While I honestly didn't mind, I nevertheless reminded them I had only come home to do my laundry.

Although Rev. Mother assured me I could enter in September, I thought it odd she would not set a date. All she said was that she wanted to wait until my parents came home to find out how soon my postulant's outfit could be ready. What a switch! Most communities set the date for the aspirant and don't wait for the aspirant's parents to give them one. At any rate, I was glad when my parents returned in early August so we could finally set the date.

I don't know what happened behind the scenes, I only found out later that on her return home, mom had a long talk with Rev. Mother that "touched her heart"–Rev. Mother's heart, that is. On my next visit to the monastery I was told that since the sisters would begin their rigorous fast September 21st, feast of the Holy Cross, and considering my bout with anemia, they thought it better if I waited until the fasting season was over before I entered. And when was the fasting season over? Next Easter! I saw through this at once. Because this fast had not been mentioned prior to my parents return, I knew mom had something to do with it, something to do with Rev. Mother's "heart problem." At first I argued that being under age I didn't have to fast anyway, but she told me this fast was not a Church ordinance, but one ordained by the Holy Rule–and I didn't want to be an exception did I?

At that point I despaired of ever entering Carmel, some aspect of my spirit fell–though I didn't know what. I only knew I couldn't fight the odds anymore, I had done everything I could and it wasn't going to happen. So now what?

I never felt any anger towards my mother, I was reminded of Christ's words, "Father forgive her because she knows not what she does." In truth, mom didn't know what she was doing. That she was standing in God's way for me is something she would never understand–and even if she had, she probably would have done it anyway. Although I'm sure her problem, in part, was having to let go her youngest chick, this wasn't all. I do believe her resistance stemmed from her strong Protestant upbringing, by her own admission she could never understand the celibate or Religious life. Once dad was talking about the hardships of the priesthood when mom said,

Mom: I'll never understand the celibate religious life–its "unnatural!"

Dad: Of course, it's supernatural! Without a special grace from God nobody can live that life, nor would they want to."

Mom: But God commanded us to increase and multiply–get married.

Dad: I'm convinced marriage is harder than celibacy.

Me: How's that?

Dad: A priest doesn't have to get in bed every night with an enticing woman like your mother.

Mom: Oh for heaven's sake, Mark, don't make me out to be a siren or something!

Dad: Don't underestimate yourself!

Mom: And don't blame me if you can't control yourself!

Dad was always quite open about his difficult sexual life, which embarrassed mom no end. In sexual matters mom was a real stick-in-the-mud, if I hadn't read books on dog breeding I'd have thought the stork dropped me off.

Apart from her inability to understand the celibate life, however, mom had a horror of the monastic life, Carmel in particular. Years before, she told me that as a young girl growing up in Baltimore, every day her path to school went past the Carmelite Monastery there. When she learned it housed a group of women who had deliberately walled themselves in and never went out, she was horrified. "Why would anybody in their right mind do a thing like that?" It stymied her brain. But here now, her own child wanted to live that way! For sure, it was her worst nightmare come true.

Nothing anyone could have said would have helped mom, but what about dad? He knew of her scheming behind my back, so why did he go along with it? Years later when I asked him, he told me, "Your mother blamed me for the whole thing. She said I had planted the idea in your head and encouraged it, thus your entering was all my fault. That's why I didn't dare say anything to you, she would have taken it as proof. I thought if you got no help or encouragement from me she'd eventually realize it was your own idea." So that explained dad's silence. But since mom's accusations were false—dad neither planted the idea nor encouraged me—his going along with her made no sense. That out of fear of being blamed he chickened out, was nothing less than cowardice.

I don't know if dad ever knew it, but mom blamed him for the others leaving home as well. Thus for Gert, Lee, Marge and myself, the only reason we left home was to get away from dad, this was her stated belief. She was convinced all along I only wanted to enter Carmel to get away from dad. Now if the others did not leave home to marry the one they loved and raise a family, then I cannot speak for them. But for myself, I could have thought of easier ways, or dug up better excuses, to leave home than entering a monastery. Dad would have been only too happy for me to enroll in any college or university of my choice, and as far from home as I pleased. No, our problem was never dad; even if he'd been dead we'd all have left home and do exactly as we did and when we did.

But no rational argument could make mom see otherwise. Perhaps she would have been supremely happy if we had all lived at home with her (without dad, of course) for the rest of our lives.

One last word on this matter. With the exception of Marge, the three of us kids certainly had our moments of butting heads with dad, no doubt there were times we felt a genuine dislike for him. In these moments, however, mom always stood by dad, never interfered, never defended us, never allowed a word of criticism against him, and never evinced the slightest sympathy for us. If she had any thoughts of her own, or ever thought dad was wrong or unfair, she never uttered them, not, at least, until long after the issue had blown over. For her to blame dad and exonerate herself was a bit too much. Whatever our disagreements with dad, she was no help to any of us, never. The truth is: in leaving home we all knew we were leaving behind a good life, a good home, and two very good people.

When time came to return to school—my senior year—it was impossible to muster any enthusiasm. A few hours before leaving I got out a suitcase and threw in a few things including the Monk. Apart from keeping the Carmelite Rule, I figured I'd somehow drift through the year. Having earned my diploma, there was no reason to study anyway, and when the year was over, if Carmel was still out of the question, I'd ask dad to build me a hermitage over the garage. That way, mom would have me at home and I could still do my own thing. As for entering some other Order, the idea was as abhorrent to me as the word "meditation." If I could not be a monastic Carmelite, I'd be a Third Order Carmelite and live the Rule in my own back yard—over the garage.

Sometime after school started I called Fr. Columbanus to make an appointment. He seemed surprised to hear my voice, "Where are you? Where are you calling from?" "I'm at home", I replied. "I thought you were in the monastery," he said, "I was even thinking of you there—so why aren't you?" I told him the situation, Rev. Mother's wanting me to wait until the fasting season was over before setting another date—for the third time no less. "I can't believe it, I don't understand, I'm going to call Rev. Mother right away. I'll talk to you next Saturday."

My call to Father was in the morning. That evening I got a surprise call from Reverend Mother, the only time I ever talked to her on the phone.

R.M.: Bernadette, I thought you'd be happy to know the community has set the date for your entrance Jan. 2nd, Feast of the Holy Name, does that sound good to you?

Me: Yes!

R.M.: Do you think you can wait?

Me: Is there any possibility I can come sooner?"

R.M: Now dear, don't you think you could give your parents the happiness of having you home for one last Christmas together?"

(Although I knew for mom it would be the worse Christmas ever, I didn't dare remind Rev. Mother of this. I didn't want her pushing the date back, but I also didn't want to sound heartless.)

Me: Yes, I'll try.

R.M.: The next time you come then, I'll show you a postulant's outfit so you can have one made—your mother might want to come with you.

Me: I'll ask her.

R.M.: I will see you then.

When I told my parents the joyful news, neither of them said a word, never even changed their facial expressions. When I told mom what Rev. Mother said about the postulant's outfit, she replied, "We'll see," and that was the end of the conversation. Mom, of course, never went to the monastery with me, in fact, from beginning to end my parents never went near the place. Given all mom's anxious calls to Rev. Mother, however, she had no need to face her.

After Rev. Mother's call, I put two and two together: my calling Father with the bad news, then Father calling Rev. Mother, and then her calling me with good news. I was sure this was no coincidence, Father must have said something to cause this sudden turn around. My hunch was correct. Later Father told me, "I told Rev. Mother that if she didn't take you as soon as possible I was going to send you to another monastery of the Order, a monastery that would be a lot further away from your parents. I also told her that if I didn't hear back in two days–that she had set a date–I would start contacting the Prioresses of other Monasteries."

I couldn't believe my ears. I never suspected Father had it in him–to talk to Rev. Mother that way. His demeanor with her had always been rather subservient and reverent, but evidently this was only skin deep. That unbidden he had gone to bat for me, well, my gratitude would know no end, from beginning to end, he had been my sole ally. It was only later I learned why he wanted me in "as soon as possible." He told me, "I knew you were about to experience the "big one" (Dark Night) and I wanted you in the monastery when it happened. The world is no place to go through this; all kinds of difficulties would only have delayed you."

Apart from his spiritual concerns, Father may never have realized how clever he had been. First of all, the next closest monastery would have been San Diego to the South or Carmel-by-the-Sea to the North, some 300 miles away; to prevent my going so far from home, my parents might have begged Rev. Mother to take me. Second, if Rev. Mother didn't want to break their hearts by taking me, she also didn't want to incur their wrath for keeping me out of the closest monastery. Then too, dad had known the community from his youth, he had even helped Fathers Enda and Patrick when they came from Ireland to establish a community of Discalced Carmelite Fathers in the diocese; refusing to take an otherwise qualified daughter–both Priests knew me–might not sit well with these Father Founders. Of itself, Father's threat had put Rev. Mother between a rock and a hard place: placate an aspirant's mother or ignore her Carmelite Confessor who was prepared to go around her. Without a legitimate excuse, Rev. Mother's back was to the wall.

The reason I had never thought of applying to a different community was because I took for granted if I didn't have the qualifications for one, I didn't have the qualifications for any. Initially, I never suspected the degree mom could affect Rev. Mother, or realize that a different Prioress might not have been so easily influenced. For sure, however, if Father's lowering the boom on Rev. Mother hadn't worked, I would have applied to another Carmelite community.

Earlier I mentioned Father's "Get Tough Program" which meant more than simply "grin and bear it." It was Father's belief that very few Nuns and Monks were, in fact, true contemplatives, which he blamed on either an inadequate understanding of the Dark Nights or their inability to "get tough." He wanted to make certain I was prepared in both categories–to be informed and understand what was going on, and be able to get tough. His concern for my entering the monastery sooner rather than later was, as he said, "I knew you were about to experience the 'big one' (Dark Night)", which is when things really get tough. Father would always refer to John's Passive Night of the Spirit as "the big one" or the "big Night", he seemed to regard the other nights as progressive approaches to the "big one" and not as discreet nights in themselves. Also, by definition, Father regarded only those who went through the Big Night as a true "contemplative." If someone did not go this route they were not, in his books at least, an authentic contemplative. They might be a saint, but not a contemplative. For him, the line between the two (contemplative and non-contemplative) was toughness, whether one could "get tough" or not, hence his Get Tough Program. Had it been up to him, everyone would be a contemplative–tough, that is.

Listening to Father, I took for granted there were basically two Dark Nights, one consisting of bouts of prolonged dryness and aridity punctuated by graced reprieves; the other or "Big" Night, a more profound, pervasive state of emptiness with no reprieves–a predicament (really a transformation) that eventually culminates in an abiding Unitive State. Although I had read John of the Cross' Dark Night a year earlier and didn't get much from it–at this time I much preferred Elizabeth of the Trinity–still, I was sure I was in the worst of Nights. But when I put it to Father, he said I had not yet come that far. On one occasion I was so convinced I was already in the "big night", I took John of the Cross' book to our next meeting and read excerpts to him–"no desires, no attachments, no will, no Presence, no love, no images, no forms, etc."–and then challenged him to tell me how it was I was not in this Night already.

He shook his head and remained silent. "If this is not it", I asked, "then tell me what it is like, how could anything be worse than this?" He would tell me nothing about it from his own experiences because, he said, it was different for everybody. Somehow I got the impression he thought I was going to have one awful time of it.

To ease any fear, he told me that for every soul the Big Night was crucial, because the depths to which a man sinks is directly proportional to the heights he reaches which he compared to bouncing a ball, "the further it falls, the higher it rises." Father thought it was a matter of the soul's capacity and that the tougher the soul the greater its capacity–which is why it was so important to "get tough." "To tame a kitten is nothing", he said, "but it takes a great rider and trainer to break a powerful steed so they can ride as one, each enhancing the power of the other." Elaborating on this analogy he said:

"After making friends with a horse, the real training begins. The horse rebels and balks and wants to run free. Many people, when they come to the Dark Night do just that, they run away, seek distractions, seek other people's affections, run from confessor to confessor, avoid prayer, they are overcome with self-hate and go to ascetic extremes, they get paranoid and think they are being persecuted by those around them, they can do hundreds of things to avoid the Dark Night, and in doing so, lose the greatest opportunity God has ever held out to them in their whole life."

Me: But surely those who truly love God can take all this and not run away.

Fr.: In the Dark Night there is no love except this toughness.

Me: Do you think I'm the type to run away?

Fr: I don't want you to so much as look away, don't even turn your head. Man must fully see his nothingness before he can see what God really is.

Me: So what am I going to do right now with all this nauseating aridity?

Fr.: (Leaning forward he said emphatically): You just sit there and take it! And after that, ask for more of the same! Apart from that, you have the rule–keep it!

Me: The problem is "how" to sit there.

Fr.: Remember, the will alone is the great faculty of love, so your determined will to sit there is an act of love itself. Do not suppress distractions–good, bad or indifferent–it's ignoring all of them, not getting caught up in them, that takes guts, toughness and diligence.

(In his view, the rebelliousness and disturbance of peace I sometimes experienced was due to my deep-seated unwillingness to squarely face my own nothingness.) Once he said,

Fr.: There will come a time when I will not be around to help you, but just remember, there comes a time in everyone's life when they must stand absolutely alone and squarely face their own misery and nothingness.

Me: So I am nothing, so what? I already know that.

Fr.: To know you are nothing is very different from being nothing!

I didn't understand that, but it sounded ominous. I did, however, understand his get tough program, in my view it was the only way to go, if there was any other choice I never encountered it; it was either get tough or drop out. No question, I felt my patience, peace of soul and generosity toward God stretched beyond even the limits I thought I had. In all this, however, Father assured me everything was on course and that despite it all, I was on the right track.

Back at school the principal once more assured me she'd see that a State diploma of graduation was sent to the monastery. As already noted, however, she never lifted a finger. Fortunately the nuns at the monastery either didn't care or just plain forgot about it. To the last, I had the impression the principal hoped I would change my mind and become a Dominican. No doubt this is why I was appointed (or elected, I do not recall) President of the Sodality that year. Next to Student Body President, this was considered an honored position. The only privilege that came with it, however, was saying the Latin responses at daily Mass. There were no altar boys, and despite a community of sisters, every morning the Priest and Sodality President were the lone voices at Mass. Whatever the Priest's pace–reverent or hurried–I matched it, knew the responses by heart. If for no other reason, my years of Latin had been worth it. Apart from this, however, at a school like Flintridge, the Sodality President had nothing to do because the school provided every spiritual need, outlet, and devotion a girl would ever need. At the start of Christmas vacation then, I was only too glad to hand the job over to Juanita–who also joined an Order along with another classmate, Camilla, who became a Dominican. Three Religious out of a class of 19 was an unusually high number, sometimes there was only one, and usually, there were none.

Until the last day of school no one but Maria and the Principal knew I would not be returning. Our final evening was the annual Christmas play which most of the parents attended–I sang in the chorus. When it was over, we said our good-byes and each went their separate ways. Those from a distance, like Maria, would fly or take a train the next morning. Maria was the only one happy to see me go. She had lived with me through all the ups and downs, thus my joy was her joy. All the changes that came about following my conversion, Maria had taken in stride as if she understood perfectly, never a question or objection. On week-ends I slept on the floor, got up at 4:30, spent hours in Church while Maria took over my part in the family. She loved to shop, go to a movie, do things with Mom, and she was the only person I ever knew who teased and joked with dad– none of us kids ever did. There was never a question of leaving Maria behind, like Sally, she was a part of my life forever.

The end of September I had brought home specifications for my postulants outfit, mom said she'd talk to the seamstress across the street who often did jobs for her. Anytime I inquired how things were going, however, mom would say the lady couldn't find the right material or that she was pressed for time right now. When nothing was done by Thanksgiving, the sisters gave me addresses of several shops that carried the material. Finally, at the start of Christmas vacation, the job got started.

My final trip to Alhambra was to see Father. Although in the monastery I would be free to see him anytime, our monthly talks were over.

After assuring me he would be available anytime I asked, he told me never to forget the motto: "Keep the Rule and it will keep you." Keeping the Rule, he explained, sets us free to focus solely on God and not on our self–with all its concerns. "We never have to ask ourselves, 'Am I in the right place, doing the right thing?' because the Rule assures us we are doing God's will at every moment; it frees us from external concerns, decisions and distractions in order to give us the interior freedom of being concerned with God alone." After telling Father of my "get tough" coping mechanisms during prayer, I ended,

Me: For sure this is the Big Night!

Fr: No, not yet.

Me: How so?

Fr: You are not there yet.

Me: What's missing? What else, or what more has to happen?

Fr: When it happens you will know it, you will remember that I told you so, and you will take heart.

These were his exact words which turned out to be prophetic. At the time, of course, I didn't understand, but the way he said them, so deliberately and definitively, I knew the subject was over. I might add, in the year and a half we spent together he sometimes said other things I didn't understand, but if I tried to probe him, he never volunteered an explanation, he knew I was not yet in the right place to fully understand. It seems that anything we think we know ahead of time is not it. Years later, however, things he said came back to me, I recognized them, understood through my own experiences and was grateful to know others had traversed the same terrain; I was not alone.

As things turned out, about five months after our last meeting, when suddenly confronted with a black hole in the center of my being, his words instantly came to mind and I did, in fact, "take heart." I also remembered his saying, "the lower you go, the higher you rise," thus I never flinched until I got to the bottom of that empty hole–in truth, "Man must fully see his nothingness before he can see what God really is." Apart from John of the Cross himself, I cannot imagine anyone in the Carmelite

Order more knowledgeable and experienced than Fr. Columbanus. I often regretted every contemplative could not have availed themselves of his wisdom, but it seems Father was one of God's hidden souls known only to a few. To be accounted among the few who knew him was one of the great graces of my life. I didn't fully realized it at the time, but the longer I lived the more I realized how rare he was. Though externally small in stature, humble and unassuming, interiorly he was a giant, a truly great and holy contemplative, a glory to his beloved Order of Discalced Carmelites.

One last thing about Father. Almost from our first meeting I noticed something about him I could never put my finger on. I detected in him a certain air of what I thought might be sadness, an air of disappointment, as if some expectation had not been fulfilled or was waiting to be fulfilled. At the same time, however, I was deeply impressed with his humility—which St. Teresa defined as "the truth"—and was never sure if what I detected in him was disappointment, humility, both or neither. Certainly he never acted sad or wanting and never said anything to indicate he was; no, it solely had to do with his view of himself and, perhaps, his own spiritual status—just my impression of course. Although I knew for certain he had already gone through the Big Night, beyond this I didn't know anything. At one point I thought maybe God had robbed him of the joys of the Unitive State—the outcome of the Big Night. It would be just like God to do a thing like that, so maybe that was it, that's what kept him so humble and a bit sad, but I really didn't know.

Down the road, however, I perfectly understood where Father was. I hate to say it, but the Unitive State is not all it's cracked up to be—at least not as glorious as the literature makes it out. While at first it's all very wonderful and spectacular, yet after years of living it, the unitive state is just one's common everyday reality: namely, that of a mature, well balanced human being, an ever Present grace to be sure, but unspectacular and unglorious. Looking back on the fervor and extraordinary graces of our beginnings, and on the mystical transforming process, the mature unitive state is a comparative let-down, it may even seem humdrum compared to what it took to get there. So once this state is fully revealed in daily life, it is a surprise to find it unspectacular and not as the saints in their initial enthusiasm had portrayed it. The usual language to describe this state is of someone newly arrived whose perspective is always comparative or relative to their previous estate–the Nights, that is. Nowhere are we told anything about what this state is like 20, 30, 40 years down the road, there is absolutely no literature on it. As it stands then, the impression is that there is no further to go and that the unitive state is a kind of heaven on earth. To disabuse a beginner of this, however, might only discourage him. At the same time, it would be a great mistake to underrate this state, after all, it is God's own doing and the true estate of man on earth; nothing is of greater value than living this life in oneness with God.

In the months before my entrance I sometimes wracked my brain to think of something, anything, I would be giving up or sacrificing by entering Carmel. That nothing came to mind was disconcerting because it meant I was giving God nothing, had nothing to give, while God had given me everything. This made giving a purely one-sided affair which bothered me greatly. Certainly I could find some little thing I would miss. As I was thinking this over, the ocean came to mind–that was it! I would never, ever, as long as I lived, be able to see the ocean again. When I was younger, in the back of my mind I harbored the idea that if something terrible happened, or I ever found myself on the brink of the unendurable, so long as I could get to the sea everything would be alright. That this last ditch would now be impossible left me no place in the world to go–it was as if someone cured at Lourdes had seen the place blown to bits. But if the ocean was the one thing I had to offer to God, the truth is, I had no real choice in the matter because I was not going to stay out of Carmel just to see the ocean! So once again I was left with nothing to give, even giving myself to God was really giving Him nothing.

The reason I bring this up is because my lack of giving anything to God, never having done anything for Him, was a deep concern that would plague me all my life. Even the offer of my whole life and being was mere lip service, always it was God who took what He wanted and did what He wanted. For my part, it was all I could do to put up with this, go along with it, make the best of it; solely of myself I could give nothing. This truth was never a satisfying or happy fact to have to live with. In the end, I think this fact is what eventually ate me up–God would take it all.

* * * * *

It was obvious mom had no enthusiasm for Christmas, she put out all the old Christmas stuff mechanically and made no attempt to make things beautiful, as she always did. There was the usual round of family get togethers and exchange of presents–though I received nothing and wanted nothing. The only things I could take to Carmel were my Bible, Missal, rosary and tooth brush. Apart from supplying bed linen and night clothes, nothing else was allowed. Though I would have liked to take my book on Elizabeth of the Trinity, I didn't ask. I already knew it like the back of my hand, and they probably had a copy anyway.

One last thing mom and I enjoyed together were the season's High Masses, so beautifully sung by the Biggs' professional choir. For many years we had returned after early Mass on Sunday to hear the choir sing High Mass at noon. If there was to be any consolation for mom she would find it at Mass; I never doubted God would more than compensate her for the sacrifice she was being forced to make.

A few days before departure I made sure I left nothing behind to remind mom of my absence, nothing in the drawers, closet, top of dresser, anywhere. For some time my room had looked like a guest room, now it was going to be one. There was just one item that concerned me, my Monk–as ever, imperturbably contemplating God. Because my parents had once packed him away, I was concerned, what would happen to him now? He was too big to sneak into the monastery like a holy card. In the back of my mind I thought perhaps eight or nine years down the road I could somehow find a way to get him into the monastery, so I asked dad "Do me a favor, don't ever throw the Monk away, someday maybe I can have him with me." "Don't worry", he replied, "I always liked that picture too, I'd never throw him away; it's your mother who didn't want him around. Don't worry, I'll keep an eye on him for you."

As for the crucifix on the wall, because of its part in my conversion experience it held a special value for me. Yet it had never been mine; like all the crucifixes in the house, it went with the territory. I knew it would stay right where it was as long as my parents were alive, after that, I'd think about it.

The morning of New Year's Eve mom went with me to pick up the postulants outfit. When I put in on and turned around to show her, I was in for a shock. She had the saddest face of anyone I'd ever seen, it didn't even look like her, it was downright frightening. Immediately I took the outfit off.

When the great day dawned, I knew when I awoke God had answered my special request, which was to experience no excitement that day–such an emotion would have ruined it. High excitement can put the mind in a daze so you go about things almost mechanically. Such a condition would not have allowed me to savor the depth and true joy in the still Center of my being, after all, it wasn't just my big day, it was "Our" big day. If I couldn't go through it fully aware of this profound Oneness then I might as well not go through it at all.

God not only answered my request, however, He did more. On awaking, the divine Center was aglow, a silent, steady glow which left me free to enjoy and focus on the externals instead of being concerned with my interior disposition, yes indeed, God had taken care of things! The way this worked was quite marvelous, I was tremendously grateful.

We were to be at the monastery at three o'clock. After Mass that morning we stopped at Gert's for a special breakfast. At noon mom fixed a light lunch, after which I put on my outfit and dad put the bags in the car. On the way there, all mom said was, "Always remember, anytime you change your mind or want to come home, all you have to do is give us a call and we'll be right there." Learning over the front seat I told them: "This is the happiest day of my life! I've had a lot of happy days in my life and will no doubt have many more, but no day will ever be as happy as this one." Now I don't want to say this was prophetic, but in fact it was the truth.

When Sr. Ignatius let us in the front door, I missed her usual exuberant greeting, both sisters seemed strangely sober and subdued. Later Sr. Ignatius told me she could feel my parents' sadness and thus could not express her happiness for me. We had come a little early so I could make a last visit in the Chapel this side of the grate. My parents came with me, but then left to visit with the extern sisters.

When Rev. Mother came to the parlor, the three of us went in for instructions. We were to stand in the hallway outside the cloister door, when Rev. Mother opened the door I was to step forward and kneel on the threshold. She would give me a candle in one hand and a card in the other, from which I would read aloud a formal request to enter the community. After a formal reply, Rev. Mother would motion me to stand up, a sister would take my candle and card and I would step inside. The whole community would be lined up down the cloister hall to greet me. I would go down the line to give the kiss of peace–actually a bear hug–to each sister in turn. In the meantime, Rev. Mother would return to the parlor to talk to my parents while the Novice Mistress and I took my suitcase up to my cell–my beloved cell!–and then we'd return to the parlor to say good-by from behind the grate.

That is exactly how it went. The three of us stood in the hall, my stoical mom on one side, my dad with tears running down his cheeks, on the other. When the cloister door opened I stepped forward, knelt down and was given a lit candle and card. After reading the formal request and receiving the formal answer, I stood up, a sister took my candle and card and I walked in, the door closed behind me.

A duck born out of water–in a desert say–knows from birth he is not at home, yet he cannot figure out what happened. The day he sees a far off pond, however, something in him responds and he sets out to investigate. The closer he gets, the more certain his step and direction; then, after traversing some difficult terrain, he finally comes to the water's edge. Who can express what he experiences as he quietly slips into the water? Who can imagine such happiness or what it is to finally be home? I think everybody would agree, for this duck at least, it must have been the happiest day of his life. And so it was for me!

WHY ME?

In the early years, several times the question came up "Why me?" Each time, however, the question was posed for a different reason. The earliest was when I realized other children did not have my experiences, but why not–why me? Though I thought myself neither odd nor privileged, because of my experiences I knew I was somehow different. Later, when it was obvious the inner Power was bent on doing its mysterious work regardless of my consent, and mindless of anything else going on in my life, I pondered why I had been the unfortunate selection. Still later, when realizing the special graces I had received, again came the question, "why me?"

It was impossible to believe when God looked over the children on earth he closed his eyes and picked one at random. Nor could he have noticed me for any particular reason since I had no special talents or intellect, and certainly never merited a thing. There was nothing to recommend me over any other child, possibly even less. Nor was there any reason for God to love me more than others, since prior to revealing Himself, I had never loved him at all, never thought about him, and didn't even desire to know him. No, there was no explanation for being singled out at an early age. Though I never doubted He was equally at work in others, I had never heard of His working in such a mysterious, yet overt, persistent manner. The only hint of a reason I could come up with was that from the beginning, God knew I would never be an easy believer, that I was incapable of accepting any truth I could not verify for myself or come to know through my own experiences. If I was ever to believe and have no doubts, then God had to be evident, persistent and tough– what other reason could there be? In the end, however, I had to admit

God's mind was inscrutable and accept the fact I would never know "why me?"

In my mid-twenties, however, the question came up one day in the silence of prayer. I simply posed the question to God and went back to my silence expecting no answer at all. To my surprise, however, I got the answer, a knowledge whose truth I never doubted, a truth so beautiful and touching, it is almost too precious to relate. Yet, because it underlies the story of these pages, it is only fitting to close with the answer to "why me?"

The answer can be found in the circumstances surrounding my birth, circumstances I only learned about, however, during a visit to a cemetery–of all places–when I was eleven and still on crutches. Every year the family made two or three visits to Calvary Cemetery, one of them was always on Grandma Roberts' birthday when my parents took Grandpa to visit her grave (she died before I was born). She was buried on the ground floor of the mausoleum where, next to her tomb in the marble wall, was an empty space reserved for Grandpa. On this day, after arranging flowers in a vase on the wall, Grandpa, as was his habit, drew up one of the prie-dieu in the hall to spend some quiet time praying before his wife's grave. On this day the only prie-dieu available was a double one, meant for two people, so mom knelt down beside him. To her surprise, Grandpa took out his rosary and proceeded to say it aloud, which meant mom had to respond, of course. Opposite the marble wall of graves were French doors leading out to a lawn, and since it was a warm day the doors had been left open. Seeing that mom and grandpa would be there awhile, dad stepped outside and motioned me to follow, "Come on, I want to show you a special grave," he whispered. When I asked "Whose?" he didn't answer, so I followed him in silence. We went down the grassy hill toward the entrance gate where he veered to the right and stopped at the first row of markers on the further side of the road. Between the first two horizontal rows he stopped, pointed to the grass between the two graves and said, "You have a little brother buried here." I was dumb struck. I never knew there had been more than the four of us kids, never heard of a brother who had died. "Why is there no marker for him?" I asked. "Because", dad replied, "he didn't live long enough to be baptized, so we were not allowed to put a marker on his grave." (This was either a rule of the Church or the Cemetery).

Dad went on to explain. "When he was born he was what they called a 'blue baby'–'blue' because he never breathed. Although the doctor baptized him immediately and tried to get him to breath, he never did. You can imagine how heart-broken we were ... (dad choked up) ... to think I have a child that will never know or see God ...." He broke into tears. With his last words I was jolted from my sadness, not for a second did I believe this infant was not in heaven, the idea was preposterous. It seems at that time, St. Augustine's theory of the unbaptized was generally accepted–namely, that unbaptized children went to Limbo, which is as happy an estate as one can experience without God. I could never understand this belief since no infant desires to be baptized anyway, the parents are the ones who desire it for him, thus whether the infant is alive in the womb or out of the womb, he is the beneficiary of the parents desire–a kind of "baptism of desire." In my view then, it made no difference if the infant lives or dies, either way his baptism depends solely on the desire of the parents, never the infant.

I didn't know what to say to my father; while I did not share his belief, this was not the time or place to bring it up, it might have implied I thought his tears were for nothing. No, his anguish was deep and touching; that what he wanted most for us children was our eternal happiness with God spoke worlds to me about the man. His heart-break was not for his own loss, but rather his child's loss of the glorious vision of God. Nothing I could have said–and later I said plenty–would ever relieve him of this burden.

After a bit, dad wiped his tears and went on with the story. "Although unbaptized infants were not allowed a stone marker they could still be buried in a Catholic cemetery. So the Sister in charge of the nursery told me to go home and get a box, then come back, pick up the baby and take it to the cemetery before it closed at six 6 o'clock. She said the man at the gate-house would understand, and together we would bury the baby. I went home, but the only box I could find was one of my old shoe boxes, so I put it in the car and came back to the hospital. At the door of the nursery Sister came out with a little bundle wrapped in a white blanket and laid it in my arms, she said ….." (I do not recall what she said to dad, only that it was something beautiful and comforting). "I just made it to the cemetery before it closed, the gate-man got a shovel and led me to this spot (pointing to the ground beneath us) where he dug the hole and I put in the little box." At this point he was totally overcome, tears streamed down his face, he couldn't say a word. It was an awkward moment, I felt bad for him but didn't know what to say. We just stood there in silence. Finally, drying his tears he suddenly threw his arms around me, "Now you know why mom and I are so happy to have you, because you too were born a 'blue baby'.

I was surprised to hear this. Although I came several years after the boy whose grave we were standing on, the fact I was also a blue baby seemed odd. Mother, however, never talked about our births or mentioned the children she had lost; all she told us was that she had long hard labors and difficult deliveries—for which she blamed the doctor. The fact mother was petite and that big fat babies were in vogue, didn't help matters, that 1weighed in at almost 9 lbs. was obviously the last straw for Mom. The only good thing Mom had to say about our births was that Dad never left her side and even insisted on being in the delivery room. This was unprecedented, at that time fathers were not allowed in the delivery room, "Believe me", she said, "he made a big stink about this rule, but in the end he got his way." Thus gowned and masked dad held mom's hand as each of us came into this world. She said she didn't know how she could have gone through it without his constant attention, dad's presence was the only good remembrance she had of our births. This is why, were it not for dad, I'd never have known anything about my birth. Here is dad's story:

"You can imagine how my heart sank when you didn't breathe. The doctor baptized you immediately and then began dunking you back and forth between tubs of hot and cold water, still you didn't breathe. I prayed: "Oh God, take her for yourself, I give her to you, I give up all the joys of having her and accept the sorrow of losing her, only take her to yourself!' Just then you cried out and I shouted for joy, 'She belonged to God before she belonged to this world!" (His meaning, of course, was that having been baptized before I breathed, I belonged to God first, and only secondly, to this world.)

This time dad's tears were tears of joy. In telling me this story he had relived one of the most anguished and joyous moments of his life, and I felt closer to him for having shared it with me. My first thought, however, was one of suspicion, I thought his real intention in telling me this story was only to remind me that I belonged to God, I thought to myself, "What would he say if I told him I had already seen God (in the Woods)? If I did, then maybe he'd stop worrying about me." But I said nothing, besides, he probably wouldn't have believed me anyway. Putting his arm around me we walked back up the sloping lawn to meet mom and grandpa who were looking for us.

I determined that when we got home I would get mom's take on dad's story. The fact she never told me anything about my birth—or the little one she lost—meant it could not have been as traumatic an event for her as it had obviously been for him. So later that evening I told mom what dad had said, she verified everything and told me that when dad shouted out in the delivery room—literally shouted—it startled everyone, after that they laughed while dad broke down in tears. In telling me this, her facial expression implied it had been an embarrassing moment for her. Then I asked, "I know what dad went through, but what did you go through, what were you thinking while all this was going on?" Closing her eyes and speaking emphatically she said, "I had only one thought: no more children, this is the last, I'll never go through this again, never!" And she never did, five times was enough (on my birth certificate, however, it says I was her sixth birth). Such, at least, were mom's first and last words regarding my birth. I should add, like myself, mom never believed in the Limbo theory. Although she never said so—she would never openly contradict dad or what the Church said—yet like a lot of Christians, she had her own private beliefs. She never suffered any lack of certitude in matters eternal or domestic, as she saw it—said it, in fact—her knowledge was divinely given, thus she never argued the issue nor doubted her little ones were in heaven with God.

Going back to that day in prayer when the question "why me?" came up. There came the picture of dad in the delivery room begging God to take me, to let me live long enough to be baptized so I could enjoy the glorious vision of God for all eternity. It was the plea of an anguished father offering God the most precious thing he had to give, a father deliberately sacrificing his own will, desires and joys, for the eternal good of his child, suffer his own loss for her gain. When he said, "Take her, she is yours, not mine", God did just that, He not only took the child, but raised her every step of the way—a difficult way since it was not her way by nature. So the answer to "why me?" was the working out of a covenant between God and a father, a covenant that worked both ways: the father gave his child to God and, in turn, God gave the child everything. Although this child could have been any child in the world, the same could not be said of the father. Not just any father could enter into such a covenant, only one who truly and deeply valued eternal life with God above life on this earth could be party to such a contract. This was not a last ditch plea or prayer of an anxious father, rather it was his whole belief system, his Faith, his life of faithful practice, all brought to bear and put on the line before God, Who alone can enact such a covenant. Had God not accepted, I would not be here to tell the story. Would that every child were the product of such a covenant between their earthly and heavenly Fathers. My life, then, has just been the working out of this covenant; and as a middle term it could be said, I am this covenant.

THE END

MY PARENTS

Several Years before their 50th Wedding Anniversary in 1969

Peg

Mark

"While every child is a product of genes and environment—family, culture, religion, and so on—this can never be the whole story of one's life. Without denying these influences, priority must be given to God's graced work in the soul, because grace is no respecter of persons, genes, environment, family, culture and so on. God does not wait for better circumstances or pamper individual temperaments, nothing can inhibit or deter His work in the soul, and thus no life is complete without this graced accounting."

(Bernadette Roberts, from the Introduction to *Contemplative*)

Printed in Great Britain
by Amazon